BASIC QUESTIONS IN THEOLOGY

BOOKS BY WOLFHART PANNENBERG
Published by The Westminster Press

The Church
Basic Questions in Theology, *Volume I*
Basic Questions in Theology, *Volume II*
Ethics
Human Nature, Election, and History
Faith and Reality
Theology and the Philosophy of Science
The Idea of God and Human Freedom
The Apostles' Creed:
   In the Light of Today's Questions
Theology and the Kingdom of God
Jesus—God and Man, *Second Edition*

In collaboration with Avery Dulles and Carl E. Braaten

Spirit, Faith, and Church

WOLFHART PANNENBERG

BASIC QUESTIONS
IN THEOLOGY

Collected Essays
Volume II

Translated by George H. Kehm

THE WESTMINSTER PRESS
PHILADELPHIA

This book is a translation by George H. Kehm of pages
202-398 of *Grundfragen systematischer Theologie*
published in 1967 by Vandenhoeck & Ruprecht in
Göttingen, West Germany.

Published by The Westminster Press®
Philadelphia, Pennsylvania

PRINTED IN THE UNITED STATES OF AMERICA
9 8 7 6 5 4 3 2 1

Library of Congress Cataloging in Publication Data

Pannenberg, Wolfhart, 1928–
  Basic questions in theology.

  Translation of Grundfragen systematischer Theologie.
  Reprint. Originally published: Philadelphia :
Fortress Press, |1970-1971|
  Includes bibliographical references.
  1. Theology, Doctrinal—Addresses, essays, lectures.
I. Title.
BT80.P3413 1983   230'.044   82-15984
  ISBN 0-664-24467-X (pbk. : v. 2)

CONTENTS

ABBREVIATIONS

ANF   *The Ante-Nicene Fathers.* Edited by Alexander Roberts and James Donaldson. Buffalo and New York, 1885–96 (American reprint of the Edinburgh edition).

BC   *The Book of Concord: The Confessions of the Evangelical Lutheran Church.* Translated and edited by Theodore G. Tappert in collaboration with Jaroslav Pelikan, Robert H. Fischer, and Arthur C. Piepkorn. Philadelphia: Fortress Press, 1959.

CD   Barth, Karl. *Church Dogmatics.* Edited by G. W. Bromiley and T. F. Torrance. 12 vols. Edinburgh: T. & T. Clark, 1936–62.

CR   *Corpus Reformatorum.* Edited by C. G. Bretschneider and H. E. Bindseil. Halle, 1834–60.

EvTh   *Evangelische Theologie*

LW   American edition of *Luther's Works.* Edited by Jaroslav Pelikan and Helmut T. Lehmann. Philadelphia and St. Louis, 1955–.

MPG   Migne, J. P., ed. *Patrologia Graeca.* Paris, 1857ff.

MPL   Migne, J. P., ed. *Patrologia Latina.* Paris, 1844ff.

NPNF   *The Nicene and Post-Nicene Fathers of the Christian Church.* First series edited by Philip Schaff. Second series edited by Philip Schaff and H. Wace. New York, 1886–1900.

RGG[3]   *Die Religion in Geschichte und Gegenwart.* Edited by K. Galling. 3d ed. Tübingen, 1957–65.

WA   Luther, Martin. *Werke: Kritische Gesamtausgabe.* Weimar, 1883–.

I

WHAT IS TRUTH?

This essay first appeared in *Vom Herrengeheimnis der Wahrheit: Festschrift für Heinrich Vogel*, ed. Kurt Scharf (Berlin, 1962), pp. 214–39. Heinrich Vogel was not able to be present when these considerations were presented to the Kirchliche Hochschule of Berlin on November 24, 1961. They are thus dedicated to this esteemed teacher in this way.

THE QUESTION concerning the essence of truth touches a profound crisis not only of theology but also of the Christian churches and Christian faith generally in the present age. Since the Enlightenment, the question of the truth of their faith has been put to Christians with constantly increasing poignancy. It is the question of its power to encompass all reality – even that of modern science, the technological control of nature, and the forms of individual life – and to claim them all as evidence for the content of the Christian message. The question about the truth of the Christian message has to do with whether it can still disclose to us today the unity of the reality in which we live, as it once did in the ancient world, which was the basis for the victory of Christianity in the ancient *oikumenē* [inhabited world] surrounding the Mediterranean Sea. Thus, the question regarding the truth of the Christian faith is not concerned with a particular truth of one kind or another but with truth itself, which in essence can only be one.[1] It asks whether the Christian faith still contains the truth that gathers together everything

[1] In taking this point of departure, my presentation touches upon Heinrich Vogel's essay "Wann ist ein theologischer Satz wahr?" in *Kerygma und Dogma* 4 (1958): 176–90; cf. esp. p. 176. I also attempt here to move toward the end point of his line of thought, albeit by a different route.

experienced as real. For this reason, the question concerning the truth of the Christian faith cannot be answered by the mere assertion that Jesus Christ is the truth, but only with regard to the whole of the reality that we experience. Only in this way is the unity of truth, which is essential to it, guaranteed. If the Christian proclamation should abandon the consideration of the totality of reality experienced by its hearers, then it would neglect "Christian solidarity with the godless,"[2] and could no longer raise a well-founded claim to be speaking about *the* absolute truth. As a result, the Christian proclamation would gradually become fit for display in a museum. For this reason, theology must ask about the one absolute truth when it sets about reflecting upon the Christian message.

In such an endeavor, Christian theology will always find itself facing an intellectual realm in which the question of truth has already been raised especially on the part of philosophy. Theology turns to this question within a preexisting context within the Western view of truth, even if it is not supposed to appropriate this context uncritically. Regardless of whether one knows and admits this or not, today, there is hardly anyone on the whole earth, certainly not the theologian, who remains outside this context when he begins to ask about truth. The Western view of truth, which constitutes the context of the theological question of truth, is not itself a homogeneous entity, however, but has a history and is appropriately perceived only in this its own history. How this history of the understanding of truth is related to the essence of truth must still be clarified.

I

The beginnings of the Western view of truth may be traced back to two roots: the Greek, on the one hand, and the Israelitic idea of truth, on the other. At the same time, both sides also held different views of reality generally. These two roots of the understanding of truth were compared with each other by Hans von Soden in his Marburg chancellor's address of 1927, *Was ist*

---

[2] Vogel, "Wann ist ein theologischer Satz wahr?" p. 176.

Wahrheit?[3] He brought to light the disparity between them, but also indicated the point on which they agree. We will first follow the path he pointed out. Then it will be shown that the tension between Greek and Israelitic ideas of truth determines the whole history of the understanding of truth in the West right down to the present day.

The Hebrew word for truth is *emeth*. The underlying verb has the meaning of standing firm, establishing, supporting, bearing. *Emeth* means the reliability, the unshakable dependability, of a thing or word, and thus also the faithfulness of persons. The words of a man are *emeth* to the extent that they prove to be reliable. Thus, *emeth* is not on hand once and for all as a timeless, binding state of affairs. Rather, *emeth* must occur again and again. Such occurrence of truth, of faithfulness, appears in its purest form as "a fully free act from persons to persons." It is "that relationship which fulfills a current expectation, specific claim, or justifies a confidence that has been bestowed on someone."[4] Thus, in the Israelitic sense, truth is "reality (which) is regarded as history . . . not something that in some way or another lies under or behind things, and is discovered by penetrating into their interior depths; rather, truth is that which will show itself in the future."[5]

It is precisely this historical feature that is completely lacking in the Greek idea of truth. The Greek verb *alētheuein* is oriented from the very beginning toward the relationship of a speaker to one being addressed. It meant, originally, to let something be seen as it is in itself; not to conceal something. Plato, Xenophon, and Aristotle all agreed in saying of *alētheuein* that it consists in "reporting what was, just as it appeared, and what was not, as not existing."[6] The same conception is expressed by Parmenides when he states: "that-which-is is, and that-which-is-not is not; that is the path of conviction; for it follows the

---

[3] Hans von Soden, *Was ist Wahrheit? Vom geschichtlichen Begriff der Wahrheit,* Marburger akademische Reden 46 (Marburg, 1927).

[4] *Ibid.,* p. 13.　　　　　[5] *Ibid.,* p. 15.

[6] *Xenophon's Anabasis,* trans. J. S. Watson (London: George Bell & Sons, 1896), p. 124 [=Xenophon *Anab.* 4. 4. 15: *ta onta te hōs onta, kai ta mē onta hōs ouk onta*]; cf. Plato *Crat.* 383 b; Aristotle *Met.* 1011b26ff.

truth.''[7] The *alētheia*, the unconcealedness, as Heidegger has translated this term, thus stands in a primordial relationship to right-speaking and comprehending. True speech must hold off that which conceals as well as the distortion that proceeds from man, the lie [*pseudos*], and also the "seeming" [*doxa* = *Schein*] which veils the genuine being of beings.[8] The Greeks were aware of the difficulty of this task, at least since Anaxagoras. Typically Greek is his opinion that the senses prevent us from discerning the truth, which is concealed from us by appearances.[9] Thus, according to ancient Greek conviction, only the logos, rational thought, has access to the being of beings in its unconcealedness. This is attested to not only by Anaxagoras,[10] but also by Empedocles.[11] Heraclitus expresses the same conception.[12] And he means that even the things men deal with in their daily rounds are alien to them, because they are divorced from the Logos, the author of the Universe.[13]

One cannot say of *alētheia* that it happens, in the sense of the Israelitic idea of truth. It is much more than this. Indeed, it is always identical with itself as that which is hidden behind the flux of sense-appearances, and which only the logos-informed

---

[7] Parmenides. 2. 3f. [The translation given here is based on the author's translation. A significantly different translation of the fragment of Parmenides may be found in Kathleen Freeman, trans., *Ancilla to the Pre-Socratic Philosophers: A Complete Translation of the Fragments in Diels, "Fragmente der Vorsokratiker"* (Oxford: Basil Blackwell, 1962), p. 42. – Tr.]

[8] See Xenophanes, frags. 34, 35 [*Ancilla*, p. 24].

[9] Cf. frags. 21, 21a [*Ancilla*, p. 86].

[10] Sextus Empiricus *Adv. Math.* 7. 90ff. [not in the Diels or in *Ancilla*, but see G. S. Kirk and J. G. Raven, eds., *The Pre-Socratic Philosophers* (Cambridge: Cambridge University Press, 1962), p. 393 (no. 536), for at least one of the passages referred to by the author, viz., 7. 90: "From the weakness of our senses we cannot judge the truth."—Tr.].

[11] Sextus Empiricus *Adv. Math.* 7. 122 [not in *Ancilla* or Kirk and Raven. –Tr.].

[12] Frags. 112, 116 [*Ancilla*, p. 32].

[13] Frag. 72 [*Ancilla*, p. 29]. For Heidegger, the linking of truth and logos first came about as a result of the Platonic subjugation of *alētheia* to the Idea (*Platons Lehre von der Wahrheit* [Berne, 1947], pp. 41f.). But truth and logos belong together even in Pre-Socratic thought. It was not only Parmenides who held that thought alone grasps true being and is thus one with it (Parmenides 3) [*Ancilla*, p. 42].

reason can uncover. Parmenides concluded from the hallmark of truth, "that-which-is is" [*Ist ist*], that true being is not subject to becoming, is indestructible, and therefore can only be singular.[14] "It Is now, a Whole all together, One, continuous."[15] The unchangeable unity of truth and of true being, which was for Parmenides the consequence of the path of the conviction that "that-which-is is," is set in opposition to the multiplicity of the shifting appearances.[16] These are thoughts which Plato developed further and transformed in his conception of degrees of truth.[17] Even in the Platonic transformation, at the highest stage the Parmenidean truth remained absolutely one, exalted above all time. This timelessness, which is related to the separation of truth from the fluid appearance of sense-impressions, is characteristic of the Greek view of truth in distinction from the Israelitic view, at least within the sphere of influence dominated by Parmenides and Plato. The event of the revelation of the non-concealed, to which Heidegger has called attention,[18] is precisely not determinative for the Greek understanding of the essence of truth. The Greek understanding of the essence of truth looks away from its occurrence as the penetration of a concealment. This feature of the Greek way of speaking about truth is something that was first struck upon by us. The Greek thinkers themselves disregarded this in that they thought of the truth as opposed to all change.

Despite the deep differences between them, the Greek and Israelitic views of truth also possess common features. It is not accidental that the Old Testament *emeth* was translated by the Greek word *alētheia*. Even the true being comprehended by logos is, for the Greek, enduring and stable; and speech about it is

---

[14] Parmenides 8. 3ff. [*Ancilla*, p. 43].

[15] Parmenides 8. 5ff. [*Ancilla*, p. 43].

[16] Parmenides 8. 53ff. [*Ancilla*, p. 44].

[17] See Heidegger's interpretation of the famous parable of the cave (*Republic* 7. 514aff.) in *Platons Lehre von der Wahrheit*, pp. 27f. On the unity of truth in Plato, cf. *Phaidr.* 247 d–248 b.

[18] "Truth means, originally, that which has been wrested from concealment. Thus, truth is such a wresting from, each time in the mode of unconcealment" (*Platons Lehre von der Wahrheit*, p. 32).

reliable,[19] in contrast to the changing, merely seeming being of the objects of the senses and the correspondingly fluid opinions of men. For this reason, von Soden rightly said that even for the Greeks "the question about truth was the question about that which endures and guarantees permanence, which protects and is protected against passing away."[20]

However, not only the fundamental features of constancy and reliability, but also the fact that the truth may be experienced, belongs to the essence of truth for Hebrew as well as for Greek thought. Through von Soden, the opinion has gained currency that the reference of truth to knowledge in Greek thought is without parallel in the Israelitic understanding of truth. Nevertheless, this assertion needs to be qualified. The Israelite, like the Greek, was interested in the experience of the true, and for him, too, this belonged to the essence of truth generally. Faithfulness, as the remaining-identical-with-itself of a thing or person, always refers to a social relationship and means that a person or thing characterized by faithfulness is also reliable for others. What mattered – for the Israelite, no less than for the Greek – was for that which is intrinsically constant to prove its constancy to him as well and thereby bestow its stability upon him. That is true which confers stability and thus proves itself as stable. Accordingly, the truth of God proves itself by the fact that ultimately he alone is able to guarantee stability. The faithfulness of God is a shield and buckler (Ps. 91:4). It is not by accident that the psalms in which the word *emeth* is used with particular frequency to express the fame of the God of Israel like to name his grace and faithfulness together.[21] In any case, the Israelitic experience of truth was shaped differently than that of the Greek. The truth of the God of Israel did not disclose itself in its fullness to the logos of cogitative comprehension, as did the Greek *alētheia*, but only when met with trust in God's faithfulness. Only the one who entrusts himself to God, who

---

[19] Parmenides 8. 50 [*Ancilla*, p. 44].

[20] *Was ist Wahrheit?* pp. 17f.

[21] Pss. 85:10; 88:12; 89:33; 98:3; 100:5; 103:17; 115:1; 117:2; 138:2; 143:1, 11f.

binds himself to him, will have stability through him (Isa. 7:9).
"Binding himself" is intended here to give the plain sense of
the Hebrew word for "faith" [*he⁽e⁾min*] which is used in this
passage, and which has the same stem as truth, *emeth*. That man
must bind himself to God in order to attain stability is once
again linked to the historicness of the truth in the Hebraic view.
It always proves itself for the first time through the future.
Therefore it is accessible now only by trusting anticipation of
the still-outstanding proof, and that means precisely, by faith.
And yet, a preliminary proof of the divine constancy is not
thereby excluded, even if this still remains open to the future.
For this reason, faith should not be set in simple opposition to
the Greek experience of stability through the logos. Previous
experience of the constancy of a man or even of God is always,
for the Israelite, a presupposition, the ground of faith. Israel
always lived from the experienced faithfulness of its God, and
precisely through this, its history, is it called to entrust itself to
its God for the future, too. This is made clear in an exemplary
way at the end of the Yahwistic account of the crossing of the
Red Sea (Exod. 14:31): "And Israel saw the great work which
the Lord did against the Egyptians, and the people feared the
Lord; and they believed in the Lord and in his servant Moses."
Even the previously cited summons of Isaiah to King Ahaz to
trust in Yahweh is not without foundation. Isaiah (7:8) points
to the fact that the "head" of the Syrian enemies is at bottom
only a human king, Rezin of Damascus, and that the head of
the northern Israelites who have joined him is only a usurper,
"the son of Remaliah," as he contemptuously puts it. This
argument tacitly implies that the head of Jerusalem, by contrast,
is Yahweh's elected successor of David (if not Yahweh himself!).[22] This is the ground of that faith called for in the sentence
immediately following. To this extent, a knowledge, corresponding to the Greek guarantee of stability through the logos,
is not to be excluded from the experience of the truth of the
constancy of God. This knowledge, too, which Isaiah wants to

[22] On this point, see the comments of Hans Walter Wolff, *Immanuel*,
Biblische Studien 23 (Neukirchen Kreis Moers, 1959), pp. 17f.

impart to Ahaz, must be maintained against a superficial appearance to the contrary, and it demands that the whole, the context, be kept in view. Certainly von Soden was right in noting that, for the Israelites, the truth confronted thought in a contingent manner, and in this sense it may also be said that it is a matter of "revelation."[23] But "in a contingent manner" does not mean absolutely "irrational," but rather that contingent events are the basis of a historical experience whose meaning is disclosed in relation to a long memory, a view which knows the great connections. The constancy of its God is thus, for Israel, also something that has already appeared, and in this respect it is not different from the stability of "what-is" for the Greeks. One would even have to say that for Israel everything and anything that has occurred up to now proves that Yahweh is constant, and that finally he alone is constant. For the Hebrew, however, that is just not self-evident. It is not the result of a logical necessity, that what-is, is. It is not to be shrunken to this abstract identity. Rather, it means that it has been previously shown in very specific manifestations that God is constant and reliable, and that this will also be shown in the future through such concrete manifestations, which, however, are by no means already established by abstract necessities of thought. The truth of God must prove itself anew in the future, and that cannot be undertaken by any logos; on the contrary, only trust can anticipate it.

The unity of truth which Greek philosophy formulated is also important for Hebrew thought in another way. For the Israelite, the truth of God embraces all other truth. It not only overshadows it, but in addition provides its basis. Of God alone is it true that his works are *emeth*; so much so that they endure forever, and his commands are completely trustworthy (Ps. 111: 7f.). Of his promises, it is said that they stand fast as the orders of his creation (Ps. 119:90f.). Thus, the all-encompassing steadfast truth of God is established in his creation and is visible in it: as the Creator of heaven and earth, he will maintain faithfulness even throughout all of the future, into the furthest

[23] *Was ist Wahrheit?* p. 18.

reaches of time (Ps. 146:6; cf. also 100:5, 117:2). For this reason, he alone can proffer a reliable future to men, as Psalm 91 extols: "his faithfulness (truth) is a shield and buckler" (v. 4). Israel is conscious of this refuge, which guarantees it stability, as its privilege among the nations: "Some boast of chariots, and some of horses, but we boast of the name of the Lord our God. They will collapse and fall; but we shall rise and stand upright" (Ps. 20:7f.). Thus, if finally God alone is constant and true, nevertheless constancy goes out from him into the orders of nature and into human relationships insofar as they rest on his authority. Through his grace, *emeth* actually sprouts from the land of Israel (Ps. 85:11). All constancy, whether it be in the orders of nature, in the life of nations, or in the individual, is embraced by the truth of God and is grounded in it.

From this standpoint, it is understandable that Hellenistic Judaism and, later, early Christianity combined that true being which Greek philosophy had inquired after as one and as divine, with the God of the Bible who is the absolutely constant one and, in his faithfulness, the all-embracing truth. The difference between the Greek and Israelitic views of truth may be understood in the main as consisting in the fact that Greek thought offers an abridged view of reality in contrast to the deeper experience of reality which is established by the God of the Bible. This assertion must be confirmed by showing that the reality which the Greeks had in view is not excluded by the biblically grounded understanding of reality, but is taken up and refined by it.

The decisive point, in this connection, is the circumstance that the Greek dualism between true being and changing sense-appearances is superseded in the biblical understanding of truth. Here, true being is thought of not as timeless but instead as historical, and it proves its stability through a history whose future is always open. For the constancy of the biblical God is not available in advance (as the timeless and therefore also "now all together" of that which always already is), but from time to time is disclosed in retrospect in a new way at every historical stage. Therefore, it is certain of the future only in the trustful self-surrender of faith – *that* faith, to be sure, which is grounded in the experience of the faithfulness and constancy of God that has already been proven by his historical guidance. The unavailability of the truth of God is thus connected with its historicness. Also grounded in just this is its personal mode, as distinguished from the impersonality of the Greek "what truly is" [*wahrhaft Seienden*]. Related to the unavailability of the truth of God is also his distinctness from all present reality. While the god of Greek thought is one with the foundation of the cosmos in such a way that he belongs to the cosmos as its ground, the biblical God is distinct from his creation as one who acts freely and contingently, since he ever again distinguishes himself from it in history. Thus, the Greek truth is superseded in principle by the biblical truth insofar as the latter includes those features of reality which the Greek idea of truth excluded, though without any less decisive interest in holding fast to the permanent and enduring.

From this angle, a view now opens up onto the path along which reflection on the essence of truth has gone in the West in the tension between the Greek and the biblical understandings of truth. The starting point of understanding this matter lies entirely on the side of the Greek concept of truth. That alongside this the Old Testament has its own distinct idea of truth hardly ever, as far as I can see, came explicitly into consciousness in the history of Western thought. One nevertheless lived with the history and ideas of the Bible. They determined the intellectual horizon in which the Greek concept of truth was appropriated and further developed. Its meaning was finally changed by this horizon, but in such a way that the impasses hidden in it now became visible. Thus, the history of the Western consciousness of truth may be understood as a path from the Greek to the Old Testament idea of truth. This path, it should be emphasized again, began with the Greek formulation of the essence of truth. The questions that pushed forward along this path were conceived from the side of the Greek starting point. But it had to be decided again and again whether an answer to this inquiry can be experienced from the horizon of a biblically determined consciousness. In this regard, it must be shown again at every new stage whether the biblical understanding of truth has the power to appropriate the Greek along with its impasses. But this means: the truth of the biblical understanding of truth had to prove itself and must still prove itself today in this critical debate. We will see how, in this connection, something of decisive importance for the solution of the problem of truth is intrinsic to the destiny of Jesus.

II

Somewhat schematically, one can say: the Greek idea of truth has two aspects, which have in particular occupied the thought of the subsequent ages. On the one hand, this means the agreement of truth with itself, its constancy. On the other hand, it means the agreement of speaking and thinking with that which is true in itself. The question of the *unity* of truth falls within the bounds of the first aspect; only that can subsist as true in itself which has nothing else alongside it contradicting it; only that which without beginning and end truly *is*, has constancy in the full sense. The question of the experience of truth and the accompanying one about its *criterion* lies within the bounds of the second aspect. Both aspects of the Greek concept of truth contain problems which, in the history of Western thought, have come to the fore within the horizon of a biblically determined understanding of human existence.

(*a*) We turn to the second aspect first, the question about the experience of truth, about the occurrence of the agreement of thought with that which is in agreement with itself, with what truly is, the ever constant.

For Plato (but also for the age before him with the exception, perhaps, of the Sophists) and for the subsequent age (for Aristotle and the Stoics, at any rate) there was manifestly no question but that the experience of truth was to be understood from the side of that which was true in itself. The Idea (as the that which truly is, the ever constant) imparts unconcealedness and insight [*noun*] to that which is unconcealed.[24] That which truly is reveals itself to the one who observes it. Observing the truth is thought of here as reception. Something similar is true for Aristotle, also. Even if he speaks of an "active reason" which affects man "from outside," in order to release the universal from the images of things impressed upon the soul and to present them as they are in themselves,[25] nevertheless this active reason produces only what it finds already present in the passively received sense impressions. Finally, even the Stoics understood knowing as reception of the true,[26] although they described the activity of the soul in the noetic process in psychological terms. Indeed, still another attitude had to join in with the received impression, which decided for the first time whether the soul would at all accept this impression. But even in this spontaneous act (the "consent" [*sunkatathesis*]) it is really only a matter of attaining the least distorted reception of something given in sense perception.[27]

In the subsequent history of Western thought, a fundamental change took place at this point, with the result that the experience of truth was no longer understood as a passively received duplication of this in the soul, but rather as a creative act of man. With this step, however, the acceptance of truth as existing independently of man and as observable only in such

[24] Plato, *Republic*, ed. R. G. Bury, The Loeb Classical Library (London: William Heinemann and New York: G. P. Putnam's Sons, 1926), 2: 130f.: "being the authentic source of truth and reason" [7. 517 c: *autē kuria alētheian kai noun paraschoumenē*]. On this point see also Heidegger, *Platons Lehre von der Wahrheit*, p. 41.

[25] Aristotle *De gen. animalium* B.3, 736 b 27; in *The Works of Aristotle*, ed. J. A. Smith and W. D. Ross, 12 vols. (Oxford: Clarendon Press, 1912), vol. 5 [correcting an erroneous citation in the German text, p. 211, n. 15. Actually, the passage cited refers only to the active reason entering the soul "from outside." On its function in relation to sense impressions, see *De Anima* 3. 7.—Tr.].

[26] H. F. A. von Arnim, *Stoicorum veterum fragmenta*, 4 vols. in 2 (Leipzig, 1903–24), 2:59; cf. *ibid.*, p. 54, and on this, Ulrich Wilckens, *Weisheit und Torheit: Eine exegetisch-religionsgeschichtliche Untersuchung zu I Cor. 1 & 2*, Beiträge zur historischer Theologie 26 (Tübingen, 1959), pp. 229f.

[27] Wilckens, *Weisheit und Torheit*, p. 230, on von Arnim, *Stoicorum veterum fragmenta*, 2. 65.

a reference became problematical. It seemed as if the subject, the understanding reason considered as creative, must regard itself as the source of truth. Nietzsche expressed this consequence in an exaggerated form when he called truth "that kind of error, without which a certain species of living being cannot exist."[28] In this way truth loses its relationship to extrahuman reality and is now only an expression of man himself, of his situation and his creative freedom. This understanding of truth has found particularly clear delineation in modern art. With the conception of truth as expression, the consequence of a long history of the understanding of truth was finally drawn. This has been shown by Wolfgang Kayser, using the history of German literature as an example.[29] The way begins in the sixteenth century with the distinction between factual truth and literary fiction, and already in Hofmannsthal reached a point which Kayser characterized as "the truth of the gesture."[30] Pure expressionistic truth is also the truth of the existing individual, as this is widely understood today under the influence more of Sartre than of Heidegger. What is sought is *my own* truth, not *the* truth generally. Since Kierkegaard, the latter is readily devalued as the universal.[31] Consistent with this, one then seeks confirmation of even the truth of faith only in the behavior of Christians, only as an expression of a mode of human existence, and no longer in that wherein faith believes.

We will not yet immediately turn to the question of whether and to what extent this subjectivization of truth is a predicament or a liberation. It is not easy to answer one way or the other. The matter is intrinsically ambiguous. The history of this change in the understanding of truth should help us to see this better. It has more the form of a sequence of several breakthroughs.

---

[28] Friedrich Nietzsche, *Will to Power*, trans. and ed. Oscar Levy, The Complete Works of Friedrich Nietzsche, 18 vols. (New York: Russell & Russell, 1909-11; reissued 1964), 15:20.

[29] *Die Wahrheit der Dichter*, Rowohlts deutsche Encyklopädie 87 (Hamburg, 1959). [30] *Ibid.*, pp. 45ff.

[31] In this connection, the corresponding twists which Kierkegaard gave matters were, in any case, taken much more as matters of principle than Kierkegaard himself might have meant them to be.

One disposition toward the subjectivization of truth already lies, as Heidegger has seen, in the Greek view itself, viz., insofar as it made thinking the norm of truth. In any event, Plato was hardly the first to make this move. Rather, it is part and parcel with the beginning of Greek philosophy itself, with the turn from myth (the word that narrates) to logos (the word that orders). Nevertheless, we have seen that it was not at all the intention of the ancient philosophers to concede to thought a superiority over being. Rather, they meant that thought was distinguished precisely in its aptitude for undistorted reception of that which was inherently being and truth.

In the long run, the decisive turning point was indeed the biblical-Christian message. It altered the position of man in the world. As the image of God, man was henceforth to rule over the world, and no longer simply adapt himself to it in awe. The truth to be received by man was limited to the transcendent truth of God. Hellenism, which was widely skeptical of the possibility of comprehending truth in thought, prepared the way for this turn. This process is certainly also connected with the political destiny of the time, with the dissolution of the Hellenistic states. For Hellenistic man, the truth became something beyond this evil, fate-dominated world.[32] The Christian message of the transcendent truth of God which had first appeared in this world in Jesus, made contact with Hellenistic thought at this point, but did not fully coincide with it. For the message of Christ claimed the world for itself as God's creation, and accordingly man was not to be released from the world, but rather proclaimed as the godlike lord of the world.

I cannot now explore in detail how this new position of man came to the fore in Augustine already, since, in his opposition to the Skeptics, he grounded the truth of knowledge upon the self-certainty of thought.[33] Augustine was not yet aware of the

[32] Cf. Rudolf Bultmann, in Gerhard Kittel, ed., *Theological Dictionary of the New Testament*, trans. and ed. Geoffrey Bromiley (Grand Rapids and London: William B. Eerdmans, 1964ff.), 1:240f.

[33] Augustine *On Free Will* 2. 8. 22ff., in *Augustine: Earlier Writings*, trans. J. H. S. Burleigh, Library of Christian Classics 6 (Philadelphia: Westminster

full scope of this act. In order for this to emerge it was still necessary to go through the critical discussions of the Scholastics concerning the process of knowing. In Scholasticism, the dominant position of man became a significant factor for the understanding of the cognitive process as early as the twelfth century[34] and, again, in Nominalism in the fourteenth century. But Ockham still limited himself to analyzing the subjectivity of comprehending thought. He, too, continued to regard the whole cognitive process as something set in motion by sense impressions.[35] Nicolas of Cusa, in opposition to this, was perhaps the first to understand thought as the creative productivity of the human spirit, independent of sense impressions.[36] He held up mathematical thought as the model of this creative productivity, understanding it no longer as a mere reflective reproduction of ideal relations, but instead as the very creation of the mind itself. Cusa explicitly grounded this conception in man's nature as the image of God. Man is the likeness of the creator of the world precisely in being the creator of an intellectual world of, indeed, an unlimited number of "suppositions" [*Mutmassungen*].

Conviction about the creative character of thought underlies the procedure of modern science. This applies first of all to the natural sciences, whose founders and inspirers were, in part, directly influenced by the thought of Cusa. Modern natural scientific thinking is characterized by the fact that it projects hypotheses which are then tested by meaningfully devised

---

Press, 1963), pp. 148ff. It is true that Augustine immediately switches from the self-certainty of the thinker to the point that the commonality of all individuals in comprehending certain contents indicates the existence of eternal truths superior to man (15. 39; Burleigh, pp. 159ff.).

[34] On this point, see M. D. Chenu, *La théologie au douzième siècle*, Études de philosophie Médiévale 45 (Paris, 1967), pp. 44ff., 52–61. The understanding of man at the opening of the twelfth century described here is intended to be regarded as background for the statements of an Abelard concerning the cognitive process.

[35] P. Boehner, "Realistic Conceptualism of William Ockham," *Traditio* 4 (1946): 307–35.

[36] Maurice de Gandillac, *Nikolaus von Kues: Studien zu seiner Philosophie und philosophische Weltanschauung* (Düsseldorf, 1953), pp. 145ff., esp. p. 151, n. 40 on the opposition to the Ockhamistic epistemology.

experiments. The second part of this procedure, that of experimental testing, goes beyond Cusa. But the first part, that of spontaneous, hypothetical construction, corresponds to his understanding of the peculiar, creative character of thought. Modern historical method has a similar structure. Its procedure is characterized by the fact that it no longer merely draws upon "sources," mixing or even purifying them, but freely reconstructs the course of events in question. It first develops a picture of "how it could have happened," in order next, by means of evidence, to solidify it or to prove it useless. Even here the conviction about the creative character of intellectual activity stands in the background.[37]

Agreement with extrahuman reality necessarily becomes a problem for this creative subjectivity of man, however. Such a problem did not arise for ancient philosophy. A type of thought that understands itself as a reduplication of the beings that are independent of man will always see agreement between things and their mental replicas as the normal result of the cognitive process, a result which always comes about when this process runs its course without interference. Nevertheless, a type of thought that understands itself as independent from the external world is exposed to the question of how it can ever bridge this gap again.

Cusa solved this problem by means of the same deiformity of man in which he had grounded his understanding of thought as a creative act: man does not, like God, create things in his thinking, but only ideas, instead. However, since he is the image of the God who created the world of things, human ideas must

---

[37] Even systematic theology, if one does not shut his eyes to what it actually does all the time, can only be understood as a creative construction, as the construction of the path of the revelation of God and, thus, of the unity of truth. Its projections, too, have to be verified subsequently, and only in this way do they attain scientific character. In the case of theology, such subsequent testing has to be viewed from two sides; on the one hand, from the standpoint of evidence for the details of its projection (here, above all, is where the Scripture proof has its place), and, on the other hand, against the total context of the current experience of reality. The relationship of systematic theology to exegesis as involving both dependence and independence can be rendered methodologically fully intelligible only from the standpoint of the constructive character of systematic theology.

therefore be similar to the things created by God, provided that human thought is precisely similar to God's. Thus, God is the presupposition from which alone the agreement of human thought with extrahuman reality can be explained and guaranteed. Since then, the truth of human thought in the sense of its agreement with extrahuman reality has been guaranteed only on the presupposition of God.

After Cusa, Descartes also took this path. For him, the truth of what is comprehended in our thinking is dependent upon the *veracitas*, the truthfulness, of the almighty God.[38] Even for Kant, the agreement of reason with the course of nature, at least with regard to ethics, could be defended only by means of the presupposition of the God who created both. Nevertheless, Kant – in distinction from Descartes, Leibniz, and even German Idealism – wanted to present *theoretical* truth as independent of the presupposition of God. The agreement of an idea with the universal laws of reason is affirmed by him as the criterion of its "objective validity" as well. According to Kant, "the objective validity of the judgment of experience signifies nothing else than its necessary universal validity."[39] But the objective validity – the agreement with extrahuman reality – does not permit of being traced back to an agreement of men among each other, quite apart yet from the error that lies in his position, that the reason is the same in all men because its basic structures are supposed to be established *a priori* and to precede all experience. Kant remained in the grip of the Enlightenment at this point in that he had not yet recognized the real root of the spontaneity of reason, which is its historicness. But even if ideas were universally accepted among men, it would still be possible that all men might be trapped in a common illusion. The "objective

---

[38] Descartes, *Meditations*, trans. John Veitch (Chicago: Open Court Pub. Co., 1901), 5:83.

[39] *Kant's Prolegomena to Any Future Metaphysics*, ed. and trans. Paul Carus (Chicago: Open Court Pub. Co., 1902), p. 55 [somewhat revised, rendering *Allgemeingültigkeit* as "universal validity" instead of Carus's "universality of application," which has too much of an empirical ring.—Tr.]; cf. *The Critique of Pure Reason*, trans. J. M. D. Meikeljohn (London: George Bell and Sons, 1884), pp. 50ff.

validity" of thought is guaranteed only on the presupposition of a common ground of the human mind and extrahuman reality. For this reason, the step beyond Kant into German Idealism, which renewed this thesis, became unavoidable. The agreement of human thought with extrahuman reality, and thus its truth, is possible only on the presupposition of God. Even the fact that natural science and technology find such agreement to be confirmed again and again is everything but self-explanatory in view of the creative autonomy of their thinking. Without the presupposition of God, truth is no longer conceivable in terms of agreement.

The modern understanding of truth from the side of the subjectivity of man remains bound to the presupposition of God, as Cusa first formulated the matter. From this point of view, however, the subjectivization of truth has to be judged as a legitimate outcome of the biblical understanding of reality. The truth, which is originally God's truth, must become perceptible in the world through man, in the sense of a responsible structuring of the world that measures itself by God. The truth of human behavior and thus the truth of expression, too, are involved in this. That truth proves itself in relationships and thus has personal character,[40] shows once more that in the subjectivization of truth, features of the biblical, historically cast idea of truth have prevailed. The truth of human conduct is not already pecided simply by its agreement with some sort of fundamental existential decision, however, but only by its agreement with God's truth, which the world as a whole has to thank for its origin, as modern thought about truth is forced to presuppose. This means, however, that the conduct of man is true only if it occurs with a view to the unity of the world; for only in this way would it occur with a view to the Creator, whose faithfulness is the basis for the unity of the world. And only in him who is the author of the unity of the world can man discover the God who is the criterion of the truth of his own behavior and

---

[40] This aspect was developed, in a one-sided way, to be sure, in Emil Brunner's *Truth as Encounter* (Philadelphia: Westminster Press, ²1964), in opposition to the objective truth of theoretical knowledge.

thinking.[41] Thus, the question about the experience of truth flows into the question of the unity of truth.

(*b*) For Greek thought, the unity of truth excluded all change from it. Change would entail multiplicity, a succession of different forms, and then the full, whole truth, the truly constant, could not be found in anything. It belongs to the essence of truth to be unchangeable and, thus, to be one and the same, without beginning or end.

However, in the contrast of *alētheia* to the concealing appearances, a historical feature is nonetheless to be found, as Heidegger has rightly noted: an occurrence of unconcealment, as is expressed in the very word *alētheia*.[42] Yet, the Greek thinkers disregarded this event character of truth from the very beginning, and not by sheet accident either. For them, it had to stand in contradiction to the permanency of truth for which they were seeking. If they had taken note of this event character of truth as *alētheia*, then their whole distinction between "permanent" truth and "changing" appearance would have collapsed. That is the hidden impasse of the Greek idea of truth.

[41] That existential truth isolated by itself is not even possible has been penetratingly set forth recently by Wilhelm Kamlah in his *Wissenschaft, Wahrheit, Existenz* (Stuttgart, 1960). "The truly possible as that to which human existence is truly summoned, is not 'self-supporting', but rests upon something like a truth outside itself" (pp. 66f.). This truth outside us is, for Kamlah, too, essentially one: "There is nothing to discuss with respect to the demand that 'the' truth, as that which grounds existence, has to be at the same time universal, that is: human existence [*Existenz*] can be certain of itself, transparent to itself, in no other way than that the world, too, becomes clear to it" (p. 90). Kamlah draws a conclusion from this which theology ought to take very seriously: "This, too, is an offense against the claim of truth that belongs to the inquiring human being, namely, that in faith man has 'the' truth and yet alongside this he also has 'the' different sort of truth of science" (p. 71). The study being presented in this essay endeavors to hold its own in the face of the problem posed in this statement.

[42] "The Greek words for 'truth' . . . are compounded of the privative prefix *a-* ('not') and the verbal stem *-lath-* ('to escape notice,' 'to be concealed'). The truth may thus be looked upon as that which is un-concealed. . . ." (quoted from the note by Macquarrie and Robinson in Martin Heidegger, *Being and Time*, trans. John Macquarrie and Edward Robinson [London: SCM Press and New York: Harper and Row, 1962], p. 57, n. 1). –Tr.]

It contains an intrinsic tendency toward a historical understanding of truth, although this is contrary to its own intention.

How did consciousness of such historicness of truth come
about? Many occasions and motives worked together in this.
Hellenistic dualism, insofar as it concentrated the truth upon
the transcendence of the good God in opposition to the evil
world, surrendered the unity of truth. But even within Christian
theology, which could not give up the unity of truth because of
its belief in creation, there arose almost insuperable difficulties
as a result of the disparate tendencies of its Greek and biblical
heritages. The situation was decisively sharpened, however, by
the modern subjectivization of truth which, in turn, first
attained its full effect through the rise of historical thought
which developed out of the criticism of tradition. Since the age
of the great journeys in the seventeenth century, it has become
clear that the truth has another form for different peoples and
ages, and since the Romantic movement it has become impossible rationalistically to separate the truth from its historically
diverse forms, since it has been learned that precisely the
rationalistic view of the Enlightenment has to be evaluated as
itself that of a limited epoch. In all these exceedingly complex
processes, the radical historicness of human thought came to
light. The question arose as to whence we really presume to
know whether our view of the world is truer than that of other
peoples and other cultures. Thereby, it becomes questionable
where truth is to be found at all. If reference to the unity of
everything real is essential to truth, then it cannot deal simply
with our present world. Its unity should instead also embrace
other peoples and cultures of distant times, for whom the whole
of reality presented itself differently from the way it does for us
today. It is impossible, on the basis of our knowledge of truth
in our own age, to reject out of hand earlier conceptions of
reality as simply untrue, since experience teaches that even
what is accepted as true today will already have changed to-
morrow. Every absolutization of a contemporary truth would
at once misunderstand the historical multiplicity of pictures of
the truth. In this situation, unity of truth can now only be

thought of as the history of truth, meaning in effect that truth itself has a history and that its essence is the process of this history. Historical change itself must be thought of as the essence of truth if its unity is still to be maintained without narrow-mindedly substituting a particular perspective for the whole of truth.

To date, Hegel's system should be regarded as the most significant attempt at a solution to this problem. It is distinguished from other philosophies of history by the fact that truth is not to be found already existing somewhere as a finished product, but is instead thought of as history, as process. "The truth is the whole."[43] That which makes this whole into a whole can become visible only at the end. All preliminary stages will be driven beyond themselves by their inner contradictions. They will first find their truth beyond themselves. The final things are true, however: "The truth of this being is the end," said Hegel in *The Science of Logic*.[44] Since the truth is understood as a gradated development, so Hegel's logic, whose real object is the concept of truth,[45] also becomes a series of stages in which, at any given point, the higher stage is constitutive of the preceding insofar as it synthesizes into a unity the contradictions of the preceding one, and thus contains the provisional whole of the entire dialectical path that had been traversed up to that point. The progress of the logic therein is not that of a deduction from a principle that already contains everything in advance, but just the opposite: a reduction, so that "progress is a return to the foundation, to that origin and truth on which depends and indeed by which is produced that with which the beginning was made."[46] However, for Hegel, the outcome that is supposed to embrace all contradictions and everything provisional, showing them to have been one-sided syntheses, is the Absolute. And this means, for him, the absolute God. The meaning of this

---

[43] G. W. F. Hegel, *The Phenomenology of Mind*, trans. J. B. Baillie, intro. George Lichtheim (New York: Harper Torchbooks, 1967), p. 81.
[44] Trans. W. H. Johnston and L. G. Struthers (London: George Allen & Unwin, 1929), 1:142.
[45] *Ibid.*, 1:60, 2:209f.
[46] *Ibid.*, 1:82ff.

whole path is the truth, and indeed, the truth "is that because the finite is self-contradictory opposition, the absolute is — just because it *is not*."[47] Hegel presented the course of history and of the history of religion in this way, and he was certainly justified in doing this to the extent that the history of the human spirit always involves the creative surmounting of the contradictions and oppositions that have arisen.

Hegel's thesis that the truth of the whole will be visible only at the end of history approximates the biblical understanding of truth in two respects. It does so, firstly, by the fact that the truth as such is understood not as timelessly unchangeable, but as a process that runs its course and maintains itself through change. Secondly, it does so by asserting that the unity of the process, which is full of contradictions while it is under way, will become visible along with the true meaning of every individual moment in it, only from the standpoint of its end. What a thing is, is first decided by its future, by what becomes of it.

At this point, however, the one earthshaking objection that has to be raised against Hegel enters into the picture. This objection is not that of pantheism, for instance. That objection rests upon a misunderstanding, in my opinion. Much more serious is the point that the horizon of the future is lost in Hegel's thought. He had to understand his own position as the end of history in order to be able to think of the unity of history. The unity of history — and thus of truth— comes into view only from its end. Theologically, this means that Hegel no longer had an open future, an eschatology, before him. In his doctrine of the spirit of the community, eschatology. is radically contemporanized. Nevertheless, this train of thought inevitably brought Hegel into contradiction with the task he had set himself of conceiving the unity of truth. For future truth is necessarily excluded from his system. This means that not all truth has been appropriated within the stages of his dialectical system. In this case, however, the unity of truth remains uncomprehended, and therefore the concept of God has also not been conceived in its truth. The other objections that should be

[47] Ibid., 2:70 (italics in original).

urged against Hegel also follow from the exclusion of the future by the construction of this thought as comprising the end of history. This is especially the case with respect to the criticism that he does not take seriously enough the contingency of events, and instead makes the logic of the notion[48] the master of reality. In spite of all his efforts to allow the particular and individual to receive their due, and to have the notion find its content only in its renunciation [*Entäusserung*], he remained fixed in the primacy of the universal. Thus, Hegel could set truth in simple opposition to external history,[49] the kind of thing that should not happen in an understanding of truth that is truly historical and oriented to the contingency of experienced reality. These defects may well be rooted in the fact that Hegel, for the sake of the unity of truth, believed he could no longer grant to the future any claim to a truth of its own. Therein lies also the root of the downfall of his own system in the history of thought.

Since Hegel, however, the question of the unity of truth has not been posed again with a comparable depth. In Jaspers' work *Von der Wahrheit*,[50] the unity of truth remains merely a goal to be striven for. In Heidegger there is indeed talk of a history of Being and truth, but it is not yet clear how having a history, especially this history – that of metaphysics – belongs to the truth itself in Heidegger's sense. Only if this matter were clarified would it be possible to preserve the unity of truth.

Can the horizon of the biblical-Christian understanding of truth perhaps once again yield a solution at this stage of the problem of truth? Can it happen again, as it has repeatedly in the history of Western thought, that impasses stemming from Greek approaches to a question found solutions accruing from the horizon of a biblically determined consciousness? The posing of this question with regard to the situation determined by the Hegelian problems – which situation has not been overcome, as was said before – is no mere postulation, but rather

---

[48] [The German term here is *"der Begriff,"* which is not to be confused with Hegel's concept of *"die Idee,"* the Idea.–Tr.]

[49] *Science of Logic*, 2:222f.   [50] Munich, 1947.

one that lies very close at hand if one compares the Hegelian with the primitive Christian conception of history. Although for the biblical tradition, too, it belongs to the essence of truth to have a history; while for it, too, as for Hegel, the ultimate demonstration of truth first occurs at the end of history; and although even for primitive Christianity the definitive revelation of God had already occurred in Jesus, nevertheless, the openness of the future remained intact for it, in contrast to Hegel. Might it be the case that from this point of departure a solution might be possible to the impasses of the Hegelian conception of truth, which breaks up on just this point?

What really accounts for the fact that in primitive Christianity, despite the ultimacy of the revelation of God that appeared in Jesus, the future still remained open, so that the truth of God was not participated in by means of the concept [*Begriff*] in the last analysis, but rather – beyond all conceptualizing [*Begreifen*] and being driven by the process of conceptualization itself – by faith alone, by trust in the coming God?

The answer lies in the proleptic character of the Christ event. That is to say, the resurrection of Jesus is indeed infallibly the dawning of the end of history for men who – like Jesus himself – lived in the apocalyptic expectation of the end. But, for them, the onset of the end had occurred only in a preliminary way, happening in Jesus himself, who by this event was confirmed in his claim that the final destiny of men is decided by their stand in relation to his message. For the rest of us, the resurrection of the dead, which already happened to Jesus, is still outstanding. To that extent, it has in the meantime been anticipatorily realized in him alone. Precisely in this way, however, the possibility is opened up to all other men, through fellowship with Jesus, with the pre-Easter way of his preaching and his destiny of the cross, of the grounded hope of attaining a share in his resurrection in the future. In this connection, it is decisive for the openness of the future that we are still unable to know at all what the expression "resurrection of the dead" really means. In the first instance, it is only a metaphor, a symbolic expression, taken from the example of awakening from sleep. This metaphor is an expression of the human hope beyond death, and in the post-Exilic period it became the content of the promise of the God of the Old Testament. Since, however, we still do not know the reality to which this image corresponds, so neither do we know what really happened in the case of Jesus. Even the disciples had only the symbolic term, "resurrection of the dead," to designate this.

Thus, the proleptic character of the destiny of Jesus is the basis for the openness of the future for us, despite the fact that Jesus is the ultimate revelation of the God of Israel as the God of all men. And, conversely, without this proleptic character, the fate of Jesus could not be the ultimate revelation of the deity of God, since the openness of the future belongs constitutively to our reality – against Hegel. Thus, because of the proleptic character of his destiny, what happened to Jesus then is, at the same time, for us always the open future toward which we go out. The unsurpassability of the Christ event is thereby expressed in a manner much sharper than Hegel – despite the best of intentions! – was able to manage, since for him the Christ event was certainly something belonging to the closed past, which might at best still continue to operate in the present in spirit, in concept, but could by no means be a still-open future.

This understanding of the destiny of Jesus was the basis of primitive Christianity's, and especially of Paul's overwhelming certainty of truth. Can we still make this our own? Doing so depends upon two presuppositions, which I can only name here without going into a detailed discussion. For one thing, there is the question whether the apocalyptic hope of resurrection still contains truth for us; i.e., whether it can still be reproduced within our understanding of the being of man in the world. I answer this question in the affirmative because I believe that it belongs to the openness of man's being to question beyond death, and because the representation in terms of which we can understand such questioning today can only be that of a bodily life, even if of a sort utterly different from our present one. Further related to this question is the fact that the structure of the proleptic as such is characteristic of all human disposition toward the future. The second presupposition is that we, too, must still understand the resurrection of Jesus as a historical event which happened at a specific time: as a reality, and not a mere hallucination, even though we can designate it only by means of images. The resurrection of Jesus is to be viewed as a historical event in this sense, namely, that the disciples of Jesus were overwhelmed by a reality which confronted them, and for which not only they, but we, too, have no other explanation and therefore no other designation than the symbolic talk about a "resurrection from the dead."

On these two presuppositions hinges the decision as to whether the primitive Christian understanding of revelation can still be carried out as our own, despite the change in our intellectual situation which is expressed, on the one hand, in a clearer consciousness of the specific character of the expectation of a general resurrection, and of the historicity [*Historizität*] of the resurrection of Jesus, on the other. Should the decision come out in the affirmative, then the proleptic revelation of God in Jesus is at the same time the solution of the impasses in the Hegelian concept of truth. This solution satisfactorily meets the legitimate objections against Hegel, since it protects the openness of the future and the contingency of events, and still holds fast to the ultimacy of what appeared in Jesus, which makes possible the unity of truth. *That it alone founds the unity of truth means, however, the demonstration of the truth of the Christian message itself.* This is the sole possible proof of its truth.

In conclusion, let us summarize the discussions of this second part in some theses:

(1) From the standpoint of the history of thought, the subjectivization of truth in the modern period is grounded in the Christian faith.

(2) Subjectivity cannot understand itself and its thought as truth without presupposing God as the one origin of everything real. In this regard, the act of adopting this presupposition can only mean having an open question, not an actual knowledge of God.

(3) Subjectivity must presuppose God as the origin and unity of everything real. Only such a God, who embraces everything, can be the truth itself. For this reason, every representation of God is to be tested as to whether it permits understanding reality as a whole, and thereby satisfies the unity of truth.

(4) Since the emergence of historical consciousness, the unity of all reality is conceivable only as a history. The unity of truth is still possible only as a historical process, and can be known only from the end of this process.

(5) The unity of truth is possible only if it includes the contingency of events and the openness of the future.

(6) For this reason, the unity of truth is constituted only by the proleptic revelation of God in Jesus Christ.

The path from the Greek to the Old Testament understanding of truth is thereby traversed. The two become one for the first time only in Jesus Christ. Here, the Greek question concerning the truth which is beyond the contradiction in the essence of *alētheia* is transcended and taken up into the truth of God himself.

2

INSIGHT AND FAITH

This essay first appeared in *Theologische Literaturzeitung* 88 (1963): cols. 81–92, in reply to Paul Althaus, "Offenbarung als Geschichte und Glaube: Bemerkungen zu Wolfhart Pannenbergs Begriff der Offenbarung," *ThLZ* 87 (1962): cols. 321–30.

IN CONTEMPORARY theology one frequently encounters the opinion that rational insight into the ground and content of faith is not only denied us as a matter of fact, but is even injurious to the essence of faith. Faith, one likes to say, must remain a risk. Against this view, I have asserted that the essence of faith must come to harm precisely if in the long run rational conviction about its basis fails to appear. Faith then is easily perverted into blind credulity toward the authority-claim of the preached message; into superstition, owing to its seeming contradiction of better judgment; or even into a tediously wrought work of faith. Therefore, it is precisely for the sake of the purity of faith that the importance of rational knowledge of its basis has to be emphasized. Naturally, this is not a matter of grounding faith in man instead of in God. That faith must be understood as something effected by God himself is not to be doubted. What is at issue here is only the matter of the mediation of such faith. The question is whether the Christian has the faith which he professes to have received from God himself, through the mediation of a supportable knowledge of the destiny of Jesus and its meaning, or whether his explanation that he owes his faith to God is only a subjective reassurance.

The article by Paul Althaus must also be evaluated within the horizon of this question. In this respect, Althaus, by raising the question about the relationship of the knowledge of revelation to faith and the Holy Spirit, has rendered the service of having singled out what is perhaps the most urgent problem of the theological tradition and the one which the volume *Revelation as History* leaves most in need of further discussion. To this extent, his discussion makes a contribution that furthers dialogue, in contrast to other positions that have been taken which only distort the matter. I will be concerned here to clarify certain, perhaps all too cursory, statements from various places in the above-mentioned volume in relation to the ideas put forth by Althaus. In this way I hope to show that some of the points of his article present only apparent contradictions. Thus, for example, there certainly is no dispute between us with regard to the confession that faith is given by God.[1] On the contrary, the real point of the controversy lies in the question about the relationship of faith and knowledge.

For Althaus, too, faith is connected with a knowledge of the revelation of God in Jesus Christ. But he is of the opinion that faith "itself *grounds* and *includes* this 'knowledge' or apprehension."[2] To be sure, faith also presupposes an "actual knowledge," too, "namely, the impression of the credibility of the *report* of facts and events (historical faith [*fides historica*]) contained in the proclamation, thus, of the factuality of the reported history. But this is not yet 'knowledge of *God's revelation*' in the events. This knowledge first comes about with faith itself."[3] All of Althaus's further remarks, if I see the matter correctly, are connected with this assertion.[4]

---

[1] Paul Althaus, "Offenbarung als Geschichte und Glaube: Bemerkungen zu Wolfhart Pannenbergs Begriff der Offenbarung," *Theologische Literaturzeitung* 87 (1962): col. 324.

[2] *Ibid.*, col. 325. [3] *Ibid.*, col. 325.

[4] The exegetical expositions of Althaus (*ibid.*, cols. 323ff.) terminate, for the most part, in the point that faith is a gift of God, which is not in dispute between us. Therefore they are unable to support Althaus's dogmatic thesis on the relationship of faith and knowledge. Althaus himself apparently claims this only for his reference in col. 326 that faith and knowledge "can be used synonymously." That these two words can be used as equivalents in the New Testament is certainly indisputable. But just such synonymity fails to express any *relationship of grounding* between faith and knowledge, whether it be in Althaus's sense, or in that asserted by me. On the contrary,

The offense that Althaus takes to the exclusive mark of faith as trust[5] would be upheld as correct only if trust were understood in a formal manner, in the sense of an isolated act of trust. But that was certainly not intended in the Reformation equation of faith and trust [*fiducia*], to which such a narrow conception of faith can appeal. An isolation of the act of trust would be improper already from the standpoint of the phenomenal characteristics of the enactment of trust in everyday life. Every act of trust reaches backwards (or forwards) to a ground of trustworthiness in the object being relied on. The individual elements of this act can be distinguished, to be sure, but they cannot be isolated from one another without falsifying the essence of trust itself. To this extent, one is by all means entitled to understand the word faith, with Althaus, in a wider sense, so that it also includes knowledge of the present ground of faith, corresponding to the concept of faith in classical Protestant dogmatics which comprised the elements of knowledge [*notitia*], assent [*assensus*], and trust [*fiducia*]. But even so, knowledge of the content of faith (*notitia* with *assensus*) remains the logical presupposition of the trust which is based upon it. Whether one follows the Reformation's linguisitic usage and concentrates the concept of faith upon the element of trust, or whether one takes it in such a broad sense that it includes the knowledge connected with the act of trust: in either case, one has to speak of a grounding of *fiducia* by means of *notitia* and *assensus*. If one takes faith and *fiducia* as synonymous, one will have to speak of a grounding of faith by a presupposed knowledge, as I have done. If one takes faith in a broader sense, it becomes a matter of

---

only the intimate connection between the two concepts is made clear hereby. On the other hand, Paul nevertheless does occasionally expressly designate knowledge as the ground of faith (Rom. 6:8f.; 2 Cor. 4:13), even if not in explicit opposition to the reverse sort of grounding which Althaus proposes. Even in the case of John there are points, like the surely deliberately formulated sequence of coming, seeing, and abiding – in the Johannine narrative of the calling of the disciples (John 1:34, 46) – which go behind the synonymity of insight and faith, and refer to a relationship of grounding which here again runs counter to Althaus's view.

[5] *Ibid.*, col. 325.

speaking of a relationship of grounding between the individual elements, i.e., of a grounding of *fiducia* by *assensus* and *notitia*. However, one may in no case eliminate in advance the question of such a relationship of grounding by means of a formulation such as Althaus', that faith "itself grounds and includes this 'knowledge' or apprehension."[6] To be sure, the maxim that, in certain respects, the whole precedes its parts, applies to the act of faith, too – a point to which we will return later. But, on the one hand, as act, the totality of faith cannot condition its content, but can at most condition the perception of its content. And, on the other hand, the reference to the conditionedness of the parts by the whole may not leap over or even suppress the question about the relationship of grounding between knowledge and assent on one side, and trust, on the other. The conditionedness of the part (e.g., knowledge) by the whole (faith [*fides*]) is not to be confused with the assertion that knowledge and assent are somehow grounded by trust which, for its part, is only one element of faith in the broader sense of the term. Such confusion is imminent, however, when Althaus says that the knowledge that belongs to faith "is first disclosed in believing reception of the message." This sentence seems to lead to the conclusion that the *decision* of faith is the ground of certainty with regard to the content of faith, and that is precisely the conception of the relationship of knowledge (with assent) and faith that I must reject, because with that the founding of faith upon a truth "outside myself" [*extra me*] is in fact surrendered in favor of a self-grounding of faith. In every grounding of knowledge [*notitia*] upon trust [*fiducia*], I can see only the perversion of a correct understanding of Christian faith.[7] Paul speaks of the reverse, of the grounding of faith upon

---

[6] *Ibid.*

[7] For this reason, distinguishing between ground of faith [*Glaubensgrund*] and "thoughts of faith" [*Glaubensgedanken*] in the way hit upon by Wilhelm Herrmann is suspect, at least in part. In any event, so long as it is a matter of the event that grounds faith, the "thoughts of faith" formulate precisely the ground of faith, even if not always in the same way but in different ways at different times. Conversely, the ground on which faith relies is accessible only by means of "thoughts of faith." But in this connection it cannot be a

a knowledge (Rom. 6:8f.; 2 Cor. 4:13). Whether this belongs to faith in the wider sense or not, there is in any case no talk of this knowledge being in turn grounded in faith; rather, the opposite is stated, viz., that faith rests upon such knowledge.

It is not thereby asserted that a man can in the course of his life attain or hold fast to such knowledge without faith. That is a new question. The logic of faith and its psychology must be distinguished.[8] What has been said holds for the logic of faith,

---

matter of thoughts that for their part arise out of faith and that have faith as the presupposition of their truth; rather, it would at the very most be a matter of thoughts of faith in the sense that these thoughts have to do with the ground of faith. Knowledge of the ground of faith must, as such, logically precede faith, however.

One may gauge against this how far off the track the criticism is which was raised by Hans Conzelmann against the symposium *Revelation as History*, according to which that volume is supposed to share with Walter Künneth the conception "that historical facts may be postulated on the basis of systematic premises" (*EvTh* 22 [1962]: 218, n. 16). Unfortunately, one can indeed find such things expressly stated by Künneth (*Glauben an Jesus? Die Begegnung der Christologie mit der modernen Existenz* [Hamburg, 1962], p. 286). Nevertheless, it should have been clear to every reader that the authors of the symposium were aiming at the very opposite. "To ground" faith "by historical facts" (Conzelmann, *ibid.*), is certainly something else than postulating such on the basis of systematic premises. The attempt to ground faith on historical facts ought, at the beginning, to have the right to have its historical claim taken seriously by a corresponding criticism, instead of having someone lay it down, without further explanation, that it deals with facts that "cannot be exhibited, but only dogmatically asserted." In any case, the collaborators of that symposium have not made it as easy for themselves in their attempts to establish their theses as Conzelmann has made it for himself in his criticisms.

It is unnecessary to go into the charge of subjectivization of the concept of revelation which was made against me by Günther Klein ("Offenbarung als Geschichte? Marginalien zum einem theologischen Programm," *Monatschrift für Pastoraltheologie* 51 [1962]: 68). That in relation to revelation a merely theoretical attitude is inappropriate, and even less so a merely subjective reflection, runs throughout the above exposition as well as my earlier statements in the symposium previously named.

[8] This distinction is misunderstood, e.g., by H. G. Geyer ("Geschichte als theologisches Problem: Bemerkungen zu W. Pannenbergs Geschichtstheologie," *EvTh* 22 [1962]: 103) when he construes sentences from my "Redemptive Event and History" (see Vol. 1 of this work, pp. 15–80) which correspond to the presentation in this article as contradicting the demand for historical exhibiting of the ground of faith.

viz., that as trust [*fiducia*] it is grounded by a knowledge [*notitia*]. In the psychological enactment of faith, both can be taken up in the same act. Trust can also arise in the expectation that the (logically, already presupposed) knowledge will later be disclosed – a fore-conception of the result that is ordinarily characteristic not only of the attitude of faith but also of the cognitive process generally. One conjecturingly anticipates the result, but must then confirm this conjecture, find verification of it. Furthermore, believing trust can also arise in such a way that the believer does not always have to prove on his own the trustworthiness of the knowledge presupposed therein. It is the special task of theology to do this. Not every individual Christian needs to undertake this task. He can trust on the assumption that things are in order with respect to the ground of his trust. This point of view presupposes, of course, an atmosphere of confidence in the reliability of the Christian tradition which has more and more been lost in the course of the last century, and not last of all by theology's reneging. This atmosphere of the reliability of what the pastor has to preach – so far as it deals with a knowledge – must always be freshly established, and one might think that theology, in full critical openness, would devote all of its energies to this task.

I would not like to distinguish the knowledge logically presupposed by *fiducia*, or which in a broader sense of the term is included in faith, from natural knowledge, as Althaus does.[9] I admit that I cannot understand any knowledge as other than "natural." And I cannot free myself of the suspicion that the distinguishing of a special knowledge of faith leads once again to the conclusion that the truth of such knowledge can be justified, in the last analysis, only by a decision of faith.[10]

Günther Klein also fails to note this distinction, and therefore holds this misunderstanding against me as a contradiction (cf. "Offenbarung als Geschichte?" p. 83).

[9] "Offenbarung als Geschichte und Glaube," col. 325.

[10] I am well aware that this demurrer runs counter to the whole tradition of distinguishing between natural and supernatural knowledge. It is worth noting in this connection that both sides of this disjunction are equally problematical. For this reason it is not a matter of simply striking out one

Reference to the message does not help here at all, since it only raises the question whether the message is true. When its truth does not convince my power of judgment, then its acknowledgment becomes just a matter of decision, and thereby we return again to the ruinous consequence that faith grounds itself, and so distorts that which is essential to it, viz., its dependence upon a truth outside itself. If the moment of decision becomes foundational for the structure of faith, then the bond with truth "outside myself" [*extra me*] is irretrievably lost. Psychologically speaking, the decision of faith can well have the form of an anticipation of future insight, or of simply resting on the presupposition of the truth of what is believed. But, logically, it must remain grounded upon possible insight.

One cannot run away from the dilemma of the question of truth in relation to the Christian message by appealing to the Holy Spirit, for instance. I opposed this misuse of the Holy Spirit in *Revelation as History*. An otherwise unconvincing message cannot attain the power to convince simply by appealing to the Holy Spirit. The fact that the one who is convinced by the message confesses that this apprehension was affected in him by the Holy Spirit[11] must not be misunderstood as if the

---

side (e.g., the supernatural). The whole that has been divided by this separation must be rethought in its unity.

[11] Perhaps I have misleadingly formulated this point in saying that the Holy Spirit is "not the condition without which the Christ-event could not be recognized as revelation' (*Revelation as History*, p. 36), as if the Spirit had nothing at all to do with the origin of faith. That this was not intended should, in any case, have been clear already from the very next sentence, which continued that the Spirit is received "by faith in the gospel, which for its part belongs to the realm of the Spirit insofar as it tells about an eschatological event" (*ibid.*). The sense in which the Spirit should not be claimed for the knowledge of faith, the sense in which its possession does not represent a condition for faith, follows from the remark on the preceding page that no "*additional* perfecting" of man's cognitive power is necessary – additional, in the sense that apart from the gospel and the power of truth emanating from it still another presupposition would be necessary in order for its truth to be apprehended. The Spirit does not join itself to the gospel as something additional. It is rather the case that the proclaimed eschatological event and, proceeding from it, even the process of proclaiming the gospel is itself Spirit-filled. For this reason, the hearer receives a share in the Spirit in attaining a share in the essential content of the gospel, in relying

Spirit were taken to be the criterion of the truth of the message. On the contrary, it is much more the assurance that one is speaking in the power of the Holy Spirit that is itself in need of a criterion for its credibility (1 Cor. 12:1f.), and this criterion is the testimony to the Lord Jesus Christ (1 Cor. 12:3), thus, the content of the message. The convincingness of the Christian message can stem only from its contents. Where this is not the case, the appeal to the Holy Spirit is no help at all to the preacher. He may, perhaps, assert that he has the Holy Spirit as warrant for the truth of what he says. But if he has nothing else to introduce by which to establish his assertions, he ought not to wonder that no one accepts them. If, however, the preacher desires to convince his audience's power of judgment, then the Holy Spirit becomes effective through his words and arguments. Argumentation and the operation of the Spirit are not in competition with each other. In trusting in the Spirit, Paul in no way spread himself thinking and arguing. On the other hand, Luther used hard words against a "bragging about the Spirit" [*iactantia spiritus*] at a point where it was a matter of establishing an assertion on the basis of Scripture.[12]

The question of whether the message that is preached to me is true can only be answered out of its content, by referring to that whereof it reports and to the *inherent* meaning of the reported event. This is the knowledge that faith (logically) must presuppose if it is not to be debased into a self-empowered decision. This knowledge is identical with "historical faith" [*fides historica*] or "historical knowledge" [*notitia historica*], in the terminology of the Reformers. In recent times, so many confusing things have been written about this concept that one must first clear away the rubbish of pre-judgments that have covered up the sense of the Reformation's rejection of a *mere* (!) "historical faith." Two points are involved here, above all.

---

upon what he has heard – and only in this way, for the operation of the Spirit of God in the creation remains utterly hidden.

[12] *Martin Luther on "The Bondage of the Will,"* trans. J. I. Packer and O. R. Johnston (Westwood, N. J.: Fleming H. Revell Co.; London: James Clarke & Co., 1957), p. 124 [=*WA* 18, p. 653].

In the first place, to the best of my knowledge, "saving faith" [*fides salvifica*] is not set in absolute opposition to the "historical knowledge" [*notitia* (also *fides* [faith] or *opinio* [opinion]) *historica*], but is regularly described by a "not only . . . but also" [*non solum . . . sed etiam*] or some similar expression.[13] This means, however, that the fundamental significance of "history" for faith remains a self-evident presupposition, so that the sixteenth century could, and in fact did, take it this way. But the *mere* acknowledgment of the history was not enough. It had to be grasped instead as an event that has a *bearing on me*. This "for me" [*pro me*] significance of the history really does not add anything to its content, for at this point it is a matter of the influence [*effectus*] of the history itself, or of the purpose that belongs to it [*finis historiae*], viz., insofar as this history has an intrinsically promissory character. One must therefore say that in saving faith, in the apprehension of its significance for me, the history of Jesus first receives the acknowledgment that it deserves and which matches its unique character. *Mere* historical faith, which is satisfied with the establishment that the event happened and does not allow itself to be grasped by this event, thus has precisely not understood aright the inherent meaning of this history, but has diminished it.

Secondly, the "historical knowledge" [*notitia historica*] comprises not only what historical positivism would allow as history, but also Jesus' resurrection from the dead and the incarnation.[14] For this reason, Luther could say in an earlier statement that

[13] So, the Augsburg Confession, art. 20, sec. 23 (*BC*, p. 44). Cf. Melanchthon, *CR* 21, p. 743: *non tantum* ["not so much"]; *ibid.*, p. 176: "*Nondum . . . sed . . . etiam . . .*" ["not yet . . . but . . . also"]; Apol. 4, 51: "*non satis est . . . nisi addimus*" ["it is not enough . . . unless we add" (*BC*, p. 114)]. Luther also spoke in a similar way, e.g., *WA* 29, p. 197; *non solum* ["not only"]; ". . . *wens 'mein' dazu* (!) *kompt, est alia fides quam absque 'mein'* " (*ibid.*) [". . . when 'my' supervenes on it (!), faith is there in another way than without 'my.' "]; cf. *WA* 27, p. 105.

[14] Cf. for instance, "*Bondage of the Will*," p. 7of., 73f. [=*WA* 18, pp. 606, 608f.] where, it is true, the *fides historica* is not directly mentioned, but rather the outer clarity of Scripture, which corresponds to it. Further, see again the Augsburg Confession, art. 20, sec. 23 (*BC*, p. 44), as well as Melanchthon, *CR* 21, pp. 176f.

"unformed faith" [*fides informis*] does not yet designate faith (as act), so much as the object of faith, that which is to be believed.[15] Thus, it does not correspond to the Reformation conception to say, as Althaus does, that the "historical faith" is "not yet 'knowledge of God's revelation' in the events."[16] The limit of the "historical faith" is not that the significance of the events is inaccessible to it, so that it is able to view these events only as bare facts. This distinction is closer to the neo-Kantian juxtaposition of fact and value than it is to the Reformation conception. On the contrary, the real defect of *mere* historical faith is that it stops at the level of historical knowledge,[17] and does not let itself be drawn into the event but instead gapes at it as if it were only a theatrical production, so to speak. The fact that such a drama is, for the Reformers – against Althaus –, an altogether divine one changes nothing with respect to the fact that by this mode of viewing man withholds himself and so does not participate in the redemptive meaning of the history. Mere knowledge of God's revelation does not yet make one a participant in the salvation included therein. Only when man relies upon this in that he trustingly takes this event as the ground on which he stands does he receive a share in that. Salvation is received only in the act of trust, which is essentially self-surrender, in the exact, literal sense of a placing of one's reliance entirely upon that to which one entrusts himself. The knowledge of that which faith believes cannot displace the act of self-abandonment in trust. But this does not alter anything with regard to the fact that faith (in the narrower sense, as trust) presupposes such a knowledge; otherwise its essence would be perverted into self-salvation by means of the so-called decision of faith. In order to be in a position to trust, one must experience as reality whatever it is he is supposed to build upon.

---

[15] *Luther: Lectures on Romans*, trans. and ed. Wilhelm Pauck, The Library of Christian Classics 15 (Philadelphia: Westminster Press, 1961), p. 18 [= *WA* 56, pp. 172f.].

[16] "Offenbarung als Geschichte und Glaube," col. 325.

[17] Luther formulated the matter this way in the *Disputation on Faith and the Law*, Thesis 17 (*LW* 34, p. 110 [= *WA* 39/1, p. 45]).

And if believing trust is to be distinguished from thoughtlessness and superstitition, then the man or event on which it is built must be found trustworthy. Nor, for instance, can knowledge of the decisive factor of the content of the Christ event, namely, its revelatory character, first be added to it by faith itself, as Althaus has it. For then we are back once again at self-salvation by the decision of faith. Only the revelation of God in this event is the ground of faith! According to the Pauline and the Reformer's conception, at any rate, the knowledge which (logically) underlies faith comprises everything *wherein* faith believes, even precisely the revelatory character of the Christ event, as was shown above. Only in this way is faith's vital interest in being rooted beyond itself, beyond its decision, secured. In comparison, Althaus's effort to hold to both a historical knowledge presupposed in faith, as well as grounding the knowledge of God's revelation in faith itself – Althaus explicitly says "grounded" [*begründet*] in col. 325! – looks to me like a combination of heterogeneous ideas.[18] Althaus' thinking here is in the tradition of C. L. Nitzsch's concept of revelation, which became highly influential through Rothe. This view accepts the idea of the supplementation of a manifestation which takes place in external occurrences by adding to this an inspiration which empowers one to appreciate the significance of the events. It must be asked here what the function of this inspiration is. Is it necessary only because the inherent meaning of the events cannot be perceived straight off, although it is possible in principle to exhibit this from the given features of the events?

---

[18] See also the statement of Bultmann, worked out from an entirely different viewpoint, that Althaus "does not make clear the origin of faith. Faith does not at all arise from the acceptance of historical facts. That would only lead to legitimizing, whereas the kerygma calls for faith. And when according to Althaus, the 'kerygmatic content of preaching' (that is, 'the confession of the *saving significance* of what has happened') touches the hearer's conscience and requires that he 'relate what has happened to (his) existence,' of what use then is historical legitimation?" (Rudolf Bultmann, "The Primitive Christian Kerygma and the Historical Jesus," in *The Historical Jesus and the Kerygmatic Christ*, trans. and ed. Carl E. Braaten and Roy A. Harrisville [New York and Nashville: Abingdon Press, 1964], p. 25.)

In this case, the inspiration does not make any substantive addition to the event. If Althaus should have only this state of the case in mind, then there is no opposition between us. The point that the revelatory event cannot even in fact be recognized as such by man without further qualification will be dealt with shortly. The situation is different, however, if Althaus means that a meaning is attached to the event by means of inspiration which could not be traced to the event itself either beforehand or afterward. Then, the inspiration would involve a substantive augmentation of what was perceived in the events, and in this case I do not know how one will be able to avoid the consequence that faith would accept the thoughts of the apostles as true without making a proper judgment. From my point of view, this line of thought eventuates at the decisive point in a sacrifice of the intellect in relation to the apostolic message, and this would be only the reverse side of the capricious kind of faith that was rejected above. To be sure, Althaus' meaning is not that the *facts* but only the appreciation of their *meaning* as the revelation of God stands in need of a supplementary inspiration. But even the meaning is not to be left, say, to the taste of the individual. If the events were understood in their context, in their connection with the history of the transmission of tradition, their original meaning would be recognizable in the events themselves. A subsequently appended significance must therefore run into competition with the original meaning inhering in the events. The pure facts of positivistic historiography are already the products of an abstraction; an abstraction from both the interest of the historian who gathers and selects the events according to their weightiness, as well from the nexuses in which the events originally stood. It is simply not the case that one can take uninterpreted, established facts and then subsequently ascribe to them this or that meaning as one wishes, so that one could, for instance, also place a revelatory meaning on the list next to other equally possible meanings. On the contrary, events always bring their original meaning along with them from the context to which they have been assigned by their having happened. With reference to the Christ event, it is a matter of the God of Israel having revealed his deity in this event – a conviction that, I admit, can be justified only in view of the universal connection of all events, and therefore always stands to come under new discussion.

The discussion up to now has not aimed at disputing the fact that – not with respect to the truth of the contents of the Christian message, but certainly with respect to the psychological process of its apprehension – an illumination is necessary in order for that which is true in itself to appear evident in this character to a man. I am completely at one with Althaus in affirming that Paul "views the fact that men have come to faith as a gift of God,"[19] nor should I want to dispute the appropriateness of this view. It is really a banal fact that men are by no means always enlightened by that which is in itself true and right, or even as having been demonstrated to be true and right. Thus, much that is true beyond any doubt, and strictly demonstrable, is accepted as true by most men only because others, and indeed the majority of those one believes capable of judgment, affirm it as true. A new and unfamiliar-sounding truth, on the other hand, even when it is strictly demonstrable, is by no means evident to all at once. Rather, they persist in non-understanding until it, as one says, has "prevailed" [*durchgesetzt*]. This shows that materially and logically impeccable grounding is *one* thing, but the consent of man is very often quite another matter. Not infrequently the way to insight into a truth that is in itself most evident is barred by pre-judgments. And the more the vital interest accompanying a specific question, the more do the pre-judgments have a habit of being stiff-necked. Yes, indeed: "measured by our natural human criteria of the knowability and clarity of God . . ."[20] the Christ event may appear obscure, and "its divinity hidden for all who confront the Gospel with the criteria provided by their religion."[21] For this reason I have said that men must first be brought to reason in order that they may also really perceive the event that reveals the truth of God's deity. For this truth,

[19] "Offenbarung als Geschichte und Glaube," col. 324.
[20] *Ibid.*, col. 328.   [21] *Ibid.*, col. 324.

as evident as it is in itself,[22] and no matter how much it may also be presented as evident – otherwise faith would be without foundation – is opposed by pre-judgments which commonly prejudice men. It is true that the sweeping away of such pre-judgments can never be a matter of rational argument alone because these pre-judgments are themselves irrationally rooted, provided that we *are* dealing with pre-judgments. To this extent, a kind of illumination is needed in order for the truth, which is clear in itself and demonstrable as true, to dawn upon the individual man, too. Nevertheless, it can dawn upon him in a way that sweeps out the pre-judgments only on the pre-supposition that it is clear in itself and is – if not yet, then still in principle and at least in the future – demonstrable as true. Without this presupposition, faith would lapse into superstition, the essence of which is the opposition of its contents to what the superstitious person knows or could very well know. The fight over the Christian faith since the Enlightenment may be

---

[22] I am alarmed by the fact that Althaus not only speaks of a "relative concealment" of revelation "measured against our natural human norms" (*ibid.*, col. 328) but also affirms, beyond this, "that the possibility of unbelief is also grounded in the manner of God's revelation" (*ibid.*). For this threatens faith's certainty. Althaus himself sees that his assertion has put him in contradiction with Paul (2 Cor. 4:3f.), who understands unbelief – precisely in the way Althaus rejected – as entirely "sinful delusion" and explicitly opposes talk of the gospel being "veiled!" The "divine incognito" was just (against Althaus, *ibid*) what was broken through at Easter by the "revelation of the mystery which was kept secret for long ages but is now disclosed" and proclaimed to the nations (Rom. 16:25f.; cf. Col. 1:26; Eph. 3:5; 1 Pet. 1:20). To be sure, even the believer is freed from delusion only by the power of God, by the power of truth in the revelatory event. And it is indeed the case that the believer, too, has to struggle against temptations which seek to darken this truth's power for him. So he, too, has an appreciation of the situation of the unbeliever. But isn't the only thing that can sustain him against collapse into unbelief certainty about the truth of the revelation in Jesus Christ? If he cannot at least presuppose this, even in hours in which it becomes opaque for him, how will he be able to withstand temptation and how should he be able to hope that the light of truth will dawn even among unbelievers? The meaning of the proof of the truth of the message in the conscience of man, of which Paul speaks in 2 Cor. 4, is in fact not primarily an *ethical* one, as Althaus seems to have assumed (*ibid.*, col. 327). It is not a matter of obedience without insight but a matter of obedience to the truth which is realized by means of conviction.

tentatively described as the fight over the question whether the Christian faith is true faith or superstition. I think that even Althaus cannot find this concern "odd."[23]

The illumination that is necessary in order to clear away the pre-judgments standing in the way of unencumbered perception of the event that reveals God thus, in the nature of the case, adds nothing substantive to the content of this event or to the content of the message that reports about it and its meaning. Even Althaus says that the operation of the Holy Spirit is "nothing else than making the Word itself effective."[24] The process of the apostolic kerygma itself may be thought of as an analogue of this. What is involved here is the occurrence in which the attested event becomes effective in human language. The Spirit, who illuminates, leads to the truth of the Word and thereby shows himself to be the power of the Word itself. This Word, however, reports about an event which comes to verbal expression in the message, and even here one will have to judge that such "coming to verbal expression" occurs through the Spirit which belongs intrinsically to the event in question – the ministry and destiny of Jesus. For this reason the Holy Spirit is called the Spirit of Christ. According to the primitive Christian conception, the Spirit is to be understood in close connection with the event of the resurrection of Jesus, in particular. The resurrection reality which has already appeared in Jesus is precisely the Spirit-reality itself, so that the body of the risen one can be called a "Spirit-body" [*Geistleib*]. For this reason, the preaching of the resurrection of the Crucified One is also filled with this new, spiritual reality, and therefore those who believe the message receive a share in this through the proclamation. For this reason, too, although the resurrection life has not yet appeared in believers themselves, they nevertheless have the Spirit already as "earnest money" of the future glory. In the context of what has been said, no special explanation is needed to understand that even faith itself is effected by the Spirit, i.e., by the eschatological reality of new life that has appeared in Christ, of which the Christian message speaks. This

---

[23] Cf. *ibid.*, col. 327, n. 5.   [24] *Ibid.*, col. 327.

means nothing else than that the hearers of the message really receive its content into themselves. It is impossible here to trace all these connections, which can be found in the Pauline literature in particular. But perhaps the references already given suffice to warn against asserting that in the theological projection, *Revelation as History*, there is no place for confession of the Holy Spirit. If the Holy Spirit cannot be spoken of in a way which has to a certain extent become a tradition, that does not by any means signify that no significance at all, or only a subordinate kind, can be ascribed to him.

The tendency toward a subjectivization and individualization of piety, which has threatened the life of our churches and wrought its divisiveness for a long time, expresses itself in an especially crass way in the usual structure of the doctrine of the Holy Spirit. The Holy Spirit is widely taken as a catchword for the view that the content of faith is present only for the pious subjectivity, so that its truth cannot be presented in a way that can claim universal binding force. This widespread attitude makes it possible to preserve only in a very impoverished way what primitive Christianity knew as the reality of the Spirit. If the Spirit is understood as the new life that appeared in Christ, and which operates in our present in a provisional and only initiatory way as our common future, then there is a safeguard against the subjectivistic emptying of the confession of the Holy Spirit. The Spirit of which the New Testament speaks is no "haven of ignorance" [*asylum ignorantiae*] for pious experience, which exempts one from all obligation to account for its contents. The Christian message will not regain its missionary power, nor church life its health, unless this falsification of the Holy Spirit is set aside which has developed in the history of piety especially in reaction against the assaults of the Enlightenment.

Revelation as history and faith? One has to concede to Althaus that the revelation of God first reaches its goal where it effects faith and so becomes manifest to someone. Actually, it reaches its goal only with the glorification of believers in the future of Jesus Christ, in whom all things will be created anew through the Spirit of God, just as Jesus Christ himself has already been raised from the dead by the Spirit of God. Not just faith, but also the glorification of believers belongs to the history of revelation. God's revelation in Jesus Christ is indeed only an anticipation of the final event, which will be the actual revelatory event. And yet, we have the well-founded confidence that the final event will not bring anything decisively new that was not already anticipated in the resurrection of Jesus. To this extent, Jesus is already the revelation of God. That which happened in him will not be substantively augmented by any further events, not even by our faith. For this reason, the matter must remain thus: revelation as history, anticipatorily summed up in Jesus Christ – but *for* faith, which lives between the prolepsis of the end in the Christ event and the universal onset of this end. The proleptic structure of faith (in the future reference of trust) corresponds to the structure of the Christ event, and it is just for this reason that only in faith is this event received in a way appropriate to its peculiar character. Even the insight we may acquire into the revelation of God that occurred in Christ always presupposes a telescoping vision that links the fate of Jesus with the end of the world that is still outstanding for us. To this extent, even talk about the revelation of God in Jesus Christ is proleptic. It occurs in anticipation of the ultimate proof of its truth through the onset of the end itself. This anticipation does not have the character of a subjectively supplementary valorization [*subjektiv ergänzender Deutung*] of a brute fact. Rather, the bracketing of the fate of Jesus with the final event is already grounded in the context of the Israelitic-Jewish tradition in which the Easter event has its original horizon of meaning. An appropriate apprehension of this event is therefore nothing else than one that traces its proleptic structure, but only in such a way that the knower allows himself to be taken up into the movement of faith.[25]

[25] To this extent, with regard to the perception of the Christ event, it is in faith for the first time that "reason fully comes to itself," as Althaus says, to my joy (*ibid.*, col. 327). Althaus rightly says that the act of perception and reception also has its particular character, corresponding to the par-

Trustful anticipation of the future is characteristic of faith, but this anticipation is founded in a corresponding proleptic meaning of the Christ event itself, as it offers itself to knowledge. To this extent, knowledge of the revelatory event establishes the believing trust in which it issues. This knowledge is not a stage that surpasses faith, as the gnosticisms of every age have held. Rather, if it is genuine, the opposite is true; knowledge issues in believing trust. Christian knowledge stands under the sign of the same "already" and "not yet" that marks every aspect of the life of Christians between the resurrection and the second coming of Jesus. But the resurrectional reality of the Spirit, which also makes all things manifest, is not only that which has "not yet" appeared in us insofar as we indeed still live in this dying form of life. Rather, starting from the resurrection of Jesus, it is for us, too, the "already" present guarantee of salvation because it is presently known truth.

---

ticularity of the Christ event – precisely to the extent that it is stamped by its content. I attempt to do justice to this point in the arguments presented above.

3

FAITH AND REASON

A lecture delivered before the theological faculty in Marburg on July 6, 1965, and in Hamburg on June 6, 1966. The introduction has been revised for publication.

THE RELATIONSHIP between faith and reason has been a problem since the beginning of Christian theology. On the one hand, theology is itself a process of thought, and one must hope that it is pursued in a rational manner. On the other hand, however, "reason," as commonly understood, can scarcely have the last word in theology without violating the exaltedness of the reality of God and his revelation above all human conceptualization. It was not by accident that the structure of the relationship between faith and reason in history has been charged with tensions. The Christian faith manifestly cannot withdraw from every kind of cooperation with rational thought. Some such cooperation is implied in the commissioning of the Christian message to all men, with the task of preaching the message convincingly as the truth which is universally binding. Yet, the Christian faith cannot thereby simply dissolve into what, in a variety of very different accentuations since the Greek beginning of our philosophical tradition, has at some given time been called "reason." Explicit reflection upon the togetherness and cooperation of faith and reason that takes place in all Christian thought must begin with the clarification of the tension that exists here. This point holds even if this relationship should be understood as a unity-in-tension [*Spannungseinheit*] and not as simply an opposition. Even someone who is concerned about the overarching unity of faith and reason will be unable to ignore the difference which is always breaking out anew between them, stemming from the duality of the spiritual roots not only of Christian theology but of our traditions generally insofar as they go back to Israel and Christianity, on the one hand, and Greek antiquity, on the other.

For Christians, the perfect unity of faith and reason has been promised for the eschaton only (1 Cor. 13:12f.). Nevertheless, Christian eschatology does not mean simply that one should keep watch for a still-outstanding future and thereby become alienated from the present. On the contrary, the Christian understanding of the eschaton turns one's view back to the present, insofar as the present is also experienced as determined by the coming reign of God. In this sense, should not even the tension between the Greek and Israelitic heritages belonging to our history which has been expressed again and again as the tension between faith and reason be considered in the light of their eschatological unity, so that this would be determinative for our thought already in the present? Is it perhaps the case that even the tension between faith and reason is possible only on the presupposition of a unity which encompasses both, namely, the presupposition of the unity of truth?

Concern about what it is that first makes possible a preliminary unity of faith and reason has a special urgency today. For the tension between faith and reason has sharpened into an opposition in the modern period and, despite all attempts to reconcile them, has finally snapped in many quarters and changed into a disconnected juxtaposition.

Harsh opposition between faith and reason had already appeared, of course, in the ancient and medieval churches. In the history of theology, Tertullian, Peter Damian, and Luther especially went down as opponents of reason. Nevertheless, all three made use of reason despite their sharp judgments upon reason and philosophy. The same Tertullian who asked what Athens had to do with Jerusalem, or the Academy with the church, and who wanted to affirm nothing that went beyond faith,[1] admitted Stoic thought into theology in a very risky way, for example, by conceiving God and the soul as special kinds

[1] Tertullian *De praescriptione haereticorum* 7 [see *ANF* 3, p. 246].

of bodies.[2] Peter Damian, who damned philosophy as an invention of the devil, at the same time used a dialectical-philosophical path to refute attacks on the omnipotence of God, and formulated the principle that philosophy should serve theology as a maid.[3] Finally, Luther could certainly term reason a "monster," "the source of all evil," and "the blind whore of the Devil."[4] He never tired of stressing that the gospel is "against all reason." However, the same Luther not only esteemed reason as the highest court of appeal in the natural, worldly realm, but also affirmed the cooperation in the realm of theology of a reason illuminated by faith and the Holy Spirit. Lastly, at Worms, Luther appealed not only to Scripture but also to the clear evidence of reason [*ratio evidens*] as the judges of his case.[5]

The relative opposition of faith and reason which was occasionally – by no means predominantly – championed in the ancient and medieval churches, was marked by the tension between free, rational insight and obligation to an authoritative norm.

Wherein lies the real reason for the fact that Christian doctrine can never be transformed completely and without remainder into rational insights, but rather must always be assigned to the custody of an authoritative norm such as Scripture or the teaching office of the church? Augustine traced this state of affairs back to the fact that the genuine truths of faith deal with historical facts.[6] The ancients were convinced that there can be no science of the historical in the strict sense

[2] *Ad Praxean* 7 [see *ANF* 3, pp. 601f.].

[3] *MPL* 145, 603D.

[4] Cf. *LW* 40, p. 175 [= *WA* 18, p. 164, ll. 25f.]; *A Commentary on St.Paul's Epistle to the Galatians* (based on the lectures of 1531, published in 1535; London: James Clarke & Co., 1953), p. 224 [= *WA* 40/1, p. 365, ll. 18f.]. On this matter see also Bernard Lohse, *Ratio und Fides: Eine Untersuchung über die ratio in der Theologie Luthers* (Göttingen, 1958), pp. 72f.; and Paul Althaus, *The Theology of Martin Luther*, trans. Robert C. Schultz (Philadelphia: Fortress Press, 1960), pp. 64ff.

[5] Lohse, *Ratio und Fides*, pp. 112f.; cf. pp. 98ff.

[6] *On True Religion* 25, 46; in *Augustine: Earlier Writings*, trans. J. H. S. Burleigh, Library of Christian Classics 6 (Philadelphia: Westminster Press, 1963), p. 247.

because science always deals with the universal, whereas historical accounts have to do with events which are always particular and occur only once. To the extent that historical knowledge does not rest upon eyewitness testimony or at least on interrogation of eyewitnesses, it is referred to the credibility, the authority, of a tradition. For this reason, then, genuine truths of faith cannot be fully transparent to reason, but must always be believed.[7] Thus, the reference of the Christian message to the historical and the necessity of belief on the basis of authority belong together, for Augustine. To be sure, this faith does not consist only in accepting what the authority says, but therein it takes the "step from the visible to the invisible, from the visible or verifiable authority of the witnesses, such as the church, to the invisible matter which the witnesses report."[8] Correspondingly, however, the eyewitnesses of the history of Christ must also have already made the step from the visible man to his invisible deity, and it is in this that faith consists. Luther placed the greatest emphasis on this aspect of the Augustinian concept of faith when he repeatedly stressed, appealing to Hebrews 11:1, that faith, in contrast to reason, is a certitude about that which man does not see. In this connection, Luther gives the phrase "what man does not see" the sense of "that which is future." "And while reason is wont to concern itself with the things that are present, faith apprehends the things that are not present and, contrary to reason, regards them as being present."[9] Luther, it is well known, set faith as

---

[7] Augustine *On True Religion* 10. 20; in *Augustine: Earlier Writings*, p. 235. On this point cf. Ephraem Hendrikx, "Augustins Verhältnis zur Mystik," in *Zum Augustingespräch der Gegenwart*, ed. Carl Andresen (Cologne, 1962), pp. 271–346, esp. pp. 321ff. See also the following additional references in Augustine: *De 83 quaest.*, q. 48 (*MPL*, Augustine 6, col. 50); and *On the Usefulness of Belief* 11. 25 (in *Augustine: Earlier Writings*, pp. 311f. [= *MPL*, Augustine 8, col. 120BC]).

[8] R. Lorenz, "Gnade und Erkenntnis bei Augustine," *Zeitschrift für Kirchengeschichte* 76 (1964): 21–78. Augustine judges differently in *On the Trinity* 15, 21 (*NPNF*, First Series, 3: 221); cf. Lorenz, "Gnade und Erkenntnis bei Augustine," p. 36.

[9] *LW* 2, p. 267 [= *WA* 42, p. 452, ll. 22ff.: *Ratio praesentibus soleat niti, fides absentia complectitur, et ea contra rationem praesentia esse judicat*]. On this

trust in the invisible in sharp contrast to mere belief on the
basis of authority, the *notitia historiae* ["historical knowledge"].
The two aspects of the Augustinian concept of faith separate
here. However, this does not happen in such a way that Luther
allows acceptance of the veracity of the history simply to be
dropped as inconsequential. Therefore, he characteristically
uses the formulation that one must look *not only* upon the history
but also upon its "fruit."[10] This *"not only – but also"* [*non solum –
sed etiam*] is often overlooked today when people appeal to
Luther's criticisms of "historical faith." His criticism by no
means aimed at making the subjectivity of religious experience,
in Wilhelm Herrmann's sense, or the existential decision of faith
independent of belief on the basis of authority. On the contrary,
Luther said: ". . . So it comes to the point that if one should
forget that history [*illam historiam*], the foundation of faith
would be done away with."[11] Thus, Luther argued for his stress
on the fruit, the significance of the history "for me," completely
within the jurisdictional limits of belief on the basis of authority.
For this reason, the opposition between faith and reason still
remained for him, too, the foundation of statements about the
relationship of faith and reason.

In the modern period, the situation with respect to the problem of the relationship of faith and reason has shifted because
of the fact that the initiative has gone over to the side of reason.
It is no longer a question of whether the authority of the
Christian source of revelation, viz., Scripture, can be accepted
by reason without contradiction. In the modern period the
question is instead whether reason, after it has shown that belief
on the basis of authority is irrational, can still allow any room

---

point, see Lohse, *Ratio und Fides*, p. 103. On the beginnings of this idea in
Luther, see Lohse, pp. 38ff., and also Reinhard Schwarz, *Fides, Spes und
Caritas beim jungen Luther* (Berlin, 1962), pp. 15ff., 50ff.

[10] "Not only the agony, but also the love which suffered for us" ["*non
solum die marter, sed etiam die lieb, quod pro nobis patitur*" (*WA* 37, pp. 22f.) –
translation mine – Tr.]. On this, see Gerhard Ebeling, *Evangelische Evan-
gelienauslegung: Eine Untersuchung zu Luthers Hermeneutik* (Darmstadt, ²1962),
pp. 232f., 412ff.

[11] *WA* 29, p. 657, ll. 3f. [translation mine – Tr.].

at all for the Christian faith. A philosopher like Hume could put the Christian faith on record precisely for its (true or alleged) character as a belief based on authority precisely in order thereby to expose its absurdity. Thus, he states: "Our most holy religion is founded on faith, not on reason, and it is a sure method of exposing it to put it to such a trial as it is by no means fitted to endure,"[12] that is to say, by searching for rational grounds for its assertions. This reference to the irrationality of Christianity is pure derision, since Hume was convinced that Christianity is committed to the affirmation of miracles, the irrationality of which he had demonstrated. For him, therefore, faith is itself a continuing miracle in the person of the believer: "And whoever is moved by *faith* to assent to it, is conscious of a continued miracle in his own person, which subverts all the principles of his understanding, and gives him a determination to believe what is most contrary to custom and experience."[13]

In the face of this modern attack upon the meaningfulness of the Christian faith, theology cannot retreat to the standpoint of authority. The difference between the modern and the medieval situations consists in the fact that the authority of the Christian tradition (be it of the church and its dogmas, or of Holy Scripture) can scarcely be viewed any longer as unproblematically authoritative. As long as the mere authority of Scripture can guarantee the truth of its contents, theology can only demand that reason simply submit to it. In the realm of modern thought, however, where even historical questions are settled not by appeals to authorities but by the new science of historical criticism, persistence in maintaining the authoritative character of faith in contrast to reason takes on a new aspect. This insistence upon an authority that is no longer generally convincing as an authority takes on the character of an external coercion, and an individual's acceptance of such a claim becomes an arbitrary decision – quite the opposite of what it was

---

[12] David Hume, *An Enquiry Concerning Human Understanding* (Chicago: Open Court Pub. Co., 1912), p. 137.
[13] *Ibid.*, p. 138 (italics in original).

earlier, when the acceptance of an authority was grounded in insight into its credibility.[14] If the authority is no longer intelligible as such, and if it no longer convinces our reason of its legitimacy, then all external maintenance of its claim is in vain. For in that case, no matter how much one may emphasize a prior authority, the believer turns himself into the ultimate ground of faith, as Hume incisively showed. For if an asserted authority is no longer able to prove itself convincing to our reason, then its acceptance can come about only by a sacrifice of the intellect and *ergo* as a work of man.

For this reason, the understanding of the kerygma has rightly been joined to faith. The obedience of faith in relation to the kerygma would be an illusory self-salvation by man if it were not motivated by understanding; if it did not mean being won over by the truth of the message. In any case, the question of the truth of the Christian message will not permit of being narrowed down to the theme of self-understanding, but must also be carried out in the realm of the understanding of the world, too, since self-understanding and understanding of the world are always correlative. Therefore the question of the truth of the Christian message involves not only ethical but also theoretical knowledge.

In the modern period, it is true, especially since Kant and Schleiermacher, the attempt has been made to overcome the hopeless opposition between authority and reason by contrasting theoretical reason with religious and ethical *experience*, instead of with an *authority* that had become unintelligible. The authority of the Christian doctrinal tradition was accepted only to the extent that it proved to be an expression of or was confirmed by religious and ethical experience. Nevertheless, the old opposition between reason and faith based on authority continued to exist. The decisive theme was the autonomy of religious experience – sometimes determined more as feeling,

---

[14] Thus, Augustine stated: "No one believes anything unless he has first thought that it is to be believed" (*NPNF*, First Series, 5: 499 [*Nullus quippe credit aliquid, nisi prius cogitaverit esse credendum* (*On the Predestination of the Saints* 2. 5)]). Cf. Lorenz, "Gnade und Erkenntnis bei Augustine," pp. 28, 31.

sometimes related more to conscience – over against theoretical reason. However, the assertion of the independence of religious and ethical experience from theoretical reason is problematical in the extreme, since religious and ethical contents are always mediated by theoretical consciousness. An independence here is at most only partial. In addition, this assertion locates the critical debate between faith and reason solely within the area of self-understanding. The universal validity of a special religious province within the human spirit is what needs to be proven. And beyond this, the peculiar appropriateness of Christian doctrine to this religious disposition must be shown if there is to be any basis for acknowledging the preeminence of Christianity over other religions. If such proofs are not forthcoming, the appeal to experience can draw upon only the experience of the individual and thereby transform the Christian faith completely into a phenomenon of subjectivity, claiming no universal obligatoriness. So understood, however, the appeal to experience once again allows faith to become a work of self-salvation, or – judged externally – the expression of a neurosis, an "uneasiness toward culture." A religious subjectivity of such a sort has found a place in our society only because the understanding of man in positivistic science overlooks this aspect of man, and therefore leaves it vacant for occupation by subjective tastes which nevertheless remain without any universally binding power.

Thus, the task of a rational account of the truth of faith has acquired an ever more acute urgency in the modern period. The appeal to the authority of Scripture and to a proclamation grounded in this is no longer sufficient to establish the legitimacy of faith. And the appeal to religious-ethical experience or to the individual's decision, taken by themselves, can only lead to a subjectivism which is not only non-obligatory for one's fellow-men, but also destroys the essence of faith, since faith is not a work of man but remains faith only as a work of God in man.[15]

---

[15] There has been much talk these days about the death of God. It is supposed that theology must adapt itself to the soil of the modern consciousness for which God is no longer a self-evident presupposition. This does not

If, however, theology admits the necessity of rational account-ability for the Christian faith, the problem we found formulated by Hume immediately arises: Is not modern reason so fashioned that it leaves absolutely no room for Christian faith other than a subjectivity which lacks any intersubjective binding force? Is not any attempt at a rational accounting of the Christian faith foredoomed to vain compromises?

The recent history of theology provides an abundance of material for such a pessimistic conjecture. However, instead of taking an inventory of the theological compromises that have been made with "the" modern reason and its understanding of the world, I want instead to ask whether there really is such a thing as "the" reason, which is so monolithic in form that theology can only be dashed to pieces against it. Are there really compelling reasons to concede to Hume and his positivis-tic followers the pathos of speaking in the name of "the" reason absolutely? Is it necessary to acknowledge as the *non plus ultra* of historical reason a certain kind of historical positivism that allows the uniqueness of events to be lost on the basis of a postulated homogeneity of all events? Theology could still have the task of inspecting more minutely such sorts of absolute claims put forth in the name of reason. Only in this way will it be possible to obtain a critical concept of reason and knowledge that will for the first time make it possible to give a rational account of the truth of the Christian message and thereby would itself already be a step on the way to such an account.

Upon closer inspection, "reason" is by no means a uniformly determined entity. For this reason, even the relationship be-tween faith and reason has been presented in very different ways, each according to what has been understood as reason. Naturally, the same applies to the understanding of faith, too. We have already spoken about that. Regarding the ambiguity

---

exclude, however, the possibility of a justification of God-talk. To this extent, the catchword "death of God" is misleading. The truth in it must be taken seriously by theology, however. Every theological statement must prove itself on the field of reason, and can no longer be argued on the basis of unquestioned presuppositions of faith.

in the understanding of reason, I will limit myself to three typical forms. We will examine *a priori* reason; the so-called receiving reason [*vernehmende Vernunft*]; and historical reason.

(1) The reason [*ratio*] of which Luther spoke was the Aristotelian-Thomistic understanding of reason. Characteristic of this understanding of reason is the distinction between and co-ordination of reason [*ratio*] and intellect [*intellectus*]. According to Thomas, reason and intellect are related to each other as movement and rest.[16] The intellect lives in serene contemplation of the truth. Reason, on the other hand, moves from one representation [*Vorstellung*] to another in its ranging about [*discursus*] in order to lay hold of the one truth that binds all truths together. The intellect does not need to engage in such discursive thought. It intuitively sees that which the reason can attain only as the result of its *discursus*.

According to Thomas, human knowledge is not yet of a perfectly intellectual sort. In contrast to angels, we are not able to have an unmediated view of the true essences of things. This is implied in the fact that the human soul is bound to the body so that all its knowledge must derive from sense impressions and not from immediate comprehension of the substance [*substantia*] of things. For this reason we need ratiocination [*ratiocinari*], discursive reasoning. But the process of ratiocination would not be possible without a firm starting point. This starting point is given in the fact that we at least possess general principles that are immediately evident. This "intuition of the principles" ["*intellectus principiorum*"] constitutes the point of departure for the activity of reason in theoretical knowing. The "practical" reason proceeds in a perfectly analogous way, its judgments likewise resting upon a knowledge of principles which, in this case, have their seat in the conscience. As the theoretical principles of the intellect are applied by the reason to sense impressions, so the practical principles of the *synderesis* are applied by the conscience to individual acts.[17]

---

[16] *Summa Theologiae*, pt. 1, quest. 79, art. 8 [in *Basic Writings of St Thomas Aquinas*, ed. Anton C. Pegis (New York: Random House, 1945), p. 759].

[17] [The term "conscience" here stands for Aquinas' *conscientia*, which

We have here a form of aprioristic conception of reason, for all knowledge occurs as an application to the data of experience of principles already contained in the intellect. It could now be shown that this aprioristic understanding of reason goes back to Augustine and was formulated by him in contrast to Plato, as by Thomas in contrast to Aristotle, in order to avoid a confusion of the human spirit with God. However, we will limit ourselves to the relationship between reason, so conceived, and faith.

It is clear that the activity of reason conceived as the application of given principles to sense impressions cannot be open to something that is not congruous with these principles. Luther's sharp judgments upon reason are to be understood in the light of this insight. The contents of the Christian faith could not be derived from these *a priori* principles. In relation to Aristotelian reason, therefore, these contents had to be regarded as suprarational and supranatural, i.e., situated beyond the natural range of reason. Thomas Aquinas had in fact related faith and reason to each other in this way. The supranatural truths of faith must step into the place of natural principles of knowledge, the light of faith in place of the light of nature, in order that the knowledge of faith may occur.[18] In a similar sense, the young Luther also accepted an illumination of the intellect by the supernatural truths of faith,[19] and later could still praise reason illuminated by faith as much as he disparaged natural

---

designates the act of applying moral principles to particular acts, in contrast to *synderesis* which is the seat of knowledge of the primary principles of morals (cf. *Summa Theologiae*, pt. 1, quest. 79, arts. 12–13). Thus, our ordinary usage of the term "conscience" to designate some kind of inherent moral arbiter in man is closer to *synderesis* than to "conscience" as used in the sentence above. – Tr.]

[18] *Summa Theologiae*, pt. 1, quest. 12, art. 5 [in *Basic Writings of St Thomas Aquinas*, pp. 98f.].

[19] Cf. Lohse, *Ratio und Fides*, pp. 38ff., on the positive evaluation of *intellectus* in Luther's lectures on the Psalms. Lohse, however, does not go into the connection between this and the scholastic determination of the relationship between intellect and reason and with the understanding of the knowledge of faith as supernatural illumination of the intellect by the truths of faith.

reason.[20] As an Ockhamist, Luther felt the opposition of Christian faith to natural reason more sharply than Thomas Aquinas. Nevertheless, their common involvement with the Aristotelian conception of reason cannot be overlooked.

Luther's evaluation of reason easily lends itself to being carried over to the Kantian understanding of reason. For Kant, too, rational activity is thought of as the application of *a priori* principles to the material of experience.[21] Thus, in relation to the Kantian aprioristic concept of reason, Luther's placing of the knowledge of faith in opposition to reason is still actual today. It would then have to be said, in any case, that to accord with Luther's sense, the Kantian reason would have to have new principles established in it by faith. In contrast to this, the usual theological Kantianisms of both rationalistic and supranaturalistic mintage, with their confinement to practical reason, to the ethical, can precisely not appeal to Luther.

In any case, the history of the relationship between philosophy and theology clearly shows that this illumination of the reason which Luther had in mind cannot result from an infusion of supernatural principles. The truths of faith imposed as supernatural principles are always felt, by a reason that understands itself as knowing by means of principles, to be nothing but fetters that have to be struck off, and not as the fulfillment of the essence of reason (which is what illumination really meant in Platonic thought).

(2) Thus, we have to ask whether another understanding of reason is possible which would open up a more meaningful relationship between faith and reason. In philosophical thought since Hamann, Herder, and Jacobi, the idea of "reception"[22] which lies in the word "reason" [*Vernunft*] has been set forth in opposition to the Kantian aprioristic form of reason. Thus, for

[20] *Ibid.*, pp. 98ff.

[21] Kant, as is well known, reversed the relationship between reason and intellect in this connection. The intellect [*Verstand*] is now taken as subordinate to the power of reason [*Vernunft*], which is taken as the higher cognitive power.

[22] [*Des Vernehmens* – interpreted from its roots, *ver-* (= "away from") and *nehmen* (= "take" or "receive") – Tr.]

example, Herder said that reason is no "innate automaton" but that the word "reason" [*Vernunft*] points to something's having been apprehended [*etwas Vernommenes*].[23] Today, the formula "receiving reason" has been renewed by Wilhelm Kamlah above all, in opposition to the self-mastering reason of the modern age which is bent on the domination of what is present at hand.[24] For Kamlah, the model of receiving reason is Platonic insight, which receives the pre-existing forms of true being through a sudden illumination. Receiving reason means in this case the reception of that which is, in contrast to the creative character of modern reason. Now such a "receptive" reason seems to be related to faith, as Jacobi already believed. Would it not also receive a supernatural revelation as such, instead of dissolving it by criticism? If one looks into the matter more closely, however, it becomes apparent that this receiving reason is oriented toward something entirely different from the Christian faith, at any rate. What it receives is, in accord with Platonic intuition, just what the Parmenidean "mind" [*nous*] received, namely, that which always is. Faith, on the other hand, is directed toward something future, or toward him who promises and guarantees something future. The future played no role in the Greek understanding of receiving reason, as Gerhard Krüger pointed out, because the historicness of thought and of truth had not been discovered.[25] The historicness of truth, however, is not something first achieved in modern times, but already constituted a fundamental conviction of Israelitic thought. Hans von Soden showed this in his Marburg chancellor's address of 1927.[26] For the Israelite, as indeed for the Greek, truth was characterized by constancy and the reliability based on this. But the Israelite did not search for this reliable reality

---

[23] Herder, *Ideen zur Philosophie der Geschichte der Menschheit*, reissue of 1st ed. (Berlin, 1965), vol. 1, bk. 4, chap. 4.

[24] Wilhelm Kamlah, *Der Mensch in der Profanität: Versuch einer Kritik der profanen durch vernehmende Vernunft* (Stuttgart, 1949).

[25] Gerhard Krüger, *Grundfragen der Philosophie: Geschichte, Wahrheit, Wissenschaft* (Frankfurt on the Main, 1958), pp. 87f.

[26] *Was ist Wahrheit? Vom geschichtlichen Begriff der Wahrheit*, Marburger akademische Reden 46 (Marburg, 1927).

behind sense appearances, as if it were an imperturbable, timelessly present reality. Rather, for the Israelite, what is reliable
and true is that which the future will bring forth,[27] namely, that
which will prove itself to be reliable. Obviously, the final future
is of decisive importance in this view. To this extent, the
Israelitic understanding of truth is, at least implicitly, fundamentally eschatological. And because the truth is futural, it
therefore cannot be comprehended by the sort of reason (*nous*,
as in Parmenides) that is directed toward what is contem-
poraneously present. Rather, it can only be grasped by faith,
which trusts in him who will in the future prove himself truly
reliable.

In the history of theology, receiving reason, in the Greek
sense of a perception of what always is, has repeatedly obstructed
understanding of the historical truth of the promising God, on
which faith depends. As opposed to this, faith which, according
to Hebrews 11:1, is oriented toward future things permits the
question of historicness to be posed to reason as well. For if the
truly constant being first comes to light in the future, then such
historicness of truth must also have an influence upon reason,
at least to the extent that every unhistorical self-understanding
of reason and of the truth toward which it is oriented could be
condemned to defeat.

(3) A historical reason is by no means a mere theoretical
postulate. Rather, the discovery of the historic character of
reason designates the main direction in which the understanding of reason has been deepened since Kant.

A point of departure for this development already existed in
Kant, insofar as the "productive power of the imagination,"
creative fantasy, constituted the genuinely vital core of his
concept of reason, since the gathering together of the manifold-
ness of experience into a unified representation, the synthesis, is
an achievement of the imagination. Kant believed that knowledge won in this way "in its beginning, indeed, may be crude
and confused, and is therefore in need of analysis – still, synthesis is that by which alone the elements of our cognitions are

[27] *Ibid.*, p. 15.

collected and united into a certain content."[28] To be sure, Kant failed to take note of the creative profuseness of the activity of imagination, which is always bringing forth something new, for the creative imagination was concerned only to educe the forms of an *a priori* reason. But should not precisely the creative imagination break out of a closed system of that sort in that it may hit upon something quite different?

That has in fact happened, and was accomplished, indeed, by means of the discovery of the reflective structure of thought that was worked out along the way that led from Fichte to Hegel. Every insight is but a stage on the way to new insight. Since thought knows not only the object known, but also knows its knowledge of its object in that it constantly reflects upon itself, it never fails to run up against the limits of its knowledge in comparison with that which this knowledge claims to know. Thus, through the movement of reflection, imagination is called upon to bring forth ever new syntheses. What appeared in Kant as a rigid, permanently fixed structure of reason was dissolved by means of the principle of reflection into a process which continually moves forward from one stage to another. Such a process of reflection determined the systematic structure of Fichte's science of knowledge and Hegel's phenomenology and logic. But Hegel still conceived this process of reflection as a progression that from the very outset was undertaken of necessity. Therefore, in his philosophy, reflection fulfilled itself by becoming absolute in the Notion [*Begriff*]. Hegel did not see that every advance to a new synthesis in his own thought had in fact the character of an irreducible achievement of imagination, in the Kantian sense of an imagination that productively generates syntheses. This reflection of ours about the nature of the Hegelian process of thought demolishes its claim of having brought this process to completion in the Notion. What remains is an open process of a reflective movement of thought in which thought continually circles back on itself, and by its own movement runs up against the difference it thereby recognizes

[28] *Critique of Pure Reason*, trans. J. M. D. Meikeljohn (London: George Bell and Sons, 1884), p. 63.

between itself and its object. This process reaches new stages by ever new syntheses which, like all earlier ones, arise as an output of the productive imagination. With the downfall of the Hegelian claim to a definitive ending of the path of reflection in the Notion, the historical movement of reason, which thrusts us into the open, has been uncovered. The investigation of this historical life of reason was the theme of Wilhelm Dilthey.

Not the acceptance of a frozen *a priori* regarding our cognitive powers, but only a history of development which stars out from the totality of our nature, can answer the questions with which we have to deal in philosophy.[29]

It is true that Dilthey neglected the reflective nature of "historical reason."[30] For this reason, his analyses strike us as somewhat superficial in comparison with Hegel. But by his investigation of the category of "meaning," Dilthey worked out the peculiar openness of the historical mind. The category of meaning in Dilthey steps into the place occupied by the Hegelian Notion. Whereas reason allegedly reaches its culmination in the Notion, the total meaning of life is always only provisionally accessible. Every individual experience has its meaning only in connection with life as a whole. This is true for the individual person as well as for a people or the human race. A meaningful whole can only be seen in retrospect,[31] however, and thus always in a merely provisional way because history is never already finished. Dilthey once said:

One would have to wait for the end of a life and, in the hour of death, survey the whole and ascertain the relation between the whole and its parts. One would have to wait for the end of history to have all the material necessary to determine its meaning.[32]

Dilthey resignedly drew from this insight – since no one stands at the end of history – the conclusion that all assertions of meaning are relative. Nevertheless, one must draw the opposite

[29] Wilhelm Dilthey, *Gesammelte Schriften* (Leipzig and Stuttgart, 1927; [2]1948), I:xviii.
[30] *Ibid.*, 7:191f.
[31] W. Dilthey, *Pattern and Meaning in History*, ed. H. P. Rickman (London: Allen and Unwin, 1961) p. 100 [= *Gesammelte Schriften*, 7:74].
[32] *Ibid.*, p. 106 [= *Gesammelte Schriften*, 7:233].

conclusion: every assertion of meaning rests upon a fore-conception of the final future, in the light of which the true meaning of every individual event first becomes expressible in a valid way. Heidegger drew this conclusion with respect to individual human existence when he spoke, in *Being and Time*, of human existence attaining its wholeness and thereby itself in anticipating its own death. But the anticipation of a final future cannot be limited to the individual human being because this one attains his significance again only as a member of a whole, a society, ultimately the whole human race – an aspect which Heidegger, unfortunately, leaves bracketed out. But not even the individual human being can attain wholeness for himself by anticipating his own death because every human life remains a fragment at death, and just for this reason cannot win its wholeness from death. The fore-conception of a final future which alone yields the true meaning of all individual events must therefore be, on the one hand, something that points beyond the death of the individual, and on the other hand, something that embraces the totality of the human race, indeed, of all reality. Only from such a fore-conception of a final future, and thus of the still unfinished wholeness of reality, is it possible to assign to an individual event or being – be it present or past – its definitive meaning by saying what it is. Thus, when some-one names a thing and says, "This is a rose," or "This is a dog," he always does so from the standpoint of an implicit fore-conception of the final future, and of the totality of reality that will first be constituted by the final future. For every individual has its definitive meaning only within this whole.

Reflection upon the historical nature of reason has led us into the horizon of eschatology. Faith is not the only thing that has a relationship to the future in that as trust it anticipates some-thing future and unseen. Rather, a fore-conception of the future is constitutive for reason, too, conceived in its historic openness, because it is only an eschatologically (because temporally) con-stituted whole that yields the definitive meaning of everything individual, which we ascribe to things and events as a matter of course by saying what this is or that is. The creative character of the productive imagination seems to draw its vitality from this fore-conception. Conversely, the eschatological structure of reason opens up room for faith's talk about an eschatological future of the individual, the human race, and the world as a whole. Such talk cannot any longer be cast aside as contrary to reason.

The question about the relationship of faith to reason must be presented differently in relation to historical reason, of which we last spoke, than in relation to the aprioristic views of reason in the Aristotelian or Kantian traditions. The antithesis between faith and reason that was meaningful there cannot be mechanically transported over to the historical understanding of reason. One cannot say that this reason, in contrast to faith, has to do only with what is visible. One cannot say without qualification that reason, in contrast to faith or conscience, is concerned only with denomination. Both these statements would signify an abridgment of reason, provided that every idea or every spontaneous flash of the imagination derives from that tacitly presupposed, anticipated totality to which Heidegger points when he speaks about the words of language coming from a "pealing of silence."

A difference between faith and reason remains, nevertheless. Faith is explicitly directed toward that eschatological future and consummation which reason anticipates while at the same time keeping behind it when it says what those things are whose essences it names. Reason is indeed not confined to such naming of present things. As a movement of reflection, it returns to its absolute presupposition, which has been shown to us to be the anticipation of a final future constituting the wholeness of reality. But reason is always concerned with present things in the first instance. For this reason, it can happen that it might forget its own implicit presupposition and understand itself on the basis of the present things with which it is involved.

The Christian faith, by contrast, is directed toward that future from which reason derives. To ask about the reason for this would take us beyond the limits of this essay, because this ground of faith is God who by his promise points to the future that he himself is, namely, the future of his reign. Faith is directed to this future which constitutes reality as a whole and thereby brings everything individual to its essential perfection. However, because this future is not alien to reason, but is rather its origin from which it implicitly always derives, faith cannot stand in opposition to reason. Much more does it remind reason of its own absolute presupposition by speaking about the eschatological future and its pre-appearance in the history of the resurrection of Jesus, from which faith derives. In this way, faith can assist reason to become fully transparent to itself in its reflections. This would be reason enough – even if there were others available – for theology not to abandon as obsolete its talk about the eschatological future. For it would thereby surrender precisely the positive reference of faith to the essence of reason. Faith can confirm itself as the criterion for the rationality of reason just by its orientation toward a final, eschatological future.

4

TOWARD A THEOLOGY OF THE
HISTORY OF RELIGIONS

This essay, published here for the first time, is a revised version of a lecture delivered in Berlepsch in October 1962, at a gathering of scholars in the fields of ancient Near Eastern studies, classical philology and history, and theology.

I. THEOLOGY AND THE HISTORY OF RELIGIONS

In his last public lecture in Chicago, Paul Tillich[1] called for Christian theology to adopt a new approach to the history of religions in contrast both to the supranaturalistic way of thinking which starts out from the utter uniqueness of the Christian revelation and therefore must lead to spiritual isolation, as well as to the Enlightenment's quest for a natural theology and religion in abstraction from the historicness and historical particularity of Christianity and of the other religions. Tillich thereby pointed not only beyond the kerygmatic theology prevailing in Germany at that time, but also beyond his own apologetic theology. Even the latter seemed to him now as still too much in the clutches of a supranaturalistic point of departure.

The program of a theology oriented around the history of religions[2] clearly harks back to the problems posed by Ernst

---

[1] Paul Tillich, "The Significance of the History of Religions for Systematic Theology," in *The Future of Religions*, ed. Jerald C. Brauer (Chicago: University of Chicago Press, 1966), pp. 80–94.

[2] In contrast to Tillich, Gerhard Rosenkranz regards "theoretical debate between Christianity and the non-Christian religions" as belonging "to a bygone era" ("Wege und Grenzen des religionswissenschaftlichen Erkennens," *Zeitschrift für Theologie und Kirche* 52 [1955]: 244). He juxtaposes the

Troeltsch. Of the two systematic theologians Tillich regarded as his teachers, and whose thoughts were combined in his work in an easily disturbed tension – Martin Kähler and Ernst Troeltsch – it was Troeltsch who finally emerged, in this last turn of Tillich's thought, as the one who had formulated the truly fundamental questions and tasks for theology in the twentieth century.[3] In view of the fact that the majority of theologians went along with the "dialectical" reaction in turning their backs on these tasks, for which after all no unlimited time is available, Tillich's shift to the questions of Ernst Troeltsch takes on the significance of an impressive omen. The longer theology persists in a kerygmatic approach that permits no questioning of the truth of the kerygma itself, the longer the urgent questions

---

work of the scientific investigator of religion, which he regards as taking place "under the law of historical knowledge," and "the kerygmatic confession" of the theologian (*ibid.*, p. 231). Through the spectacles of the latter, the religions appear to be only man's "vain efforts" to "render the 'passages' of his life (birth, puberty, marriage, death) safe, and to overcome the misery, enigmas and catastrophes of his existence" (p. 244). Anyone who would like to know upon what basis Christianity is exempted from such a characterization seeks in vain for an answer if he is not willing simply to accept the theologians' "kerygmatic confession." Then, with the support of this kind of solid foundation, Nathan Söderblom's endeavor to achieve a theology of the history of religions (see below, n. 23) is unceremoniously rejected as "theologically false" because it sounds too much like the venerable patristic doctrine of the "seminal reasons" [*logoi spermatikoi*] (p. 237; cf. p. 253) and thus deviates from postwar Protestant orthodoxy. In contrast to this, Rosenkranz, in his earlier work *Gibt es Offenbarung in der Religionsgeschichte?* (Leipzig, 1936) knew how to evaluate Tillich's reference to the "seminal reasons" in a thoroughly positive way (*ibid.*, p. 44). In general, Rosenkranz' earlier attempt to connect the exclusivity of Christianity in comparison with other religions to its place in the history of religions as their heir, in the sense of Heb. 1:2 (*ibid.*, p. 43), deserves to be given preference over his later position. Rosenkranz would not have felt himself compelled to reject the Barmen theses at that time (so, *ibid.*), if only he had been clear about the fact that the loose concept of revelation, unfortunately the one usually found in the religious sciences, that he used, and which permitted finding divine revelations everywhere in the history of religions, is structurally different from the theological concept of revelation found in the Barmen declaration and therefore does not at all immediately exclude the latter.

[3] See also the judgment of Ernst Benz, *Ideen zu einer Theologie der Religionsgeschichte* (Wiesbaden, 1961), p. 39.

concerning Christianity as a religion among the religions, first brought to light in a comprehensive way by Troeltsch, are put off, the greater must be the devastation that will occur when it awakens from its kerygmatic dreaming.[4] The recent discussions about a Christian atheism provide a foretaste of this. Alongside this sort of theology, Troeltsch's alleged sell-out of Christian doctrine could present itself as the epitome of conservative circumspection. In its own way, i.e., on the basis of official decisions, Catholic theology is today trying to do justice to the fact that the Christian religion exists as one religion among many, no matter how much it may always remain different from them. If Protestant theology also does not once again face this fact openly and without dogmatic restrictions, then general critiques of the phenomenon of religion will inevitably further undermine the credibility of the Christian message as well. The Christian faith cannot for a moment so easily detach itself from the whole realm of religion and the religions as might conceivably appear today to be opportune. For this reason, where theology continues to leave out intellectual debate with critical study of religion, this neglect will boomerang upon Christianity.

To be sure, a return to Troeltsch would also mean a return to the impasses of his position – impasses which occasioned the counter-movement of kerygmatic theology. The theology developed by Troeltsch on the basis of the history of religions could no longer ascribe any "absolute" or ultimate truth to the

---

[4] Theological claims that Christianity is not a religion but rather the "annulment" and "overcoming" of the religions (as most recently still Ulrich Mann, *Theologische Religionsphilosophie im Grundriss* [Hamburg, 1961], pp. 59f.) must seem to atheists to have no more validity than merely contrived assertions, which nevertheless are unable to pull Christianity out of the reach of general critiques of religion. And in relation to the non-Christian religions, such sovereign gestures already give decisive indication of a controversy that is to be carried on precisely by theology itself, namely, the controversy about the true faith. In his *Ideen zu einer Theologie der Religionsgeschichte*, p. 36, Ernst Benz spoke of the "frightening isolation" into which Christianity had fallen through the unfounded claims of dialectical theology and from the internal difficulties of a position that calls upon Feuerbach's illusionism in order to shake off the competition of other religions, but which has to postulate a non-religious status for the Christian religion – against which Feuerbach's critique was chiefly directed (p. 37).

Christian revelation. Unquestionably, Troeltsch failed to take seriously enough the fundamental Christian conviction of the *presence* of the eschaton in Jesus and in primitive Christianity. The possibility of any theology at all seemed to collapse along with that of the idea of an eschatological revelation having occurred in Jesus. The kerygmatic reaction was certainly justified on this point. The question remains, however, whether its boasting about the claim of a revelatory word really succeeded in getting beyond that subjectivism which Troeltsch saw as the weakness of the Ritschlian school and dubbed its "theology of claims."

Paul Althaus's demand for a theology of the history of religions[5] may be mentioned as an example of a kerygmatically grounded way of laying claim to the history of religions. It wants to explicate Christianity's "claim" of "unconditional validity for mankind" by means of a "missionary understanding" of other religions, in counteracting the abandonment of this claim and therewith also of the missionary goal "that the whole world become Christian" on the part of the scientific study of religion. Nevertheless, Althaus believes that the "legitimacy of the Christian certainty of being commissioned" is not something that can be confirmed by "historical proof." This knowledge is instead "given solely to the decision of faith."[6] Thus, it is no wonder that Joachim Wach could discern in such a theology of the history of religions only a subjectivistic construction from the standpoint of a particular religious faith.[7] Wach could concede to Christian theology the right to "construe the facts of the history of religions in harmony with its own view,"[8] but he stressed all the more that such constructions lack binding validity from an objective standpoint. The redemptive-historical theology of religions recently developed by

[5] Paul Althaus, "Mission und Religionsgeschichte," *Zeitschrift für systematische Theologie* 5 (1928): 550–90, esp. pp. 561, 585ff.

[6] *Ibid.*, p. 588.

[7] Joachim Wach, "Und die Religionsgeschichte? Eine Auseinandersetzung mit Paul Althaus," *Zeitschrift für systematische Theologie* 6 (1929): 484–97.

[8] *Ibid.*, p. 484.

Roman Catholic theologians[9] has also failed as yet to overcome that sort of intellectually non-obligatory, merely subjectively accepted supranaturalistic standpoint. Still, it has made great advances beyond older conceptions since it is able to combine a positive evaluation of alien religions with the idea of the historical particularity and ultimacy of the Christian revelation. The ultimacy of the Christian revelation can be illuminating, not as a supranaturalistic presupposition, but only if it can result from an unprejudiced understanding of the total process of the universal history of religion.[10] A theology of the history of religions can count on being taken seriously outside its own community of faith only to the extent that it appeals to what are termed by Wach the "facts of the sciences of religion" and is able to argue from these. It may then expect its arguments to be discussed no matter how the subjective faith-stance of the

[9] An example of this can be found in Heinz Robert Schlette, *Towards a Theology of Religions*, Quaestiones Disputatae V. 14 (New York: Herder & Herder, 1966). Schlette's position is based on Karl Rahner, "Christianity and the Non-Christian Religions," in *Theological Investigations* (Baltimore: Helicon Press, and London: Darton, Longman & Todd, 1966), 5:113–34 (on this, see Schlette, *Towards a Theology of Religions*, pp. 77ff.). Schlette, like Rahner, detaches the sacred history around which his theology of the history of religions is to be oriented (*Towards a Theology of Religions*, p. 31; cf. pp. 65ff.) from the ambiguities of profane history which "purely of itself cannot cause sacred history to stand out from it and become visible" (*ibid.*, p. 70). Although, taken absolutely, sacred history and profane history are "coextensive" (*ibid.*, p. 68), nevertheless "the coming to consciousness or reflective self-awareness of sacred history" (*ibid.*, p. 70) requires a special revelatory history which, as such, is not accessible from profane history. The element of supranatural construction introduced here leads Schlette to the noteworthy admission "that the introduction of theological principles infringes objectivity as this is understood by the 'secular' science of religion" (*ibid.*, p. 60). Such a retreat from the struggle for universally binding truth seems to me neither self-explanatory nor unavoidable. It necessarily hands over the statements of theologians about other religions (and even about their own) to the criticisms of bias and substantive irrelevance.

[10] Ernst Benz writes in a similar vein: "The genuine universality of a religion is first attained where this religion, in its message of salvation, establishes a positive relationship with the total development of the human race, which is to say with the universal history of mankind, especially with the general history of religion from its earliest stages" (*Ideen zu einer Theologie der Religionsgeschichte*, p. 49).

theologian might be regarded. The decisive point in gaining such a hearing is that the theologian's arguments do not presuppose, for instance, specifically Christian beliefs as their logical point of departure. If they did depend on such a presupposition, then they would only articulate the presupposed faith perspective and would remain substantively irrelevant. Where, nevertheless, arguments bring into view specific aspects of the disputed state of affairs, there the question of which subjective standpoint determines the horizon in which this aspect sprang to light as a meaningful and occasioned formulation of the arguments becomes secondary – at least with respect to the substantive discussion. In such cases, it is justifiable to consider it immaterial if the discussion partner rejects the argument thrown up against him as merely an expression of an opposed standpoint instead of confronting it in its substantive weightiness. In this way, it would be possible to conceive a theology of the history of religions which would not deny its Christian perspective and would also not use its Christian presuppositions as arguments, but would appeal instead to observable states of affairs. There are many tendencies today in the direction of such a sober involvement of theology with the history of religions, and perhaps the theologian might expect that under these circumstances even the professional historian of religion will overcome his distrust – all too justified by previous experience – of the arguments of theology that are pertinent to the discussions of the sciences of religion.

Tillich's demand for a new theology of the history of religions manifestly called for research of such a kind, which is obligated to the phenomena without being bound to any sort of premises that would be exempt from critical testing. His methodological account of the execution of such research emphasizes structural comparison between the different religions. Nevertheless, it is not exactly clear how in this way a *theology* of the history of religions should be possible, which would be devoted not only to the religious disposition of man but also to the appearance of the divine reality to which this attitude is directed.

In addition to this, it seems doubtful that the phenomenological procedure proposed by Tillich, with its typologizing abstraction from the process of history, can suffice to grasp the particularity of Christianity within the world of the religions. It could be the case that the religious particularity of Christianity would itself first come into view through its function in the process of the history of religions. This point of view has been applied most impressively by the Catholic side of the development of the modern theology of redemptive history, despite its supranaturalistic orientation. That such an investigation of the function of Christianity in the historical process of the history of religions was suited, even without supranaturalistic presuppositions, to elucidate the peculiarity of Christianity in the sphere of the other religions was demonstrated by van Leeuwen a few years ago.[11] On the other hand, the phenomenological attitude toward the structural features isolable from the historical process stands under the suspicion of from the outset systematically concealing the dimension of historical change and transformation among the religions. This methodological problem cannot fail to attract special attention from the theologian who – thinking along the lines of redemptive history – is inclined to search for the peculiar historical function of Christianity within the historical process itself. Nevertheless, this is a matter of a methodological question of general significance, and as such should constitute the point of departure for our further considerations.

II. PHENOMENOLOGY AND HISTORY OF RELIGIONS

The relative youth of the modern sciences of religion might have something to do with the fact that the division of subordinate disciplines still coincides to a large extent with the varying accentuations in the directions of interest and the way problems are formulated.[12] If one distinguishes the systematic

[11] Arend T. van Leeuwen, *Christianity in World History: The Meeting of the Faiths of East and West*, trans. H. H. Hoskins (New York: Charles Scribner's Sons, 1964).

[12] On the following discussion, cf. Gustav Mensching, *Geschichte der Religionswissenschaft* (Bonn, 1948).

arrangement of information about an alien religion from its collection and preliminary description, then one may well say that the topical labels Philosophy of Religion, History of Religion, Psychology of Religion, Sociology of Religion, and Phenomenology of Religion designate not only distinct disciplines existing alongside each other, but also, and more originally, different perspectives under which – in this order – the systematic treatment of religiously informative material has been acknowledged since the previous century. Today, the phenomenological method is obviously the dominant one among the sciences of religion. This does not exclude the continuation of concomitant studies in the psychology and sociology of religion, or even the history of religions in the narrower sense as the investigation and presentation of the historical course of individual religions or religious epochs. Still, these are more like subdisciplines, and hardly methods for the fundamental, systematic ordering of the materials of the sciences of religion. The situation of philosophy of religion appears particularly difficult today. Hegel's philosophy of religion could still combine into a total picture all the aspects which have since gone their separate ways – psychology, phenomenology, sociology, and history. In particular, his philosophy of religion was still directly united with his projection of the history of religions. In the ensuing period, empirical knowledge of alien religions, which, to be sure, Hegel had already worked over in what was for his time astonishing breadth, made tremendous advances, swelled the fund of religious data, and gave rise to the demand for greater differentiation in its systematic ordering. However, the idea of evolution made it possible for a time to continue to develop different theories about the total history of religion, which at the same time implied a comprehensive understanding of religion as a whole, its origins and highest development. Only with the repudiation of total conceptions of the course of religious history did the history and philosophy of religion finally split apart. The latter henceforth concentrated on the character and truth of religious experience – whereby it soon found itself in competition with the psychology of religion and then with the sociology of religion. The history of religion turned its attention to the history of individual religions and their reciprocal influences on each other, even though the framework in which the different religions were represented as stages in a process of development persisted a while longer. Nevertheless, within the work in the history of religions a significant shift of accent had been going on for some time with the rise of the so-called *comparative* approach to religious history. Through its clear impulses toward the criticism of tradition, this approach had had a lasting effect upon the older theological research in the history of religions. Its special interest was now the appearance of similar motifs in different religions, especially, of course, in biblical religion, on the one hand, and its environing religious world, on the other – "parallels," suited to correct dogmatic theses about the utter uniqueness of the biblical revelation, as illustrated, for example, by the "Babel-Bible" controversy that excited the spirits around 1900 with its discussions about the Babylonian parallels to the biblical creation story. The genetic question about the causal connections between the parallels that were discovered was of decisive importance for such comparative study of religion. On the other hand, there was a tendency to evaluate the appearance of parallels as already a sure index of genetic connection as well (e.g., between the Persian "Primal Man" idea and Hellenistic Gnosticism and the Mysteries, as well as between these and New Testament "parallels"). Consequently, such a comparative way of looking at things had a peculiar way of shrinking genuine *historical* interest in religion – the question about the growth of individual religions – to the pointing out of analogous structures. This detachment of interest in comparison, in structural analogies between widely separated religions, from the question of the place of these religions in the process of history, undoubtedly contributed to what then appeared on the scene as the phenomenology of religion. The phenomenology of religion detaches the forms in which the religious life is expressed from their historical contexts; treats the latter as inconsequential; and co-ordinates similar forms of religious representation, cultic

behavior, and religious institutions into a systematic structure
of the "phenomenon" of religious life as such. In this way,
Asclepius, Apollo, and Jesus can be named side by side as
"savior figures."[13] The accolade and circumcision,[14] formulations from the Upanishads and from twentieth-century Catholic
pastoral letters,[15] are taken without further ado as comparable
phenomena, just like "the Pope or the Dalai Lama."[16] Similarly, Mircea Eliade can say that "a sacred stone, an avatar of
Viṣṇu, a statue of Jupiter, or an appearance of Yahweh" are
examples of the fact that "the sacred expresses itself through
something other than itself" because "viewed in isolation, they
are all equally meaningful (or illusory) simply because in every
case the sacred, in manifesting itself, has limited and incarnated
itself. This paradox of incarnation, which makes hierophanies
possible at all – whether the most elementary or the supreme
incarnation of the Word of Christ – is found everywhere in
religious history."[17] The question has to be raised here whether
such generalizations do not lead us astray.[18] Are not the motifs
that have been named alongside one another so different within
their respective concrete contexts that the common features
illustrated by this coordination are hardly of any substantive
interest at all for the determination of their historical peculiarity?[19] A criterion is needed to distinguish deeper mutualities,

---

[13] Gerardus van der Leeuw, *Religion in Essence and Manifestation*, trans.
Hans H. Penner, 2 vols. (New York: Harper Torchbooks, 1963), 1: 100–114.
[The precise order of names cited by Pannenberg does not appear in the
English text, but the pages cited are pertinent to his point. – Tr.]

[14] *Ibid.*, p. 195.   [15] *Ibid.*, pp. 220f.   [16] *Ibid.*, p. 220.

[17] Mircea Eliade, *Patterns in Comparative Religion*, trans. Rosemary Sheed
(London and New York: Sheed & Ward, 1958), p. 26. [Translation slightly
revised, to accord with German text cited by Pannenberg. – Tr.] For
further examples, see below, n. 24.

[18] One must take seriously the judgment of Klaus Koch that "no greater
contradiction to the historical point of view can be found than this sort of
phenomenology, which selects ostensibly common religious endowments
from different times and lands and arranges them into a potpourri" ("Wort
und Einheit des Schöpfer-Gottes in Memphis und Jerusalem: Zur Einzi-
gartigkeit Israels," in *Zeitschrift für Theologie und Kirche* 62 [1965]: 286).

[19] Joachim Wach, *The Comparative Study of Religions* (New York: Columbia
University Press, 1958), p. 26, appeals to Dilthey's assurance that typo-

which point to an inner kinship between the phenomena involved, from superficial similarities that are beside the point or else utterly fruitless when it comes to grasping the peculiar character of the phenomenon being used as an example, and which only too easily shift one's attention away from deep-going contradictions among apparently common properties. A fundamental defect in the method of the phenomenology of religion may be seen at this point. The more it abstracts from the historical particularity of its material, the less it is able *empirically* to distinguish between superficial and essential mutualities. The only criterion that can serve to distinguish between relevant and irrelevant structural features is the anthropology of religious conduct which tacitly or explicitly guides the systematics of the phenomenology.[20] The structure of the religious life is usually not understood by the phenomenology of religion as historically alterable. Rather, religious representations, cultic forms, and institutions are construed as modes of expression of "the" religious life. In favorable cases, this can be done in a very differentiated way, but it always stands under the presupposition that the structure of "the" religious life has remained essentially the same throughout

---

logical distinctions are "only intended for a better understanding of history from the point of view of life" (cf. Wilhelm Dilthey, *Gesammelte Schriften* [Leipzig and Stuttgart, 1927; ²1948], 8:100). One must nevertheless be skeptical of this confidence that such typologizing serves the understanding of history *in its historicness and unrepeatability*. It is no accident that the later Dilthey abandoned his earlier attempts along the lines of Schleiermacher to develop a psychological typology grounded on the concept of life, because he recognized that human life is itself changed in the historical process in which it expresses itself in history.

[20] To this belong not only the subjective forms of religious acts, but also their mode of reference to their objects, like the distinction between the sacred and the profane; the delimitation of holy places and times; the forms of the cult; and, finally, even the general forms of the intentional object of the religious attitude, in other words, the concept of the holy power (which becomes defined, upon reflection, as the infinite); as well as objective appearances of the holy power (or powers) in the media of predesignated finite forms of being making up the great constants of man's experience of the world: mountains, sky, stars, storms and rain, vegetation, and even social institutions like kingship.

time.[21] The genuine meaning of religious phenomena can scarcely be sought in their historical particularity on the basis of this presupposition.

The observation that the phenomenological way of looking at religion implies an anthropology of religious experience requires a discussion of its relationship to the psychology of religion, which in fact deals thematically with the structure of religious experience.[22] Like the psychologist of religion, the phenomenologist wants to understand the subjectivity of the religious man, who lives in the rites, representations, and institutions of a specific religion. But the phenomenologist takes a different route to this goal. He does not begin with introspection and questioning of others regarding their religious experience and feeling, but begins with the more readily accessible external life-forms and representations, which he takes as expressions of human attitudes and thus may be questioned with respect to the intention expressed in them. This reversal of the psychological approach to the problem – inquiring back from the outer expressions to the inwardness of the attitude, instead of beginning immediately with the inwardness animating the forms of religious conduct – is something the phenomenology of religion shares with the phenomenological method generally. It makes it possible to discover expressions of the universally human even in apparently scurrilous rites and representations

[21] So even Rudolph Otto, *Vishnu Nārayana* (Jena, 1917), p. 150, cited by Rosenkranz, "Wege und Grenzen," p. 232. Joachim Wach, too, in his criticism of A. Jespers's contribution to the Bertholet Festschrift [*Festschrift Alfred Bertholet zum 80. Geburtstag*, ed. Walter Baumgartner, Otto Eissfeldt, et al. (Tübingen, 1950)], explicitly emphasizes his agreement with that person's attempt to "describe an 'original type' of religion as an unalterable structure of religious experience" (*ibid.*, p. 52).

[22] The work of Robert Winkler, *Phänomenologie und Religion: Ein Beitrag zu den Prinzipienfragen der Religionsphilosophie* (Tübingen, 1921), esp. pp. 13ff. shows how difficult it originally was to delimit phenomenology from psychology in the study of religion. Winkler speaks of a phenomenological method of religious psychology (p. 17 passim.), which, as an intuition of the essences of intentional meanings (p. 20), he contrasts with an empirical, factual psychology that deals only with the psychic form of a religious act instead of its intended contents (pp. 20f.). See also Joachim Wach, *Religionswissenschaft: Prolegomena zu ihrer Grundlegung* (Leipzig, 1924), p. 193.

of an alien religiousness. It is true that certain specific assumptions about the psychology of the religious attitudes are always presupposed in this. To this extent, the psychology of religion cannot be completely dropped and replaced by phenomenology. But the empirical control of such assumptions rests much less upon introspection or the observations of others than upon the multiplicity of the historical objectivations of the religious attitude which are to be interpreted as expressions of the intentions of religious subjectivity. The multiplicity of these phenomena demands therewith an extensive differentiation in the interpretation of the forms of the religious attitude and its objectivations.

Thus, in point of fact the phenomenology of religion makes a significant contribution to a preliminary anthropology of religious experience. It deals with *anthropology* to the extent that phenomenological investigation construes religious data as expressions of "the" religious life, in other words as expressions of a human attitude, even if the intention of such is directed toward an extra- or suprahuman reality and deposits itself in objectified representations and institutionalized modes of behavior. The phenomenology of religion only makes a *contribution* to the total task of an anthropology of religious experience because it must presuppose the fundamental categories for such a description of the religious attitude as having already been provided from another quarter. It will be most appropriate to carry out this task in contact with general anthropological research, and thereby its connection with psychology is also established. The contribution of the phenomenology of religion to an anthropology of religious experience is *significant* because of the fact that in view of the multiplicity of forms in which the religious attitude has objectified itself, an extensive differentiatedness must be worked out in the categories used to describe it and the reality intended by the religions, which is most often represented as "divine." Hence, the phenomenology of religion has been of great service in the clarification and criticism of the conceptuality to be employed in the sciences of religion. Nevertheless, its work can at best provide only a preliminary anthropology of religious

experience. The reason for the limitation of the phenomenological method suggested thereby lies in the fact that man is a
historical being and changes in the process of history, so that all
assumptions of an ever identical structure of human behavior
remain problematical. Every anthropology that faces up to the
radical meaning of the historicness of man must ultimately
eventuate in the interpretation of the concrete history of individual human beings in relation to their societies, including
their traditions, forms of life, and experience, and within the
whole of human history. For it is only through historical por-
trayal that one comes as close as possible to the actual course
of the concrete life of man. In contrast to this, all general forms
of anthropology, be they biologically, psychologically, or socio-
logically oriented, remain preliminary abstractions, which are
indeed indispensable for a first approximation to an understanding of human behavior but can nevertheless have only a pre-
paratory character, and must pass over to the phase of a
historical representation if the science of man wishes to reach
the concrete actualization of human existence. For this reason,
historical writing is called upon to complete the anthropological
task as far as this is humanly possible. Thus, even the anthropology of religion worked out by means of phenomenological
methods needs to be completed by the presentation and interpretation of the history of religions. A phenomenological anthropology of religion which takes full account of the historicness
of man would from the start see to it that only the history of
religions would be able to achieve the closest approximation to
an adequate understanding of religious experience possible for
a methodical mode of comprehension.

For this reason, a phenomenology of religion that operates
on the assumption that the structure of religious experience and
religious behavior is always the same in its fundamental features,
so that the historical differences between the individual differences thus possess no essential significance for the structure of
religious experience itself, is questionable already on phenomenological grounds. It necessarily leads to violent distortions
of the phenomena and to the affirmation of deceptive mutuali-

ties that have no basis in the concrete intentionality expressed in the religious phenomena. One will only then attain an understanding of these phenomena, especially of religious texts, when one devotes himself to the indispensable comparative study of the historical particularities of these phenomena, even with regard to their apparently common features, within the framework of their historical contexts.[23] This is already necessary for the phenomenological ordering of the fund of religious data,[24] but in addition to this leads to the further systematic task of a presentation of the history of religions.

From the standpoint of the history of religions itself, every conception remains inadequate which treats the individual religions as self-enclosed, more or less unalterable types, and allows them to be linked only by means of a historical succession. Hegel construed the history of religions in this way. His philosophy of religion set up each of the great religions as a specific type of religion as such, through which it passed on the way to its historical self-realization from the religion of nature to the

---

[23] Thus, Nathan Söderblom confessed that he had become increasingly skeptical of the quest for analogies and parallels in the fund of religious data. For "here as in every branch of human knowledge, further analysis shows differences which seem at first sight to be only somewhat divergent specimens, but which bring out very soon to the careful eye characteristics which prove them to be rather of an essential and genetic character" (*The Living God: Basic Forms of Personal Religion* [Boston: Beacon Press, 1962], p. 323).

[24] Mircea Eliade, in distinction from other phenomenologists of religion, tries especially in his book *Patterns in Comparative Religion* to document his theses about the structure of religious phenomena first of all by means of material from an individual religious tradition, in order immediately thereafter to trace this same aspect in the realm of other religions or cultures. Nevertheless, even he, under the pressure of the typologizing approach – which in this case is dependent upon Carl G. Jung's doctrine of archetypes (p. 58) – succeeds, for example, in classifying Yahweh under Storm-, Rain-, and Fecundation-deities (pp. 93ff.; cf., on this type, pp. 82ff.) without giving a thought in this context to the opposition between Yahweh and Baal, who was mentioned only a short time before (pp. 90f.). And if it could have happened in Christian art that the cross of Christ was portrayed as a tree of life (p. 292), this was hardly because of its being analogous to the herbs of vegetation mythology which were supposed to reawaken the dead (*ibid.*), but rather because of the historical event of the resurrection of Jesus. And this event was probably never conceived as the effect of the miraculous power of the wood of the cross.

religion of the spirit, in a process of the gradual elevation of the spirit over nature. There was hardly a word in Hegel about the history of the individual religions themselves. The demand for a thoroughgoing historical treatment of the individual religions first arose around the turn from the nineteenth to the twentieth centuries.[25] By contrast, contemporary understanding of the task of the history of religions places this problem in the foreground,[26] as well as "the historical dependence and mutual influence of the religions upon each other." And in this connection it is "essentially a matter not of parallels and comparisons, but rather of the particular and irrepeatable." Only in this way can one acquire the basis for a substantively appropriate comparison between different religions in their totality, as for instance between the religion of Israel and the religions of the ancient Near Eastern peoples. Current research no longer regards the religion of Israel as something that at some time suddenly appeared in the world in finished form, but views it rather as the result of a process of historical growth. Only when the religions of Israel's environing world are understood in their historical growth in accord with the same fundamental principles as are applied to its history can a comparison that is really appropriate to their essential content be undertaken.

III. THE UNITY OF THE HISTORY OF RELIGIONS

An investigation that concentrates on the development and changes of individual religions must seem problematical to the usual attempts at conceiving the unity of the history of religions. It is certainly no accident that the work in the history of religions in the last decade has been predominantly *historical* in the nar-

[25] In the postscript to his lecture "Die Aufgabe der theologischen Fakultäten und die allgemeine Religionsgeschichte," Adolf von Harnack spoke out in this way against the demand for a general history of religion in order to give priority to specialized research into individual religions (*Reden und Aufsätze*, 7 vols. [Giessen, 1906–30], 2:183ff.).

[26] So W. Holsten, *RGG*[3] vol. 5, cols. 986–91, esp. 987f. The shift noted in the text is discussed in col. 988. Gustav Mensching also says that it is not religion but the individual religions that are the real object of the history of religions (*Allgemeine Religionsgeschichte* [Leipzig, [2]1949], p. 9).

rower sense of the term, and has been devoted to monographs on individual religions,[27] or occupied with concrete interactions between specific religions. This is understandable for a variety of reasons if one remembers the peculiar limitations of older conceptions of unity of the history of religions.

Above all, it is no longer possible to coordinate, with Hegel, any particular religion with a single stage of the total process of the religious development of mankind, once one has become aware of the profound changes one and the same religion undergoes in the course of its history. Once its historical growth has come into view, no religion permits of being reduced, without doing violence to it, to a single "type" so that it could then be inserted into some tendentious typology which is proffered as the structural frame of the religious development of mankind. As a rule, the growth of religions has taken place in the form of adjacent processes, sometimes in mutual interaction, less frequently as a succession in which one religion accomplishes the dissolution of another; but even then not in such a way that a sequence of religious types could be established, construed as a path from the religion of nature to the religion of the spirit, as in Hegel's philosophy of religion, or from primitive demonology to monotheism, according to a later conception.

To be sure, the conception of the history of religion as a "development" permeating all religious life, from primitive beginnings to higher forms of polytheistic culture religions and finally to monotheistic religion, is not bound to the construction of a sequence of religious types. The idea of development can acknowledge or even demand that in the beginnings of even highly differentiated "culture religions," so-called primitive features may be found, so that the evolution of mankind from magic and animistic belief in demons into culture religion and monotheism is documented in the history of every individual religion, although not all of them have advanced the same distance along this path. The charge of progressivistic optimism does not touch this view of the history of religions. This view has no need to shut its eyes to the phenomena of decadence and

[27] This is emphasized by Holsten in *RGG*[3] vol. 5, col. 990.

brutality in the history of religions. That in the actual course of history "in spite of many periods of stagnation and retrogression . . . a great, steady progress, a gradual self-unfolding of higher forms and a more intensive life in which religion too has participated"[28] may be discerned seems, after two world wars and in view of the possibility of a nuclear catastrophe affecting the whole of mankind, to be more dubious today than it was in 1904. The history of the human race conceived as a continuous development hardly contains *within itself* the guarantee of perpetual progress. Nevertheless, it is unnecessary to dispute the fact that the need for an encompassing unity that makes it possible to experience even the multifarious as a positive wealth is so deeply rooted in human existence and in the structure of human reason that it inevitably brings up the question of the extent to which this religion or that can provide a basis for a universal unity in the experience of reality, which is very likely the criterion of its relevance and saving power – and thus, perhaps, of its truth, too. Therefore, one need not regard the abstract idea of God, to which the Enlightenment so eagerly subscribed, as the final wisdom of the scientific study of religion. The integrative power of a religion is not simply to be read off from its idea of God. It is expressed in the whole of the religious understanding of human existence, so that whether (or to what extent) an idea of God is representative of a religion and can be taken as the gauge of its saving power and truth depends upon its place and significance within that whole. An ever so universally conceived high god who remains an inconsequential background force having little or no relation to the world of present experience and is unable to reconcile the lawless and absurd aspects of existence, is certainly no index of an especially high stage of the religion in question. This reason alone already shows that it is inadequate to construe the course of the history of religions as a process of evolution from chaotic demonism to monotheism.

[28] Wilhelm Bousset, *What Is Religion?* trans. F. B. Low (London: T. Fisher Unwin, 1907), p. 8. See also Tiele-Söderblom, *Kompendium der Religionsgeschichte* (Berlin-Schöneberg, ⁵1920), p. 11.

Nevertheless, there are two special difficulties burdening such kinds of evolutionary conceptions, and which have led to a growing skepticism about the possibility of carrying out an evolutionary construction of the totality of the history of religions.

In the first place, systematic application of the idea of evolution demands a knowledge of the initial stage from which the development proceeded. For this reason, efforts at an evolutionary construction of the whole history of religions have devoted special attention to the question whether this initial point of departure is to be found in animism, with belief in the dead, or in the totemistic identification of the hunter with the power of an animal, or, finally, in the more many-sided experience of power found in the Melanesian belief in mana. However, it is just the beginnings of the histories of the different religions that are the most difficult to illuminate. The attempt to utilize the methods, outlooks, and customs of "primitive" peoples existing today as witnesses for an early stage of the religious history of mankind remains at least very hypothetical, and in every case requires confirmation by means of the religious texts of ancient cultures. Thus, it seems risky to attempt to figure out the explanation of the whole history of religions on the basis of a hypothesis about its beginning, which is just what is least accessible to us.

If this difficulty is of a methodological kind, the second one has the form of an empirical contradiction to the evolutionary conception that views the appearance of a universal "monotheistic" deity as the outcome of the evolutionary course of religious history. Andrew Lang's discovery of the so-called "high gods" in primitive religions in 1887 gave rise to the theory, conceived by him and later worked out by Wilhelm Schmidt, of a primordial monotheism, which reversed the evolutionary view. True, this inverse evolutionism is untenable because – as was shown by Nathan Söderblom in particular – these primeval creator figures are often neither singular nor even clear cases of gods,[29] and even as gods they usually appear only as "power

[29] Nathan Söderblom, *Das Werden des Gottesglaubens: Untersuchungen über die Anfänge der Religion* (Leipzig, [2]1926), pp. 93–156, esp. p. 124.

and will in the background,"[30] leaving the field of everyday
reality to the other powers upon which, because they are dan-
gerous or favorable to man, cultic activity is concentrated.[31]
Nevertheless, the high gods or primeval creators cannot be
traced back to experiences of other kinds of power or to
animistic representations, and thus contradict evolutionary
theories that attempt to derive them from such. As Söderblom
stressed, primeval creator figures, experiences of mana, fear of
taboos, belief in spirits, and reverencing of natural beings all
appear alongside each other,[32] just as still later high gods and
special deities are venerated side by side. Already in the experience of primitives, reality seems to be characterized *as much*
by unity *as also* by multiplicity.[33] A unified source of everything
that exists and a multiplicity of presently effective powers do
not mutually exclude each other. Which aspect predominates
cannot be decided in general, but changes from religion to
religion, and even within the history of individual religions.

Such considerations rule out the evolutionary thesis according
to which monotheism developed out of belief in mana and/or
animism, as well as the reverse conception of a primal monotheism, which sought for that which constitutes the common
element permeating all religions and thus their unified origin
in a knowledge of the one god that preceded the devolution into
polytheism.

Despite such difficulties, the question about the history of
religions as a whole is not superfluous, nor does it appear to be
absolutely insoluble. It is not superfluous because phenomenology of religion alone, with its typological abstractions, is unable
satisfactorily to provide the needed panoramic view of the fund
of religious materials since it is precisely the reciprocal relation-

---

[30] Van der Leeuw, *Religion in Essence and Manifestation*, 1:159ff.

[31] The latter is especially emphasized by Eliade, *Patterns in Comparative Religion*, pp. 64f.

[32] Söderblom, *Das Werden des Gottesglaubens*, p. 139.

[33] In this connection, at least in specific cases, even the alternatives of monotheism and polytheism are inapplicable, as Klaus Koch has shown for Egyptian religion ("Der Tod des Religionsstifters," *Kerygma und Dogma* 8 [1962]: 121).

ships of the religious traditions that it leaves out in its abstractive procedure. On the other hand, the intertwining and reciprocal influences of the religious attitude and its objectivations necessitate directing one's attention beyond the investigation of particular religions toward wider historical connections. Thus, the exegesis of individual biblical texts compels one to ask about their relationship to the environing religious world.[34] The presence of such reciprocal relationships indicates, at the same time, however, the possibility of concrete studies in the history of religions beyond the sphere of individual religions in which such reciprocities are not only given passing notice but become thematized as a historical process. This process of the history of religions moves apace with the historical confrontations of nations and their politics and economics. Alongside the cults and religions that have no meaning outside narrow kinship boundaries, especially in the case of preliterate cultures, others arise whose history is coupled with the formation of extensive states, and finally even such as detach themselves from the confines of the political commonwealth in which they arose. The latter sort can themselves become the basis of new political unities without being bound to their existence. Their attractive power can spread out over continents, as the example of Buddhism shows for Asia. In the Western world, Hellenism afforded an especially favorable climate for such religious movements to arise, the most successful of which were Mithraism and finally Christianity, which inherited from and succeeded all the others.

The processes of reciprocity and integration in the relationships between cults, myths, individual gods, and whole religions might be designated as *syncretistic*, were it not for the fact that today – in contrast to its status when originally coined by Plutarch[35] – this term is burdened with a bad reputation. Still, perhaps the pejorative sense in which the word has been used

[34] The scope of this state of affairs has recently again been rightly emphasized by Koch, *ibid.*, pp. 100–123; cf. also the article by Koch mentioned in n. 18. That such insights still cannot be taken as self-evident in German theology was made clear by F. Baumgärtel's criticism of Koch in *Kerygma und Dogma* 9 (1963): 223–33.

[35] Plutarch *Moralia* 490 B.

in modern religious studies and in classical philology is rooted
in a biased judgment about the phenomenon it designates. In
this case it would make sense to hold on to the word and to
revalue it.

The religious world of Hellenism may be taken as syncretistic
in the narrower sense of the term, the purity of the different
types of religion within it seeming to have been effaced by their
mixing. This characterization of Hellenistic religion presupposes, in the first place, that in pre-Hellenistic times the religions that later became mixed (especially the Olympian)
existed as pure types; and, secondly, that such purity is worth
striving for, whereas mixture, on the contrary, is reprehensible.
Both assumptions are questionable. When a religious tradition
combines with others, if it maintains itself as the dominant
factor, it can express its assimilative and integrative power,
while purity can mean sterility. In point of fact, most of the
supposedly pure original features of the different religions, at
least in all highly differentiated religious cultures, probably
arose through the fusion of originally heterogeneous elements.
This can be studied especially well in the history of the great
god-figures. Not last of all does the Israelitic idea of God press
for consideration as an example with which to illustrate this
assertion.[36] At least three or four different streams of tradition,
which are in part still further differentiated within themselves,
have grown together into the form we know from the Old
Testament as the God of Israel, viz., the Kenite Yahweh of
Sinai (if it should be the case that the connection between
Yahweh and Sinai is original); then, the god of the Exodus,
who was perhaps not originally identical with the god of Sinai;
further, the gods of the Patriarchs (the god of Abraham, the
god of Israel, and the god of Jacob); as well as the god of
heaven, El (or different El figures), who mediated the function
of creator to the God of Israel. The driving force behind the
fusion of all these figures may well lie in the manifest exclusivity
that characterized Yahweh from the very beginning. This
characteristic could mean, in confrontation with other deities,

[36] On the following, see Koch, "Der Tod des Religionsstifters," pp. 107ff.

either identification or struggle, since the way to a pluralism of gods mutually supplementing each other was closed. In relation to El (or some El figures) as well as to the gods of the Patriarchs, identification was possible under conditions that can only be conjectured today. Baal, on the other hand, was bitterly opposed, but Yahweh seems to have been able to gain the victory only by usurping specific functions Baal had possessed. Thus, the growth of the biblical figure of God has actually the form of a syncretistic process; and this could likewise be shown for the history of the Egyptian Amon and other Egyptian gods, for Marduk of Babylon, and even for Greek gods such as Apollo or Zeus. Not only is the history of god-figures syncretistic, however, but so is the very mode by which a religion asserts itself and expands. From this perspective, the mixing of religions in the Hellenistic period seems to be only a special instance of a general rule, and its particularity consists at least partially in the severing of religious traditions from their particular, native political rootage, committing them to migration within the whole inhabited world of Alexander, the Diadochi, and later, the Roman Empire. Christianity, however, affords the greatest example of syncretistic assimilative power. This religion not only linked itself to Greek philosophy, but also inherited the entire religious tradition of the Mediterranean world – a process whose details have still not been sufficiently clarified, but which was probably decisive for the persuasive power of Christianity in the ancient world.[37]

[37] In this sense, Hermann Gunkel was justified in saying: "Christianity is a syncretistic religion" (*Zum religionsgeschichtlicher Verständnis des Neuen Testaments* [Göttingen, 1903], p. 95). This classification touched off many protests since it was understood as a threat to the uniqueness of Christianity. Thus, Max Reischle wrote: "One may legitimately speak of syncretism only where elements of different religions are being combined as having equal rights, but not where the views of an earlier religion somehow still continue to operate or where individual bits of related or combated religions are taken over and incorporated" (*Theologie und Religionsgeschichte* [Tübingen, 1904], p. 36). This judgment obviously underestimates the significance of the Hellenistic material for the formative process of the religious history of early Christianity. Ideas of epiphanies, mystery-type conceptions of the sacraments, platonizing doctrines of God, were by no means only incidentally taken over and turned into statements that were somehow completely

The unity of the history of religions has actually appeared in the historical interaction between the different religions; or, better, this process is still in progress today as a competition between the religions concerning the nature of reality, a competition grounded in the fact that the religions have to do with total views of reality. Only in this way can they provide a basis for the orders of human existence or, in another way, mediate salvation to man. By coming into contact with the devotees of other gods, however, they run into conflicts with their religions, which can be smoothed out or peacefully settled in various ways: by the relativization of the universal claim of one's own as well as of the alien religion to merely that of a given circle of devotees;[38] by means of interpretation or – under corresponding political conditions – even cultic fusion; and, finally, by displacement. Where the conflicts are peacefully settled, usually the question involved is whether and to what extent a divine figure, together with its cult and the myth that legitimates and propagates its meaning, is able to become convincing to other groups or peoples beyond the original local circle of devotees as

independent of such contents, but rather became constitutive – or co-constitutive – elements of the specifically Christian understanding of revelation. To this extent, the statement about the syncretistic character of Christianity is correct. But this concept does not assert that the different religious elements have equal rights (against Reischle). Rather, in Plutarch's interpretation of the term, as designating a confluence of differing elements – an interpretation which is supported by the older verbal form, too – an integrating principle prior to the different elements is presupposed. This function is fulfilled in the Hellenistic world by the philosophical logos as the common denominator of the different religious symbolizations, while in Christianity, on the other hand, it was fulfilled by the person of Jesus and the redemptive event of his death and resurrection – in other words, by the logos incarnated in Jesus. The latter formula expresses the universal relevance of what happened in Jesus, and the inexhaustible assimilative and regenerative power of Christianity corresponds to this. The fact that Christianity is syncretistic to an unusual degree thus expresses not a weakness but the unique strength of Christianity.

[38] Thus, in concluding a treaty, each side expects of the other that he will swear by his own god. The parallelization of alien gods with one's own gods of similar character goes a step further. In addition to the relativization of the gods to their function, there is also expressed in this a pressure toward religious unification, whose systematic formation was accomplished in Hellenism – not by accident – in coalition with philosophical reflection.

the powerful source of reality as they experience it. The answer depends on the concrete circumstances of the situation in which the confrontation of cults and deities takes place. This may be connected with political processes in which a place, along with its local cult, succeeds in becoming predominant over a large political realm, as was frequently the case in ancient Egypt. Even a cultural collapse can play a role, as in the history of Marduk, which is still to be mentioned. Nevertheless, the decisive factors are the possibilities already inherent in the historically developed form of a specific deity, in its myth and cult, for mastering new situations and which permit combinations with new aspects. For all the special conditioning of a given historical situation by what are today called non-religious factors – e.g., of a political or cultural sort – the growth or fixation, retrogression or disappearance of religious motifs, the fate of god-figures and of whole religions, is ultimately decided by their religious convincingness or lack of it; by the power over reality in relation to the horizon of experience of the current historical situation which either emanates from them or fails to appear. Thus, it should always be asked where in the experience of reality of a group or a people the occasion for a change of its religious representations and rites is to be found. As has been said, this does not mean explaining religious changes on the basis of other sorts of change, social or political, for instance. For the men of ancient cultures, changes in the social and political world as well as natural events were all alike primarily religious events, the power or weakness of their gods being exhibited therein. "Power or weakness" in this context should never be taken as dependent simply upon the sort of profane meaning of events to which we, too, have access, such as the victory or defeat of a nation, the growth or decline of its order of life, but decisively upon whether the event in question in some way permits being taken as an effect of the power of the god in question, and consequently as a manifestation of his attitude toward his worshipers. In every change in the history of religions, then, it is not only a question of its *occasion* in particular experiences which alter the understanding of reality, but also of the *reasons* for the mastery or non-mastery of the situation that arises thereby – reasons that are to be found in the ability of the current religious traditions themselves to disclose new aspects in the face of new constellations.

The Upper Egyptian deity Amon seems to have possessed an extremely high degree of such an ability. He could not only coalesce with Re and Ptah of the Middle Kingdom, but proved superior even to the Aton religion of Amenhotep IV – not only because of the social power of the Amon priests but also because the god, Aton, possessed no such broad spectrum of attributes as to be able to fit the complexity of the Egyptian understanding of reality. Thus, the lack of an illuminating relationship to Osiris, the god of the dead, may have contributed to the inferiority of Aton. Amon, on the other hand, could coalesce even with Osiris in the late period. And, as the principle of the all-permeating air, Eusebius in the fourth century A.D. could even explain him as a preliminary stage of the Christian "Spirit" [*Pneuma*].

Another example is provided by Marduk, whose peculiar attractive power made it possible for him to assert himself even after the downfall of the ancient Babylonian empire. It is certainly not self-explanatory that a god should with undiminished esteem outlast the downfall of the society that was originally the bearer of his worship. A similar phenomena is found in the way faith in Yahweh outlived the destruction of the kingdom of Judah by the Babylonians in 587 B.C. Nevertheless, while here it was only the Jewish people themselves, clinging to the previous prophecies of doom, who held fast to their god despite the loss of the old salvific blessings, in the case of Marduk it was the Assyrian conquerors who were so overcome with fascination for his divine character that the efforts of Sennacherib to replace him by Assur in the creation epoch – the way Marduk had himself taken the place of the Sumerian, Enlil – met with no success among the Assyrians. Here we have an impressive example of the diffusion of an old culture into a younger, conquering nation.

A further example might be found in the characteristic of the figure of Mithras as a victor. He would seem to be scarcely conceivable apart from the combination of the Persian god of war with redeemer figures that arose to meet the longings of the men of the Hellenistic age and then again in the late period of the Roman Empire with its economic and political decline. The point of departure for such redeemer figures, which presumably were developed by Near Eastern magicians for motives unknown to us, is to be found in any case in the many-sided cosmic relationships of the figure of Mithras as the deity of the nighttime heaven *and* of the sun, as well as in his primary aspect as the god of the contract. These characteristics made Mithras suitable as a mediatory figure.

The mutual interaction of religious traditions which has resulted in the furthering of such competitive struggles among the gods over the nature of reality is not to be deduced from any sort of principle, but to be understood only by reflecting upon the way it actually took place. The process of the history of religions cannot be constructed nor even periodized *a priori*. One cannot allow, not even for a moment, a fundamental distinction between folk religions and universal religions, as if up to a specific historical epoch there were only folk religions, and thereafter universal religions also came into existence.[39] Religions having a universal tendency did not arise for the first

[39] So, Gustav Mensching, *Volksreligion und Weltreligion* (Leipzig, 1938). Both of the main distinctions developed by Mensching – that world religions arise from individuals, not from peoples; and that the primary occasion for them is a state of disaster, not of prosperity – do not establish any strict disjunction between the two types since both characteristics can be found in the contrasted type as well. Recently, Mensching (*RGG*³ vol. 5, col. 967) took his distinction between folk religions and world religions as the principle for dividing the history of religions and connected it with Karl Jaspers's attempt to establish the unity of human history by orienting it around an "axial period" (*The Origin and Goal of History*, trans. Michael Bulloch [New Haven: Yale University Press, 1953], pp. 1ff.). This attempt, as Jaspers himself noted (*ibid.*, pp. 278f.) was based on observations made by Alfred Weber (*Kulturgeschichte als Kultursoziologie* [Leiden, 1935], p. 24). According to this view, important and fundamental changes in the spiritual posture of mankind, affecting subsequent generations right down to the present, occurred simultaneously in the four most important cultural spheres of the ancient world – the Near East, Greece, India, and China –

time only after the beginning of the first millennium before Christ. Even ancient Sumerian religion and culture seems to have had a universal character, at least from the standpoint of its symbolism, although its actual spread remained limited to the southern area of the Tigris–Euphrates valley. And the Israelitic universalism which is claimed as an example of the new universal form of religiousness has its roots in the second millennium, in the heavenly creator-god, El, on the one hand, and in ancient Egypt, on the other – to the extent that it is connected with special Jerusalemite traditions like world rule, which Psalm 2 ascribes to the Davidic king. Thus, with regard to their spiritual posture, folk religions and universal religions are not so easily separated. In the sense of actual expansion, however, the distinction can hardly be made on the basis of an axis that is supposed to have been established at such an early date. The genuinely universal *propagation* that arose from the Israelitic heritage in the religions of Christianity and Islam falls in a later millennium.

Thus, even here one finds no handle for a fundamental division of the history of religions. All that is left to us is to follow the actual course of the debates, splits, growth or decline, fusion or supersession of individual religions in their relationships with one another. Can we discover some sort of unity in these mutual interactions that would permit us to speak of a common history of religions?

The religions of mankind have as little unity at the outset as

---

between 900 and 500 B.C. That is certainly a noteworthy matter. But that a "threshold" (an expression taken from John Cobb) in the development of mankind was crossed over here still does not justify systematizing this epoch into the "axis" of world history. This step is already problematic insofar as Jaspers admits that he wants to replace the axis which the Christian understanding of history has provided up to now by a construction accessible to non-Christians as well (*Origin and Goal*, p. 19). It may be questioned, however, that the presuppositions for such an analogical transfer are really present in this case. The segment of time in which everywhere the subjectivity of the individual made its breakthrough lacks the homogeneity that is to be expected of an axis of history, and aside from this, the subjectivity of man may be too ambiguous in itself to be able to qualify as the axis of history.

mankind itself. The different religious traditions seem rather to have had a multiplicity of different starting points among the different tribes and peoples. In another sense, these independently originated religious traditions had a universal character from early on, namely, as ascriptions of universal meaning [*universale Sinndeutungen*] to existence. Such an intended universalism stands in contrast to the actual pluralism of religious origins. But this conflict becomes conscious only to the extent that communication develops between the individual groups. A common history of religions arises only when suitable conditions bring about a competition between the different religions stemming from a collision between their competing intentions of universal meaning, and proceeds hand in hand with the onset of the political and economic integration of man. One can begin to speak of a global process of integration for the first time in relation to the history of Christian missions and the Islamic conquests. Christian missionary activity especially, which proceeded apace with the expansion of Western civilization and technology in the last century, drew together the different, more or less isolated religious traditions into a world history of religion. The unification of the religious traditions of mankind taking place in this process does not appear for the first time with the displacement of other religions by Christianity. Rather, the simple fact of the different religions moving into relationship with each other mainly through the impact of the Christian missions brought to the fore a unity in the religious world situation, albeit one filled with tension. In just this way conflict and debate between the different religions became unavoidable since now the religious traditions find it less easy to remain encapsulated alongside each other. Up to now, the inevitable religious conflicts have been concealed by a tendency toward relativizing every kind of religious faith as a result of a secular understanding of human existence. But this secular understanding of human existence which has brought about an unheard of homogenization among the various cultures is in itself, once again, a product of Christianity. Thus, by means of its thrust toward a universal mission, Christianity has become the ferment for the rise of a common religious situation of the whole of mankind. And only in relation to this is it possible to speak of a general religious history of mankind. The unity of the history of religions is therefore not to be found in their beginnings, but rather in their end. At present, it has only the form of a tension-filled unity of the common religious situation of mankind, which is characterized by competing religious claims. But the struggle of religious traditions with each other points beyond the present to another form of religious unity which is trying to take shape in such struggles. Such a unity has always attained a merely particularistic form in the history of religions up to now. But it would seem to be the most distinguished task of religious-historical research to investigate the occasions and motives that have from time to time contributed to such developments, since the unity of the history of religions is not simply to be presupposed as given – that would be a fiction – but to be inquired after in its growth within the processes of history.

In this connection, the history of Christianity is of special interest in the history of religions on account of its specific contribution to the rise of a worldwide religious situation. The rise of Christianity as a religion already presupposes the religious and cultural unification of the ancient Mediterranean region by Hellenism. Christianity, as could be shown in detail, took possession of the heritage of this whole, complex cultural and religious world. Thus, the process which was bringing about the fusion of the cultures of the ancient Mediterranean world temporally as well as substantively paved the way for the ascent of Christianity as a world religion, and in this double sense constitutes its historical footing.

This provides a point of entry for a presentation of the unity of the history of religions as a unity that proceeds from the processes of historical interaction between the different religions. It is not necessary to take as such a point the obscure, scarcely discoverable beginnings of religion. The path to the religious unity of mankind can be attacked from many points of departure, but the critical process of integration begins in the comparatively bright light of historical knowledge, with the religions of the ancient Mediterranean world and of the Near East, with the Egyptians and in the Tigris-Euphrates valley, with the Persians and their Indian kin who then went their own way for quite a while. The overlapping and coalescence of the most varied religious traditions is evidenced with particular intensity in the history of Israel and then of the Greeks – and more than ever in primitive Christianity, in which the Jewish and Greek heritages were united, and in the expansion of Christianity throughout the ancient religious world, which was saturated with Hellenism. The process of religious integration was at first interrupted by the rise of Islam at the borders of the Christian world, only then to maintain a development that was nonetheless in many respects parallel to it. This process advanced farther in the outreach of the Christian missionary movement beyond the Hellenistic realm, especially by the conversion of the Slavic and Germanic peoples to the Christian faith, and then by the colonization of America, and finally by encountering the religions of the Far East and the illiterate cultures of Africa and Australia, which at that time along with their histories entered the stream of the world history of religion which the Christian mission had mediated. Finally, in this century, the diffusion of the secular culture of the West altered the traditional form of the Christian mission itself after this had led – not to the conversion of man, of course, but in another sense – to a common religious situation characterized, on the one hand, by the confrontation of all the religious traditions of mankind with the Christian tradition, and, on the other, by the secularized form of human existence in industrialized society.

It is possible in such a way to trace how the unity of the history of religions takes shape in the history of particular religions, and how therein – this has still to be shown – the unity of the divine reality itself is operative, upon whose appearance the religions depend. This path of a progressive religious integration of mankind – in ever new surges, even if not without interruptions, defeats, and new splits – is possible because from the very beginning different peoples understood their gods as powers determining the totality of reality. Only because of this can the controversy between the religions about the nature of reality arise, the result of which is the progressive unification of the history of religions, even if in a plurality of differently articulated religious perspectives.

IV. THE REALITY-REFERENCE [*Wirklichkeitsbezug*] OF RELIGIOUS EXPERIENCE AND ITS SIGNIFICANCE FOR THE UNDERSTANDING OF THE HISTORY OF RELIGIONS

Observation of the growth and alteration of religions in their reciprocal relationships with each other permits no answer to the question of the specifically religious truth inhering in religious myths and rites unless a judgment about the relationship of religious experience to reality is already presupposed. Research into the history of religions has for the most part attempted to dispense with the pros and cons of such a judgment – not only about the truth claim of this or that specific religion, but also with regard to the truth of any sort of religious experience whatever – and to construe religious phenomena simply as expressions of human attitudes.[40] It nevertheless remains a question whether such abstention permits the process of the *transformation* of religious images and forms of life to be appropriately described, viz., as motivated by religious upheavals that are not simply identical with political or social shifts, and by experiences with the specifically religious power of inducing the convictions which have been deposited in new religious forms. Since such processes of change in the religious

[40] Nathan Söderblom says this himself: "The comparative study of religions in general leaves the question about revelation open. He who practices it may be inspired by the conviction that a supranatural reality is lying behind the phenomena of religion. Or he may deny the belief in the spiritual which is fundamental for religion. Or he may remain inquiring and uncertain about the revelation, certain only of the impossibility of knowing anything about it. Or he may lack interest in the question about the truth of religion" (*The Living God*, p. 384). Söderblom's own personal perspective was completely determined by the acceptance of a progressive revelation in all religious phenomena. On this, see Rosenkranz, "Wege und Grenzen," pp. 235ff.

consciousness are repressed for the most part, the specialist in religious studies is thrown back upon his own categories in trying to describe them, and cannot be content simply to play back the religious convictions of others. His description of the historic transitions involved in the religious transformations remain unsatisfactory, however, if it is incommensurable with the religious character of the phenomena that constitutes their starting point and end point; in other words, when it tries to explain the religious change simply in terms of political and social changes. For this reason, when trying to understand religious transformations it is not as easy to bracket out the question of the specific reference to reality [*Wirklichkeitsbezug*][41] of religious phenomena as it is in the case of mere phenomenological analysis of the forms of behavior and images that have been developed and intended by other men as expressions of their faith. At least in hypothesis it is necessary to introduce assumptions about the peculiar character and reality-reference of religious experiences in describing religious transformations as religious processes.

The question about the truth content of religious experiences, insofar as they derive from encounters with suprahuman powers that cannot be exhaustively understood by means of the natural occurrences that stand in the foreground of such experiences,

---

[41] I prefer this expression to talk about the truth of "the" religion (on this, see the third book of Heinrich Scholz, *Die Religionsphilosophie* [Berlin, 1921], pp. 331–443: *Die Wahrheit der Religion*). To be sure, every religion or every religious assertion may be questioned as to its truth – in the limited sense of the word as the truth of judgment (*ibid.*, pp. 333ff.). But when it is a question of the truth of "the" religion, it must immediately be asked *which* religion is meant in this case, since the claims of the various religions conflict with each other and cannot all be "true" at the same time. Thus, absolute truth can only belong to a specific religion, if to any at all. This does not necessarily exclude all truth *content* from other religions, nor, above all, does it deny that any other religion may perhaps in an inadequate or distorted way refer to the same *reality* as the religious assertions acknowledged as "true." Thus, when it is a question of whether all religions, regardless of their differences and opposition, are not mere products of fantasy but have to do with a suprahuman supraworldly reality, one should rather speak of the *reference to reality* expressed in their experience or of the *truth content* [*Wahrheitsgehalt*] of their assertions, instead of speaking flatly of their "truth".

cannot be unpacked here to its full extent. In the context of this exposition, it must suffice to open up the question whether the reality-reference of religious experiences can be decided by an analysis of these experiences in themselves, or whether the judgment about this depends upon other perspectives.

For years, people believed that the problem raised by Ludwig Feuerbach's illusion theory whether religious phenomena generally were grounded in some sort of extrahuman reality or whether they consisted of mere projections of subjective human states could be settled by deeper psychological understanding of the religious consciousness or of religious experience. Along these lines, even Ernst Troeltsch held that "in the analysis of religious needs an objective referent is always co-posited, from which the former proceeds." The therein documented presentiment of an infinite and absolute is "not something we learned from reality and bestowed our wishes upon by imagination, but rather a non-arbitrary, original datum of consciousness co-posited in every religious feeling."[42] As a purely psychological argument this contention would hardly be able effectively to meet Feuerbach's theory of projection, any more than William James's appeal to the persuasiveness of the feelings of reality in the processes of religious experience.[43] An ever so intensive feeling of reality can be completely erroneous, and likewise there are doubtless also non-arbitrary illusions, if it does not belong to the essence of illusions to be non-arbitrary. Nor can the theory

[42] Ernst Troeltsch, "Die Selbständigkeit der Religion," *Zeitschrift für Theologie und Kirche* 5 (1895): 406. For the argument concerning non-arbitrariness, see esp. pp. 408ff., and also the whole line of argument beginning on p. 400. Troeltsch himself designates Eduard Zeller's essay "Ursprung und Wesen der Religion" (in *Vorträge und Abhandlungen: Zweite Sammlung* [Leipzig, 1877], 2: 1–92) as the source of his debate with Feuerbach ("Die Selbständigkeit," p. 410). Troeltsch expects the psychology of religion which, it is true, he did not distinguish from religious anthropology but whose task he saw as consisting precisely in "establishing the place, origin, and meaning of religion in human consciousness," to convey "what can be made of the question of the truth of religion generally" (*ibid.*, p. 370).

[43] William James, *The Varieties of Religious Experience* (New York: Modern Library, 1902), pp. 72ff. Cf. the arguments of Scholz, *Religionsphilosophie*, pp. 131ff., that religion rests upon an "experience" [*Erlebnis*] of the divine, not upon needs.

of illusion be disarmed – as Troeltsch saw[44] – even by pointing to the fact that the gods of the religions are not merely embodiments of human wishes, as the early Feuerbach had asserted, but that fear in the presence of unknown powers is a fundamental feature of religious experience, which emerges with particular force in "primitive" religions.[45] That the pre-givenness of the holy that has appeared to it is intended by the religious subjectivity itself cannot be denied, but that does not exclude the possibility that subjectivity deceives itself here as it occasionally does elsewhere regarding what in fact is going on. A decision on this question cannot be attained by means of psychological description since the problem consists precisely in whether or not the psychic intentions so described do not rest upon an illusion. The settlement of this question depends at least partially upon grasping the fundamental anthropological structures of human behavior [*Verhaltens*] which manifest themselves in the psychologically observed modes of behavior [*Verhaltensweisen*] but may also be concealed by them. Feuerbach developed his argument on this level. His thesis states that the fundamental structure of human behavior generates the religious illusion. Such an argument cannot be countered by

[44] In "Die Selbständigkeit," p. 407, Troeltsch rightly remarked that the priority of fear over wishing in religious experience, which Karl C. Holsten (1886) had emphasized, indeed disposes of the theory of pure wishfulness, but "not without further qualification" the theory of illusion. In his *Lectures on the Essence of Religion*, Feuerbach took full account of fear in the presence of natural powers as the root of religion. Only he was of the opinion that in the course of development "heightened longing transformed the terrifying deities into friendly fulfillers of human wishes" (Troeltsch, "Die Selbständigkeit," p. 408).

[45] Bousset, *What Is Religion?* pp. 17ff. One thinks of Rudolf Otto's description of the *mysterium tremendum* in *The Idea of the Holy*, trans. John W. Harvey (London and New York: Oxford University Press, 1948), pp. 12ff. Against Schleiermacher, Otto rightly says that it is not the feeling of dependence that is primary in religion, but that it rather "has *immediate* and *primary* reference to an *object outside itself*" (*ibid.*, p. 10 [italics by Otto]). This priority of "an *objectively* given numinous object" (*ibid.*, p. 11) in religious experience expresses itself fundamentally in "the feeling of its 'absolute superiority (also unapproachability)' ", which is already presupposed in the feeling of dependency (*ibid.*) and to which the numinous is present precisely as "terrifying mystery" [*mysterium tremendum*].

psychological observations, but only by statements that pertain to the same level, the level of anthropological structure. Troeltsch's early sketch of a psychology of religion was basically scaled to this level, too. Its whole approach is more that of a philosophy of spirit; more metaphysical than that of an empirical, descriptive psychology. But Troeltsch still lumped both of these together. Not until a few years later did he separate the anthropological question about the structure of the human spirit from psychology, which was now also limited to the observation and analysis of phenomena.[46]

We do not need here to go any further into the problems that arose from the fact that the question about the fundamental anthropological structure of religious behavior, now distinguished from psychological analysis, first emerged in the unfortunate form of theories about a "religious *a priori*."[47] In order

---

[46] In his *Psychologie und Erkenntnistheorie in der Religionswissenschaft* (Tübingen, 1905), pp. 17f., Troeltsch expressly states that psychology is incompetent to decide on the question of the truth content of religion.

[47] This theory, first developed by Ernst Troeltsch in 1905 (in the work mentioned in the previous note), was further elaborated by Rudolf Otto and – partially in criticism of both of these men – finally by Anders Nygren in *Die Gültigkeit der religiösen Erfahrung* (Gütersloh, 1922). On the further development of Nygren's ideas see Bernard S. Erling, *Nature and History: A Study in Theological Methodology* (Lund, 1960).

The unfortunate thing about the concept of the religious *a priori* is not so much the alleged, much discussed impasse of how it might be possible for one to speak of a rational transcendental structure of what is nevertheless an irrational religious experience. All experience includes pre- or nonrational elements, and their thoroughgoing rationalization usually is first brought about by means of reflection. But what is unfortunate is the idea of an *a priori* structure of religious experience, because this necessarily misses the character of such experience as the divine reality's manifestation to man. If religious experience were grounded in an *a priori* capacity of the human spirit, then it would be the creature of this capacity. The human spirit would dictate its laws to God, as does the mind to nature in Kant's philosophy. Religious experience nevertheless understands itself, on the contrary, as the recognition of an appearance of the divine over which man has no power to dispose, so that it is a demonstration of a divine favor not only in its "that" but also in its content. How this view can coexist with the insight into the thoroughgoing spontaneity of all acts of our subjectivity, which has prevailed since Kant, may constitute a serious problem. However, it will not be solved by analogizing application of the Kantian apriorism to the

to do justice to the substantive interest of this theory it is necessary to see that it does not mean simply capitulation to the neo-Kantian spirit of the times, but rather an attempt, clothed in these garments, to establish that religious life is a necessary element in the structure of man's existence, so that religious phenomena can no longer be dismissed as products of a self-deception on the part of man who mistakenly takes his own being as an alien entity. Understood in this way, and freed of their Kantian terminology, such considerations are still pertinent in contemporary anthropological discussion.[48]

Where it is a matter of the reality perceived in religious experiences and thus of the truth of religious assertions, even the anthropological argument has its limitations, however. To be sure, only within the realm of anthropological discussion can one decide about a hypothesis such as Feuerbach's, according to which – at any rate under certain social conditions (if one follows the Marxistic extension of the theory) – it belongs to the structure of human existence to produce illusory objectivations to which the religious phenomena compiled by religious studies correspond. If this or other similar hypotheses, such as Freud's, are able to maintain themselves against all criticism on anthropological grounds, then for modern man, who can no longer find divine powers directly present in nature, all assertions of such a kind - even if they are declared to be "non-religious" - would collapse. Thus, the anthropological argument is decisive for the atheistic criticism of religion. The situation is not so simple for the opposite side, the side that makes a religious – or even "non-religious" – assertion of the divine reality. True, even here the anthropological theme is indispensable. Only on the condition that hypotheses *à la* Feuerbach do not have the last word can talk about God or divine powers or even of merely a dimension

---

holy, as if this were a realm of experience of the same character as experience of the world. At this point, the protest of dialectical theology was justified in its time (Karl Barth, *Die Christliche Dogmatik im Entwurf* [Munich, 1927], pp. 52f.).

[48] On this point and the following discussion, see "The Question of God," below, pp. 201ff.

of the holy be taken seriously as intellectually honest. In addition, such assertions must positively prove themselves worthy of belief[49] if they are to be able to claim universal relevance. Religious assertions, just like others, can win credibility only by means of a positive relationship to the experience of the rest of reality. For modern man, however, whose relationship to nature is determined by the modern natural sciences, there is no longer any direct way from the facts of nature to the idea of God. Even if reference to the world is unavoidable for religious assertions, and even indispensable for their very credibility, nevertheless the world cannot be the point of departure for their grounding. In any case, anthropology would provide such a point only if it could be shown that the idea of God or – to put it impersonally – of a mysterious ground of all reality transcending one's own and all other finite existence, is so implied in the movement of human existence beyond everything finite that man finds himself referred to this transcendent mystery and can have a well-founded hope for the fulfillment of his existence only from it.[50] As long as this kind of argument deals only with

[49] As Augustine wrote, "No one believes anything unless he has first thought that it is to be believed" (see above, p. 52, n. 14).

[50] On this point, see Max Scheler's anthropologically grounded philosophy of religion – which in its middle phase conceived the reference of man to God personalistically, although later it shifted to impersonal terms – and its further influences in Catholic theology. Even the later Scheler spoke of an indivisible structural unity of world-, self-, and God-consciousness: "At the moment . . . when an attitude of world-openness originated and a never-ceasing urge to penetrate without limits into the revealed sphere of the world and to stop at nothing in the world of facts . . ., at this moment man was also driven to anchor his own central being in something beyond this world" (*Man's Place in Nature*, trans. Hans Meyerhoff [New York: Noonday Press, 1962], p. 90). The continuing influence of Scheler in Catholic philosophy of religion has been set forth by Heinrich Fries in *Die katholische Religionsphilosophie der Gegenwart* (Heidelberg, 1949). The work of Karl Rahner in the philosophy of religion is given special prominence here, along with Rosenmöller and Wust. In his book on the foundations of his philosophy of religion, *Hörer des Wortes* (Munich, ²1963), Rahner explained, from the standpoint of the phenomenon of fore-conception [*Vorgriff*] in every judgment of general truth (pp. 75ff.), that "the finite spirit, by virtue of its transcendence, experiences itself as grounded with reference to the absolute" (*ibid.*, p. 111], and that this absolute being confronts us as a person [*ibid.*, p. 112]. Later, Rahner spoke somewhat more

statements about the structure of human existence, the question about the independently existing reality of God or of divine powers remains still open.

For this reason, the decisive step first occurs with consideration of the fact that the abstractness of statements about the anthropological structures can be overcome. If it belongs to the structure of human existence to presuppose a mystery of reality transcending its finitude and to relate oneself to this as the fulfillment of one's own being, then in actuality man always exists in association with this reality.[51] True, he does not associate

---

reservedly about the presence of a holy mystery in the "finite spirit's transcendence, which is directed to absolute being" (*Theological Investigations*, 5 vols. [Baltimore: Helican Press, 1967], 4:49). Gerhard Ebeling has recently related the word "God" to "the mystery of reality" in a specific way, namely, by referring to the phenomenon of language as the medium of experience of reality (*God and Word*, trans. James W. Leitch [Philadelphia: Fortress Press, 1967], p. 31).

[51] This might be explained in greater detail by referring to the fact that as an ec-centric being, man always has a relationship to himself, to the totality of his existence (including that of his world), and thereby also to that ground which constitutes human existence as a (non-present but anticipated) whole. It is this that first makes intelligible the fact that the divine mystery is not merely an unconscious presupposition of the structure of man's existence, but rather something man finds himself confronted by and is always associating with. The concept of association [*Umgangs*] goes beyond Rahner's statements in *Hörer des Wortes* according to which man "is always a listener for a possible revelation of God" (p. 115; cf. pp. 112, 184, 185ff.) and must reckon with something of that sort (p. 116). Since Rahner here projects his analysis of anthropological structures only toward the occurrence of the one Christian revelation in its true form, conceiving this not within the context of a historical process but rather as something that is supposed to "intersect human history in its spatio-temporal extension in a pointlike manner" (p. 194), the history of men's actual associations with this mystery, insofar as they have always experienced themselves as in one form or another constituted by it (provided that this does belong to the structure of human existence) is always passed over, so that the revelation envisaged as something pointlike always retains the appearance of something extraordinary and without continuity with the process of history. Later, Rahner (esp. in *Theological Investigations*, 5:97–134, 157ff.) included the Christ event more clearly in a process of human history as redemptive history. He even ascribed to the non-Christian religions the significance of being mediators of salvation for pre-Christian men, analogous to that of the Christian revelation (*ibid.*, pp. 128ff.). Nevertheless, reflection upon the *mediating*

with it as one object of his conduct *alongside* others. Rather, in all his experience of finite reality he at the same time, in one form or another, reaches out beyond its finitude and in this way is expectant of the infinite mystery that is present in it. And granted that what is at stake for man in his being referred to that mystery is essentially the wholeness of his own being and therefore of the universal truth that unites all men, as well as the unity of the world and the correspondence of his existence with this, it follows that this mystery will confront him particularly in events which illuminate a wider range of his experience of existence and in fact will encounter him as a power over at least one *aspect* of his existence and of his world as a whole.

The *reality* of the mystery of being, to which the structure of man's existence points, must be demonstrated in such actual *association* with this mystery. In this sense, the reality of God or of divine power can be proven only by its *happening* [*Widerfahrnis*], namely, in that it proves itself powerful within the horizon of current experience of existence. That is the element of truth in the position that wants to ground the truth of religious experiences in their self-evidence. But religious experiences do not possess such self-evidence as isolated events, but by their reference to the whole current experience of existence. The gods of religion confront men as realities distinct from themselves because they are experienced as powers over the whole of man's existence including the world.

What does it mean to say that the gods or god prove their reality by the happening of their power over the existence of

---

function of the history of mankind and especially of the history of religions for the revelation of Christ is lacking. This is probably connected with the fact that redemptive history in a narrower ("official") sense is first constituted by a supplementary, specially revealed divine interpretation (*ibid.*, pp. 106f.), so that a dichotomizing element remains in the relationship between redemptive history and world history. Is the history of man outside this official interpretation seen as anything else than an expression of the transcendental disposition of man for God? Is it looked at as a process of association with this God in which thereupon even the perversion of his appearances and the shattering of such perversion takes place?

man in the world? This statement has a thoroughly unmytho-
logical meaning. Where the god transmitted by tradition from
earlier generations, or remembered from one's own previous
experience, or even as never before so conceived – or even the
impersonal, hidden mystery of human existence – suddenly becomes relevant for the experience of human existence in a
concrete situation, at that point there takes place a happening
of *the* reality to which religious language and, implicitly, all
human behavior is related in its transcending fore-conception
beyond itself and everything finite. This is what in Christian
terms is called an act of God.

Now if it is the case that the question about the reality of
that which is presupposed in man's fore-conception toward the
truth transcending everything finite and which is attested by
religious experiences permits of being answered only by the
occurrence of their powerful happenings, then the question
about the truth of religious assertions of the reality of divine
powers is in a surprising way referred to the history of religions.
Happenings of divine reality are historical events, first of all
with regard to the act of their happening. As powerful events
they – or the power experienced in them – illuminate the
experience of existence of the men who encounter such happenings. But since men's experience of existence – their picture of
nature and their historical world - succumbs to progressive
transformation, thus even the experienced happening of divine
reality does not automatically retain its power over men. It
grows pale – whereby, with its sinking into the past, even its
deity can become doubtful – or else it may find a continuation
in new happenings. Even in this sense the individual happening
of divine reality is historic. As an individual event, it becomes
a member of a series of other such happenings. The peculiar
character as well as the reality of the divine mystery to which
man is referred in the transcending movement of his existence
comes into play again and again in the succession of such
events. To this extent, the question about the *existence* of a god
is inseparable from that of his powerful *appearance* and of his
revelation – in the sense of his definitive appearance.

The historicness of the appearance of the divine reality, which by no means always confirms its earlier appearances but often contradicts them, can be understood on the basis of its infinity and by its correspondence to the historicness of human existence.[52] To the infinity of the divine, which is presupposed by man in his transcendence over the world (as the sum of everything finite), there corresponds an uncloseable path of religious knowledge,[53] because every individual step demonstrates that it was once again finite, no matter how much the universal truth that stands in contrast to all finite appearances may also be formulated in it. And, nevertheless, that infinite mystery does *appear* on the stages along this way. Every new stage, as long as its limits remain concealed, exalts itself as an appearance of the all-embracing, infinite mystery. For this reason, time is the condition and measure of the appearance of the infinite in the finite because the difference between the future and the present conceals the limits of what is present and allows the infinite to shine forth in it in full luster as long as its time continues. The power encountered in the current experience of reality in its totality – as world – and which appears as the unifying unity of this whole, is the reality with which the religions are concerned, and which alone may be called "God," if it manifests itself in a personal mode.[54] But just as the world and the life of man in their temporality are unclosed, so the whole of finite reality appears – provisionally – different at each point in time.

---

[52] Karl Rahner also saw this connection since he characterized the history of man, which is posited along with his transcendence toward absolute being, as the "place" of a possible revelation (*Hörer des Wortes*, p. 143). "Man is a historical being. And this in and because of the orientation of his openness for being generally toward God and thus toward a possible revelation" (*ibid.*, p. 198). Missing once again is the process character of this history as a sequence of appearances of that being for which man is open. No entity can persist in an empty openness, but lives instead from the appearance of that for which it is open.

[53] Gregory of Nyssa had already recognized this as a consequence of the infinity of God. Cf. Ekkehard Mühlenberg, *Die Unendlichkeit Gottes bei Gregor von Nyssa* (Göttingen, 1966).

[54] Thus, Luther's *Large Catechism* states, in explaining the first article of the creed: "Apart from him alone I have no other God, for there is no one else who could have created heaven and earth" (*BC*, p. 412).

If that were not the case God would not be infinite, i.e., he would not be God, and the reference of man toward God would not be an infinite task in which his destination can ever again become an open question which therefore also keeps room open for his possible freedom. Only in the mode of history can the destiny of man for fellowship with the infinite God take shape.

The path of this history is characterized not by the lack of, and the continual delay of its goal, but rather by the appearing of its goal – the divine mystery and the destination of man for life in the presence of God – in the stages along the way, although only in provisional form. It is not completed, and the goal seems often to be unattainably distant, and yet history knows of provisional realizations. This was characteristic of Israel's history of promises, with their provisional fulfillments which became the pledge of a still greater hope. But the presence of provisional fulfillments of the divine mystery is experienced in every human life. It characterizes the history of religions, too, in another way, of course, than it does Israel's history of promises because in distinction from the promises of Israel the myths of the religions are not inherently determined as provisional, as transitional stages to a greater future, but are instead related to the primordial time and thus closed to the future and to their own transformation.[55]

Related to this temporal closedness is the fixation of the

[55] It is true that even Israel's faith in the promise of God was still restricted in its openness to God's future. The very structure of promise implies its provisionality in relation to the announced future, but the Israelites seem by no means always to have been conscious of the provisionality of both the form and the content of the promises in relation to the future which they anticipated. Obviously, the promises were widely regarded as the measure of the future rather than as pointers to it. Thus, the great prophets had to inveigh against the assurance with which their contemporaries adhered to the promises regarding the future of Zion and of David's house. However, it was precisely faith in the word, widely shared even within the prophetic movement, according to which the prophetic word itself *effected* the future it announced, that stood in the way of recognition of the fact that the promise was only a provisional pointer to the announced future. Nevertheless, the word of promise – and the word of threat accompanying it – opened up experience of the difference between present and future, and thereby the experience of the provisionality of the present and thus of its historicness.

divine mystery on a specific divine medium of its appearance. From the presence of the divine mystery in a mountain, the sun, the wind, or a wise government, there arise the mountain god, the god of the sun or of the wind, the divine king, or the god of wisdom. With the finitization of the divine mystery there appears a fragmentation of the divine power into many powers, even though there is seldom a complete lapse of awareness that in each of these powers one is dealing with a single all-determining divine mystery or at least one of its aspects. This alone can account for the fact that every such form of deity has a tendency to attract other forms of manifestation to itself and in this way to become as universal and many-sided as possible. Still, this tendency is again restricted by the limited representational ability of every finite medium through which the divine mystery might manifest itself. This double finitization, by fixation onto a finite medium, and by splitting into a multiplicity of divine powers,[56] constitutes the presupposition for dividing the profane from the sacred, which is confined to specific times and places. This development for the first time releases efforts to secure the safety of the profane by means of the assistance of sacred power, that attempt to manipulate the divine power which dialectical theology so one-sidedly declared to be the hallmark of all religion. Such an attempt at manipulation totally contradicts the intention of the cult to serve this power and yet it permeates cultic behavior because of the dialectical nature of sacrifice which makes it a self-assertion at the same time.

It can be shown that the finitization of the divine power and the possibility of having it at one's disposal that arises thereby – which becomes explicitly intended only in the practice of magic – is conditioned by the temporal closedness of the re-

[56] Finitization is not primarily accomplished by means of images of the gods, which seek to make visible the proper form of the divine power that remains hidden in its primary manifestations. Images of gods indicate a consciousness that the divine power is not revealed as such in its normal medium of appearance. This runs precisely counter to the finitization of the divine power through fixing it onto a specific medium of appearance. Only when this has been seen is it legitimate to point out that the cult image signifies a new finitization, this time of the god's hidden, proper form.

ligions to the future of their own transformation, which expresses itself in the fact that the myth of the epiphany of the divine mystery thinks of it as the appearance of the perfection of the primordial time. As Eliade has shown,[57] men protect themselves against the dark power of the future by cultic conjuring up of the primordial time related by the myths. In this respect, myth is the original form of what today is affirmed as tradition – constitutive tradition – and even present-day traditions still show a tendency to endow themselves with the mythical features of the archetypal. Nevertheless, whoever lives on the basis of the archetypal and strives to achieve for the present only its optimal participation in the archetypal reality, lives unhistorically. To this extent, archaic peoples close themselves off from the historic future. But in actuality, and against their own wills, all religions stand within a process of history that does not allow the allegedly archetypal contents of their myths to continue to exist as perfect exemplars, but alters them and in this way unmasks their provisionality.[58] The history of religions, as it becomes visible to the historian in retrospect, already accomplishes a critique of the religions because it shows how the archetypally suspended consciousness contradicts itself in its actual behavior. In the repetition of ever renewed critical revision of every one of its stages, the history of religions is the unending path along which the infinite destination of man for the infinite God moves toward its appropriate realization and, indeed, even comes to be manifested – contrary to the self-consciousness of the religions. To be sure, this thesis can be maintained only on the presupposition of the reality of the infinite God. If all speech about God were misguided, not only

---

[57] Mircea Eliade, *Cosmos and History: The Myth of the Eternal Return*, trans. Willard R. Trask (New York: Harper Torchbooks, 1954), esp. pp. 105ff., 111ff.

[58] To be sure, this unmasking usually occurs first from within the perspective of the historian, because as long as they adhere to their gods and myths cultic fellowships as a rule repress every alteration, and project backward into the primordial time any newly developed features of a deity. Thus, even in Israel legal convictions developed later were projected back into the situation of the revelation of the law of God at Sinai.

that which is involved in anthropomorphic finitization but even that which corresponds to the infinite divine mystery, then it would also be meaningless to think of the history of religions as the "coming-to-appearance" of the destination of man for this God. Speaking about God, then, presupposes the appearance – indeed, the *definitive* appearance, i.e., the revelation – of the divine reality as infinite. It may seem as if the very idea of a definitive appearance of God is already involved in hopeless contradiction with the previously emphasized historicness and openness of religious experience. But the truth of the matter is that just the appearance of the divine reality *as* infinite – if this can at all occur in the realm of finitude – is precisely the one thing that could have a definitive character because it would not displace but would instead *disclose* the openness of the future, the noncloseability of the history of mankind *even with respect to its knowledge of God.*

I return here once more to the question of the reality-reference of religious experiences. The result of our study has been that this question cannot be settled by merely psychological investigation. Nor can it be decided yet on the basis of the formal structure of human existence, but rather only in men's association with the transcendent mystery that is always presupposed in the structure of human existence and which proves in the actual course of life whether it is sustaining or not, powerful or impotent, reality or nonentity. The reality of the gods – and of God – is at stake in the process of the history of religions in which gods collapse and newly arise. Therefore, an interpretation of religious experiences and concepts will be able to do justice to them only on the condition that it does not construe the religious life as, on the one hand, a mere epiphenomenon of profane – psychological or social – processes or, on the other hand, as an expression of a divine presence that is independent of the history of its appearances. The religious event moves between these alternatives because the reality of the gods is itself risked or even made debatable in the history of religions. The individual religious appearances are to be understood as arguments in this controversy, arguments – more or less strong – for the reality of the power of the divine mystery. This applies not only to the individual religious happening,[59] but also to religious transformations. Even the transformations of religious ideas, rites, and institutions in the course of their history – for instance, the transformations of a divine figure or of a cult – should not be viewed entirely as functions of political or social upheavals. It is just the transformations of religious phenomena that become intelligible only as the expression in men's existence – no matter in what form – of the presupposed divine mystery *in its debatability*. Naturally, political or social changes play a great role in this since the religious life indeed concerns the understanding of the whole of reality and what makes its wholeness possible. And political and social relations and changes are of considerable importance for the whole of human experience of existence.[60] But they themselves are not unqualifiedly this whole. They may provide the *occasion* for religious transformations – which, moreover, they could never provide were they merely profane states of affairs. However, political and social changes can hardly ever automatically produce religious transformations; rather, they signify a challenge whose mastery or non-mastery remains a matter of the inner strength, the inner health and adaptability of the religious tradition itself at that time.

The result of such reflections is that the history of religions is not adequately understood when it is taken as only a history of the representations and behavior of specific men and groups which in themselves might also be described in purely profane

[59] This expression is always to be understood in the sense of the presence of the encompassing mystery of existence in a particular event, or even in an enduring state of affairs; but it is not to be related to, say, a special gift, usually not communicable to mortals, of seeing ghosts.

[60] To this extent, society and the state do not constitute profane spheres of existence in the usual sense, as if they had nothing at all to do with the religious theme. This is not to recommend any ostensibly theocratic "sanctification" of these realms of life. But it can be shown that it belongs to the revelation of the infinite God through Jesus Christ that the opposition between sacred and profane is negated since precisely the sanctification of the world for this God can occur only by means of its – rightly understood – release into secularity.

categories. More appropriate to its content is a history of religions understood as the history of the appearing of the divine
mystery presupposed in the structure of human existence, whose
reality and peculiar character, however, are themselves at stake
in the process of this history.

Clearly, this mode of observation requires no dogmatic assertion of the reality of God. But in spite of this does it not concern
a *theology* of the history of religions? Certainly not in the sense
of deriving from the history of religious propositions of one sort
or another by means of an undiscussable, presupposed standpoint of faith. But "theology of the history of religions" is a more
appropriate expression for the mode of observation only prepared for here, since the reality of God (or of the gods) is
precisely the object of its occupation with the history of religions.

In addition to this, the Christian perspective will not permit
the rejection of such a theology of the history of religions. This
is not to say that such a point of view needs to argue from a
standpoint of faith instead of appealing to the actual phenomena
of the history of religions. The notion of understanding the
history of religions as the history of the appearances of the divine
mystery indeed did not arise by chance. If this perspective, as
I hope, comes closer than others to the logic of the essential
content of the phenomena of the history of religions, it is nevertheless not *produced* by these phenomena; rather, it is this perspective that first allows the phenomena to be discovered. And
reducing it to its proper *concept*,[61] could hardly be accomplished
without commitment to the God of the Bible and his eschatological revelation in Jesus Christ. For if the processes of religious
transformation are to be thought of as the history of appearances
of the divine, then it is certainly necessary to have an understanding of God that lies beyond the scope of the thought of
almost all the religions under investigation as to their changes,
so far as just these remain closed to the process of their own
transformation. If it is impossible for a religion that is oriented
toward the primordial and archetypal to acknowledge the

[61] In other words, engaging in (the most thorough possible) reflection
upon its logical presuppositions.

changes in its contents, then the understanding of such changes manifestly requires a vantage point beyond the sphere of this ban.

In contradistinction to other peoples and their religions, Israel, in the light of its particular experience of God, learned to understand the reality of human existence as a history moving toward a goal which had not yet appeared. A painful process of historical experience opened the way for the radical reorientation involved in this knowledge. If in the early period of the monarchy Israel still relied upon the redemptive facts of the past, which it had to thank for the foundation of its independent national existence – the gift of the land and the election of Zion along with the Davidic dynasty – so it was by the loss of these saving endowments that its hope was turned completely toward a future, definitive redemptive act of Yahweh. Thereby it came to interpret world history as the path through the present misery to that salvation which was still to appear; as the manner in which the God of the future salvation was already powerful in the present. Nevertheless, Israel continued to seek the fundamental revelation of its God in the events of the past, in the giving of the law at Sinai, and not in the future of God's reign. It was Jesus who first turned this relationship around, departing from the religious traditions of his people where it seemed necessary to do so for the sake of the coming reign of God. This reign was no longer expected as the complete dominance of traditional norms and conceptions of salvation – as the ultimate realization of all that had been included in the election of Zion, or as the delivery of men to their destinies corresponding to their attitude toward the law of God handed down by the tradition. Understood in this way, the coming of God would only be the full realization of a principle already given elsewhere. Thus, who or what God is could not be understood from the side of God's coming. The message of Jesus brought about this change, however, so that now trust in the coming God was to be the sole decisive factor for the salvation or doom of the individual regardless of how his behavior might have appeared from the standpoint of the other traditions of

Israel. Certainly when Jesus spoke of "God" he meant the God of Israel. But he did not think of God's future as fixed by the religious traditions of the Israelitic people, as those who adhered to the piety of the law did. Rather, this future compelled him to do the reverse: to criticize the established and the traditional, and to make a life in love the determining basis of life in the present.

The God of the coming kingdom is thereby understood not only as the author of historical change – as was already the case in ancient Israel – but also as the power for altering his own previous manifestations. As the power to be conceived from the standpoint of its futurity, from the side of its future coming, he can no longer be superseded by any other future or any new experience of God, but instead new happenings of the divine mystery will be only further manifestations of himself in new forms of appearance. For this reason, in the God of the coming reign, who was proclaimed by Jesus, the divine mystery is revealed in its inexhaustibility. And yet it is powerful in the present. His infinity does not make him an indefinite, powerless backdrop of present reality, but rather someone who appears in the changes of history through the repeated break-up of existing religious forms of life and their displacement by new ones. Jesus is the *revealer* of the infinite God only because he in his own person pointed the way to the coming reign of God. He did not bind the infinite God to his own person, but sacrificed himself in obedience to his mission. Christianity indeed gives the appearance of having deified Jesus and thereby of not always having avoided a new finitization of the infinite God, although the christological dogma of the church opposed this danger by means of its distinction between the divine and human "natures" in Jesus. The history of Christianity is burdened by a great many dogmatic finitizations which lose sight of the provisionality and historical mutability of all forms of Christian life and thought. The hierarchical structure of the church and its dogmas especially try to secure a false ultimacy that misplaces its true ultimacy – which is to be found in the historical openness made possible by Jesus. Nevertheless, in the origin of the Christian tradition which remains its norm – with Jesus' message of the coming of God and with the appearance of the divine mystery in his resurrection from the dead – the critical element of historical change in the light of the still-open eschatological future gained entrace into the substance of the Christian religion itself.

As the power of the future, the God of the coming reign of God proclaimed by Jesus already anticipates all later epochs of the history of the church and of the non-Christian religions. From this standpoint, the history of religions even beyond the time of the public ministry of Jesus presents itself as a history of the appearance of the God who revealed himself through Jesus.

But even looking back at it from the standpoint of Jesus, the history of religions permits of being understood as the appearance of the God revealed by him. The alien religions cannot be adequately interpreted as mere fabrications of man's strivings after the true God. Ultimately, they have to do with the same divine reality as the message of Jesus. To be sure, one may observe in the religions man's peculiar resistance to the infinity (non-finitude) of the divine mystery. The forms of religious finitization that result from this, images of God and the cult, may be described, with Paul, as a radical confusion of the infinite with the form of the finite. The deepest reason for this might be found once again in the temporality of the religious attitude. The non-Christian religions perceived the appearance of the divine mystery only in a fragmentary way because they were closed to their own transformation, to their own history. Insofar as the process of religious transformation – described by the historian of religion – takes place behind the backs of the religions, they exemplify in ever new ways the fixation of the infinite God onto the finite medium of its appearance at some time, a fixation over which the infinity of God prevails by means of this process of transformation.

Research in the history of religions that undertakes investigation of the temporal appearances of the divine mystery presupposed in human existence as something under debate in the religious forms of life and their transformation by no means needs to argue in a dogmatic way on the basis of the position of Christianity in the history of religions just mentioned above. As far as it is concerned, it is subject to determination and testing by religious-historical research of the sort that has been described. If such research leads to results similar to those indicated above, that would then indeed – *from the standpoint of the examination of Christianity as a phenomenon in the history of religions*, without any additional supranaturalistic principles – present the history of religions in approximately the way that was suggested above. Nevertheless, it would only be necessary to explicate that where Christianity and its place in the history of religions itself is the theme of the investigation. The investigation of non-Christian religions along the lines of the methodology proposed here is in no way obliged to derive its statements from the Christian revelation. In any case, research in the history of religions should not shut its eyes to its own historical relativity, namely, that its historical way of formulating its questions is conditioned by the discovery of the historicness of human existence in Jewish and Christian historical thought. In addition to this, the specialist in the study of non-Christian religions ought not simply on methodological grounds to resist the *possibility* that examination of the message and history of Jesus by means of this same methodology could lead to the conclusion that at this point in the history of religions – even that of Christianity itself – the ever debatable reality of the divine power in its infinity, which manifests itself in the transformations that take place in the history of religions, appears in a definitive way and becomes revealed.[62] The possibility of such a finding, which of course should not be fundamentally ruled out on methodological grounds even in the study of non-Christian religions, would be allowed not only as a merely subjective *way*

[62] This possibility is by no means a trivial matter for the mode of inquiry into the history of religions which is being discussed here, since – as was mentioned above on p. 109 – it is the reality of the divine mystery, that is to say, of its definitive appearance which overcomes if it does not yet fully remove its debatability, that first makes it meaningful to inquire seriously into the appearance of divine reality in the religious experiences and transformations across the broad field of the history of religions.

of construing the phenomena – which remains exrtinsic and arbitrary in relation to the facticity of religious phenomena – but also as a possible result of research into the message and history of Jesus in relation to the appearance of the divine mystery that had occurred in them, such study being required to hold strictly to the same methodological rules as are applied to any sort of non-Christian religious phenomena. Nevertheless, the kind of openness of the methodology of the history of religions being considered here in relation to the question of the place of Christianity in the history of religions does not mean – assuming that the investigation of the message and history does in fact come to such conclusions – that the description of the non-Christian religions must then be developed as if seen through Christian glasses, so to speak. On the contrary, a direct application of the actual but only subsequently discovered – often only after the continuity of the history of religions as a whole has come into view – relationship of a religion to Christianity would not do justice to the specific situation of that other religion and to its relationship with the divine mystery. Respect for the immediacy of the other religion to the divine mystery is also required of the revelation: it corresponds to the manner in which Jesus, in his message, pointed away from himself to the God he proclaimed.[63] In harmony with this, the characteristic contribution of Christian theology to the history of religions should consist not in some sort of construction developed from the standpoint of Christian dogmatics, but rather in working with an unprejudiced openness to create space in the history of religions for the appearing of the divine mystery *and* for its debatability. Such openness will steer clear of the common attitude which takes it for granted that a non-religious understanding of reality equips one with an ostensibly standpoint-free objectivity which modifies the truth claims of the religions into mere matters of subjective faith positions and registers them only as such. It will

[63] It should be recalled here once again that this gesture of Jesus – and the corresponding self-sacrifice of his individual existence for the sake of his mission – is a decisive condition for the infinite God becoming revealed through him. See my *Jesus – God and Man*, (Philadelphia: Westminster Press and London: SCM Press, 1968), pp. 252ff., 334–7.

also keep itself free of merely subjective sympathizing with the truth claims of one religion or another. Instead of this, it should be tested in every case to what extent the underlying experience of the divine mystery expressed in a religious phenomenon is able to illuminate the reality of existence as it was experienced *then* and as it presents itself in *contemporary* experience, and therewith to confirm its claim to open up an access to the divine mystery.

5

THE APPROPRIATION OF THE
PHILOSOPHICAL CONCEPT OF GOD
AS A DOGMATIC PROBLEM OF EARLY
CHRISTIAN THEOLOGY

This essay originally appeared as "Die Aufnahme des philosophischen Gottesbegriffs as dogmatisches Problem der frühchristlichen Theologie" in *Zeitschrift für Kirchengeschichte* 70 (1959): 1–45.

IN THE golden age of the writing of Protestant histories of dogma around the beginning of our century, a markedly negative judgment about the theological contribution of the earliest Christian Apologists became standard. The fundamental acceptance of philosophical ideas and conceptual schemes into Christianity accomplished in the second century, most strikingly in the area of statements about God's essence [*Wesen*] and attributes, was supposed to portray the beginning of a "hellenization" of Christianity, to use Harnack's famous catchword. According to this view, the Apologists effected an accommodation to the Greek spirit which, while understandable in view of the situation of persecution, nevertheless adulterated the essence of Christianity. Characteristic of this view is the judgment of Friedrich Loofs that the Apologists "did not recognize the disparateness of religious faith and philosophical knowledge or views" and therefore mixed the two together in a disastrous way. This mixing was supposed to have occurred in such a way that religious faith was "degraded" to the level of philosophy.[1] According to Harnack, the Apologists did indeed retain the apostolic tradition in an external way, but in actuality they

[1] Friedrich Loofs, *Leitfaden zum Studium der Dogmengeschichte*, ed. Kurt Aland, 2 vols. (Halle-Saale, ⁵1951–53), 1:88ff.

turned Christianity into "a deistical religion for the whole world."[2] Their "dogmas concerning God are set forth not from the standpoint of the redeemed church, but on the basis of a certain conception of the world on the one hand, and of the moral nature of man on the other; which latter, however, is a manifestation [of] the cosmos."[3]

The dogmatics of Albrecht Ritschl underlies such historical judgments. In the period in which philosophy and theology were in retreat in the face of the advance of natural scientifically oriented positivism, Ritschl endeavored to preserve a special sphere of religious experience, in which he was aware of being allied with the interests of ethics. Precisely in the name of the purity of religious experience, which was not to be confused with world-apprehension, theology ought to eliminate from its tradition the "metaphysical" elements which were also exposed to the critique of positivism. In a remarkable way, the interests of genuine religious life and the positivistic views of the time regarding theoretical knowledge of the world seemed to coincide, in contrast to the traditional metaphysical doctrine of God. Thus, Ritschl saw in the concept of God as the "limitless, indeterminate being, a conception which is already current in the earliest Apologists,"[4] a "metaphysical idol."[5] Here, indeed, was an unholy confusion of religion and a theoretical view of the world. According to Ritschl, this concept of being was "simply the general conception of the world,"[6] and to apply "the title 'God' to this metaphysical postulate is . . . a deception,"[7] and its use in Christian theology is "an unheard-of interference of metaphysics in the religion of revelation."[8]

[2] Adolf von Harnack, *The History of Dogma*, trans. Neil Buchanan, 7 vols. (Boston: Brown, Little & Co., 1897–1900; reprinted by Russell & Russell, 1958), 2:224.

[3] Adolf von Harnack, *Outlines of the History of Dogma*, trans. E. K Mitchell (Boston: Beacon Paperback, 1957), p. 125. [Translation revised slightly – Tr.]

[4] Albrecht Ritschl, *The Christian Doctrine of Justification and Reconciliation*, 3 vols. (Edinburgh: T. & T. Clark, 1900), 3:226.

[5] Albrecht Ritschl, *Theologie und Metaphysik* (Bonn, 1887), p. 20.

[6] *Justification and Reconciliation*, 3:226. Cf. *Theologie und Metaphysik*, p. 11.

[7] *Theologie und Metaphysik*, p. 10.   [8] *Ibid.*, p. 18.

This dichotomization of religion and metaphysics is expressed in the adverse judgments of Harnack, Loofs, and others upon the Apologists of the second century. The thesis that religious and metaphysical understandings of God are irreconcilable and the corresponding assessment of the early Christian doctrine of God are still widely taken as self-evident today, especially in the field of dogmatics, and in fact hardly any less by Werner Elert than by Emil Brunner.[9] Karl Barth's critical reservations about all programmatic apologetics,[10] as well as his fight against everything he calls "natural theology," is likewise in many respects an extension and radicalization of the battle position set up by Ritschl.

In what follows, the complex problems facing us here will be discussed in detail in relation to the example of the early Christian utilization of the philosophical concept of God. It

[9] Emil Brunner, *The Christian Doctrine of God*, trans. Olive Wyon (Philadelphia: Westminster Press, 1949), pp. 153ff. Even Werner Elert, *Der christliche Glaube: Grundlinien der lutherischen Dogmatik*, ed. E. Kinder (Hamburg, (1956), p. 198, views the Apologists' concept of God as intelligible only "in their bitter struggle against all the malicious slanders coming from the surrounding social environment," but does not evaluate it as theologically legitimate. Cf. also Gustav Aulén, *Das christliche Gottesbild in Vergangenheit und Gegenwart* (Gütersloh, 1930 [original in Swedish, 1927]), pp. 28ff., and the more recent publication of Hermann Diem, *Gott und die Metaphysik*, Theologische Studien 47 (Zollikon-Zürich, 1956), pp. 10ff. The influence of the antimetaphysical character of Ritschl's doctrine of God and of his view of the early Christian doctrine of God upon circles that otherwise stood apart from him was probably conveyed through Herman Cremer's *Die christliche Lehre von den Eigenschaften Gottes* (Gütersloh, 1897), pp. 14f.

[10] In his *CD* 1/2, pp. 32f., for instance, Barth sees the dilemma of such apologetics in the fact that it either deceives the unbelieving party in the conversation by alleging to negotiate on the same level with him, or else – in the event such an assurance should really prove true – betrays the essential content of theology (cf. *ibid.*, pp. 392f.). Nevertheless, Barth can also speak positively of a "supplementary, incidental and implicit" apologetics (*CD* 2/1, p. 8). Kurt Aland in *Apologie und Apologetik* (Berlin, 1948) attaches great importance to this. Martin Doerne ("Das unbewältigte Problem der Apologetik," *Theologische Literaturzeitung* 75 [1950]: col. 259) is critical of the defamation of apologetics. And Paul Tillich expressly characterized his theology as "apologetic" (*Systematic Theology* [Chicago: University of Chicago Press and Welwyn: James Nisbet, 1951], 1: 6f.) in contrast to Barth's "kerygmatic" theology.

will have to be considered whether the Apologists' appropriation
of philosophical elements into the Christian doctrine of God
ought not be judged, even from a theological standpoint, in at
least a fundamentally more positive manner than has been
meted out to it since Ritschl, no matter how much criticism
still has to be entered against the way in which the details of
this undertaking were carried out. In so doing, the question
about the competition between these viewpoints, which the
history of dogma has viewed predominantly as a watering down
of the original Christian substance, will appear of itself, so to
speak, at the periphery of the discussion. But first the structure
of the philosophical concept of God on which the Apologists
fastened will have to be examined. Then we must clarify what
the task was which Christian theology set for itself with regard
to the concept of God it encountered in the Hellenistic intellectual world. Finally, there will remain to be investigated the
extent to which the Apologists of the second century mastered
this task.

I. THE PHILOSOPHICAL CONCEPT OF GOD

It was from Platonism, above all, that early Christian theology borrowed the conceptual tools for its reflections upon the
nature of God. In so doing, it did not so much fasten on Plato
himself[11] as on the so-called Middle Platonism, instead. This
has only recently been clearly recognized.[12] We will not within

[11] This was still assumed by J. M. Pfättisch, *Der Einfluss Platos auf die
Theologie Justins des Märtyrers* (Paderborn, 1910).

[12] Hal Koch (*Pronoia und Paideusis: Studien über Origenes und sein Verhältnis
zum Platonismus* [Berlin and Leipzig, 1932]) had already recognized Middle
Platonism, with its peculiar characteristics, as the philosophical background
of Alexandrian theology (on the concept of God, see *ibid.*, esp. pp. 256f.).
Carl Andresen ("Justin und der mittlere Platonismus," *Zeitschrift für
Neutestamentliche Wissenschaft* 44 [1952–53]: 157–95) pointed out Justin's
Middle Platonic background in which one already finds that fusion of
Platonic with Aristotelian and, in part, also Stoic ideas which at once both
raises and makes insoluble the problem of which of these philosophical
systems Justin is to be connected with. Cf. also Andresen's statements on
the Middle Platonic character of Celsus's concept of God (*Logos und Nomos:
Die Polemik des Kelsos wider das Christentum* [Berlin, 1955], pp. 135ff., 157).

the limits of this essay compile once more the statements about God made by Platonists of the first and second centuries. On the other hand, in order to reach the goal set by our theme it is necessary to indicate the inner coherence of the main features of the philosophical concept of God, which in fact were not worked out for the first time in that period. Only in this way can it be shown that in its encounters with philosophy, early Christian theology had to take issue not only with this or that isolated assertion, but also with an indeed variable but nevertheless self-contained mode of inquiry into the reality of God. The theories that had arisen in Greek philosophy concerning the divine reality by no means present a chaos of unrelated, merely adjacent opinions. On the contrary, these opinions grew out of a common formulation of the problem and constitute different variations on one and the same theme. This is why one can speak meaningfully, and without effacing or trivializing the differences between the different systems, of *the* philosophical idea of God. Naturally, this cannot be set forth in its full extent in what follows, but it will instead only be sketched with a few broad strokes.

1. God as Origin

The beginnings of philosophical theology offer the best access to the formulation of the question which is the underlying basis of the unified character of the philosophical idea of God and precedes the various doctrines about the divine. In his *Theology of the Early Greek Philosophers*, Werner Jaeger pointed out that pre-Socratic philosophy is to be understood not as primarily a rudimentary form of natural science but rather as essentially a quest for the true form of the divine. The early Greek philosophy intended to be "natural theology" in the sense of a discipline that inquired into the God who by nature, by virtue of his essence [*phusei*], *is* God, in contrast to the deities of popular belief who are *esteemed* as gods only on the strength of human consensus and convention [*thesei*].[13]

How such a formulation of the question could have come

[13] Werner Jaeger, *The Theology of the Early Greek Philosophers* (Oxford: Clarendon Press, 1947), pp. 2ff.

about in Greece has not yet been investigated. True enough, the specific understanding of God in Greek religion belongs to the historical background of the question about the true form of God, and it appears as if this question is structurally related to a peculiar feature of the Olympian deities, viz., their peculiar immanental character, their being integral to the normal order of events.[14] Homer's gods manifest themselves not in extraordinary, miraculous events, but in precisely the occurrence of the normal, the "natural." Nevertheless, the happening of that which regularly occurs and is completely normal as a fact was intelligible to the Greeks only as something wrought by the gods.[15] The fact that the gods are the origin of the reality encountered in normal experience is not in itself anything specifically Greek but a widespread conviction. But that their essence is exhausted in this function, and does not have a hidden side,[16]

[14] This feature of the Greek understanding of God has often been emphasized, as, recently, by Bruno Snell, *The Discovery of the Mind: The Greek Origins of European Thought*, trans. T. G. Rosenmeyer (New York: Harper Torchbooks, 1953), pp. 25ff.; and Walter F. Otto, *Theophania*, Rowohlts deutsche Enzyklopädie 15 (Hamburg, 1956), p. 29.

[15] Snell (*Discovery of the Mind*, p. 30) provides an excellent example of this: "At the very opening of the *Iliad*, when the quarrel between Agamemnon and Achilles has flared into view, Agamemnon demands that Achilles deliver Briseis over to him; this angers Achilles so much that he clutches his sword and wonders whether he ought to draw it against Agamemnon. At that critical point Athena appears to him, and to him alone we are expressly told. She holds him back and warns him not to fall victim to his wrath; in the end it will be to his advantage to have restrained himself now. Achilles at once obeys the command of the goddess and places his sword back in the scabbard. The poet, we feel, had no special need of the divine apparatus at this juncture; Achilles simply controls himself, and it would have been sufficient to explain his failure to rush upon Agamemnon from his own mental processes. From our point of view, the intercession of Athena merely confuses the motivation rather than making it plausible. Homer, however, could not do without the deity. We might substitute a 'decision' on the part of Achilles, his own reflection and his own incentive. But Homer's man does not yet regard himself as the source of his own decisions; that development is reserved for tragedy."

[16] On the notion, in the religions of the ancient Near East, especially in Egypt, of a second, hidden form of a deity who is manifested in a natural occurrence (e.g., in the rays of the sun), cf. Hermann Kees, *Der Götterglaube im alten Ägypten* (Leipzig, 1941), p. 346; as well as Hubert H. Schrade, *Der verborgene Gott* (Stuttgart, 1949), pp. 128ff.

which is reserved for special revelation, is a peculiarity of the Olympian deities. For this reason, "the self-testimony of the deity on which we place so much confidence, which begins with the words 'I am,' is unthinkable in the mouth of a Greek god."[17] The Greek gods need no special revelation in order to make their essence known, for they "are a necessary part of the world."[18] That is their "immanence."

Philosophical theology's point of departure becomes intelligible from this standpoint. If it is the characteristic function of the divine to be the origin of normal events, then – under possible historical conditions which need not be discussed here – the reversal of this lies close at hand: the truly divine can be no other than the origin needed to bring about the familiar reality, and which every explanation of this reality presupposes. In this way it becomes possible to reason back from the normal states of affairs encountered in ordinary experience of the world to the true nature of the divine. Whatever is most illuminating and offers the most comprehensive understanding of how the known processes and things come to pass must be the truly divine. Whatever else has been handed down about the gods must be judged as a restricted human conception of the truly divine. Motifs such as adultery, strife, and deceit must be culled out of the myths. Xenophanes had already turned against such features as being incongruous with the divine "perfection." Later on, offensive features were reinterpreted allegorically.

The presupposition that had determined the philosophical question about the original reality since the time of the pre-Socratics was that the divine must be understood as the ultimate origin of what is present in the world and that for this reason the truly divine can be grasped by means of an inference from the known state of reality back to its unknown origin. The answers of the systems varied, as is well known. Thales apparently was still aware of the connections between his questions and the religious tradition, since he combined the thesis that water was the first principle [*archē*] with a reference to the myth that the sea gods Oceanus and Tethys were the primordial

[17] Otto, *Theophania*, p. 29.   [18] Snell, *Discovery of the Mind*, p. 25.

progenitors of the world.[19] Anaximenes suggested that the *archē* was something ethereal. He thought of it as "breath" [*pneuma*] and thereby became the predecessor of a long line of later thinkers who defined the true *archē* as pure spirit.[20] Xenophanes had already expressed himself along these lines. Anaxagoras attempted to explain the cosmological influence of the spirit and, following him, Diogenes of Apollonia was the first to explicitly identify air, spirit, and the divine.[21] Diogenes was also the first to utilize the idea of the purposeful order of the cosmos as an argument for its origin being a thinking, planning mind.[22] This argument, later called the "cosmoteleological" argument, was not at first intended as a proof for the existence of a deity. That was hardly in question. But that the divine must be of an *intellectual* nature could be proven only by pointing to an arrangement of the world that was explicable only on the basis of an *intellectual* origin. According to Xenophon's report,[23] this argument was also put forth by Socrates. It is encountered in Plato,[24] and its significance for Stoic natural theology is well known.

2. *The Unity of God*

The question about the true God as the origin of present things and normal processes led with a certain stringency to the idea of the unity of God. In his dialogue, the Apologist Justin had the Platonist put forward an argument that was common in Middle Platonism: there cannot be a plurality of ultimate

---

[19] Thales A 12 (Aristotle *Metaphysics* 983f27ff.).

[20] Anaximenes B 2 [cited by Jaeger, *Theology of the Early Greek Philosophers*, p. 79]. According to Minucius Felix *Octavius* 19. 4 [*ANF* 4, p. 183], Thales had already accepted a spiritual first principle, which had formed everything out of water. Cf. also Athenagoras's *A Plea for Christians* 23. 2 [*ANF* 2, p. 141].

[21] Cf. Otto Regenbogen's review of the previously mentioned book by Jaeger in *Gnomon* 27 (1935): 305ff. Regenbogen expresses doubts about calling Anaxagoras's cosmological principle of spirit "divine" without further qualification (p. 313) and stresses the importance of Diogenes (p. 314).

[22] Jaeger, *Theology of the Early Greek Philosophers*, pp. 165ff.

[23] Xenophon *Memorabilia* 1. 4. 4ff.   [24] *Philebus* 29b ff.

principles, for there would be a difference between them, and every difference presupposes a ground of the differentiatedness. Thus the accepted principles would not yet be the ultimate origin.[25] This argument first occurs in the second century A.D., but the idea that reason inexorably strives toward the greatest possible unity of understanding, which this formulation expresses, was influential throughout the whole development of philosophical theology. The Ionian philosophy of nature was obviously already concerned to limit the number of original principles. Expressed in this is a striving, operative in all man's pursuit of knowledge and related to his vital interest in the unity of his own being, to discover an ultimate unity as the ground of all multiplicity. Anaximander was the first to provide a conceptual derivation of the unity of the origin. He saw the *archē* in the "inexhaustible reservoir or stock from which all becoming draws its nourishment."[26] This boundless origin cannot itself have an origin, otherwise it would be limited by that. For the same reason, it must also be imperishable. By means of the divine character of this predicate, Anaximander established the identity of the one origin with the truly divine, and by means of this identification he "refused to let the divine nature take the form of distinct, individual gods."[27] The contradiction this tendency toward the unity of the divine set up in relation to the humanized deities of popular religion was openly declared by Xenophanes: "One God is highest among gods and men; in neither his form nor his thought is he like unto mortals."[28] Since Parmenides then contrasted the One, as the truly imperishable being, to the transitory Many, the theme of the unity

[25] Justin Martyr *Dialogue with Trypho* 1. 5. 6 [*ANF* 1, pp. 197ff.].

[26] Jaeger, *Theology of the Early Greek Philosophers*, p. 24.

[27] *Ibid.*, p. 42.

[28] Xenophanes, frag. 23 [translation from Jaeger, *Theology of the Early Greek Philosophers*, p. 42] (fragment found in Clement of Alexandria *Stromata* 5. 109 [*ANF* 2, p. 470]). Cf. from a later period, the maxim of Antisthenes, frag. 24: "according to custom, there are many gods; but one, according to nature" [*kata nomon einai pollous theous, kata de phusin hena.* Translation mine – TR.] (cited in *Friedrich Überwegs Grundriss der Geschichte der Philosophie*, vol. 1, *Die Philosophie des Altertums*, ed. Karl Praechter, 12th ed. rev. [Berlin, 1926], p. 165).

of the divine no longer faded away. In the final draft of his doctrine of ideas, Plato set forth the One as identical with the Good in being the ontological ground of the ideas.[29] Aristotle and the Stoics also maintained the unity of the divine. One sees, particularly in these two lines of development, however, that such a unity of the divine may not be claimed as "monotheistic" without qualification. It can be combined with polytheistic popular religion in many ways.

3. The Otherness and Unknowability of the Origin

Just as essentially tied in with the philosophical question of the true nature of God as the tendency to prove the ultimate unity of the divine origin is an increasing insight into its inaccessibility to human conceptualization. This is connected with the fact that the one, ultimate origin of all things must be totally different from the everyday environing world. The more exactly the structure of these things was grasped, the more it became evident that everything in them was involved in their multiplicity and transitoriness. Thus, it could not but become ever clearer that nothing that might be represented by analogy with the many and with transitory things can be the essentially unitary origin at which the philosophical question about the true form of the divine aims. Insight into the otherness of the divine origin was thus not something first introduced into philosophy through the influence of Oriental mystery religions, although the religiosity of late antiquity doubtless encouraged the development of this element of the philosophical idea of God. Nevertheless, the insight into the otherness of the divine was already rooted in the initial tendency of the philosophical question about God. Only because this was so could the motifs of the Oriental mystery religions be understood as allusions to and illustrations of the metaphysical situation of the incomprehensibility of the divine origin.[30] It is certainly true that

[29] Julius Stenzel, *Zahl und Gestalt bei Platon und Aristotles* (Leipzig and Berlin, 1924), pp. 63ff.; cf. 12f.

[30] Erwin R. Goodenough (*By Light, Light: The Mystic Gospel of Hellenistic Judaism* [New Haven: Yale University Press, 1935], pp. 12f.) argues con-

Hellenistic philosophy first formulated the idea of the incomprehensibility of God in a radical way. Even if this was affirmed in Middle Platonsim, in an appeal to the famous statement of Plato's that it is a difficult undertaking to discover the Maker and Father of this universe and impossible thereafter to impart him to all men,[31] the precise term "incomprehensible" still goes beyond the meaning of the Platonic utterance. But does it express something totally new within the tradition of philosophical theology? Is not what was new only the religious accent which Hellenism attaches to just the notion of incomprehensibility and which establishes an interest in radically sharpening the philosophical situation? However, the tendency toward insight into the incomprehensibility of the divine was already contained in the recognition of the otherness of God. The idea of the incomprehensibility of God is hardly something introduced into philosophical theology as a novelty by Gnosticism, as Hans Jonas asserts,[32] or by Judaism, as Wolfson believes.[33]

---

vincingly that the oriental mythologies in Hellenistic philosophy, for example in Plutarch's *De Iside et Osiride*, are not utilized in a way that is fundamentally different from Plato's use of Greek mythology; in both cases the mythological portrayals are only illustrations of metaphysical contents. For Plutarch, the Greek Orphic-Bacchic traditions and the new Oriental myths of the Great Mother and the Pleroma were "interchangeable typologies for the same reality," viz., for the path of the soul out of the bonds of the body into an immaterial, immortal life (*ibid.*, p. 20). If that was true of the doctrine of salvation, it was probably all the more the case that mystery piety played no other than an illustrative role for the philosophical concept of God.

[31] *Timaeus* 28c. On the spread and use of this citation in Middle Platonism, cf. Andresen, "Justin und der mittlere Platonismus," p. 167.

[32] Hans Jonas, *Gnosis und spätantiker Geist*, vol. 2/1 of *Von der Mythologie zu mystischen Philosophie* (Göttingen, 1954), pp. 78f.

[33] Harry A. Wolfson, *Philo*, 2 vols. (Cambridge: Harvard University Press, 1948), 2:111ff. Wolfson's contention that the older philosophy, including Plato, had not designated the deity as precisely incomprehensible, is certainly correct. And in fact it is unusual that Philo – only once, to be sure (*De Mutatione Nominum* 2. 7) – designates God as beyond the reach of even the mind [*nous*]. Wolfson's thesis that the idea of the incomprehensibility of God was an original insight of Philo's is nevertheless burdened with the difficulty that the Middle Platonists, in whom one does find this concept, would in this case have to have been literarily dependent upon Philo (cf. Goodenough, at the place cited by Wolfson, *Philo*, 2:158, n. 65).

The otherness of God was already expressed by Xenophanes, who said about the One God that "in neither his form not his thought is he like unto mortals." God's otherness was at first understood as consisting above all in the contrast between himself and physical-visible things. Anaximander recognized that the divine origin cannot be mutable like visible things. Everything that is mutable and subject to movement is limited[34] and therefore cannot be the ultimate origin. Xenophanes likewise understood the One God to be immutable and motionless.[35] He neither dies nor is born, but simply is.[36] Corporeality, too, is linked to mutability as among the attributes from which Xenophanes says the One God is free.[37]

Since Xenophanes, it was believed that the otherness of the One God in contrast to the physical-visible might be conceived in a much more positive way as intellectuality [*Geisthaftigkeit*], and so the divine was described as mind [*Geist*] or as world-ordering reason. Plato, too, took over this idea of Anaxagoras'.[38] That for Plato the intellectuality of the divine was nevertheless an expression of its otherness is shown by the fact that according to him, the divine, like the ideas, is extremely difficult to know just because of its intellectuality.[39] For in our conception the intellectual element remains always bound up with the ideal. Thus, owing to our corporeality, we are barely able to grasp that which is purely intellectual. The idea of the Good, in

---

Wolfson's assertion about Philo's pioneering originality with respect to the namelessness of God is even less convincing. Plato says, in *Cratylus* 400 d, that we do not know the true names of the gods with which they name themselves. This means, however, that we have no access to the term that designates the essence of the deity. And that we can speak about God by means of inadequate expressions gained from his effects among creatures, not even Philo disputed.

[34] Jaeger, *Theology of the Early Greek Philosophers*, p. 28. Anaximander B 2 and 3 [see G. S. Kirk and J. G. Raven, eds., *The Pre-Socratic Philosophers* (Cambridge: Cambridge University Press, 1962), pp. 106f. – Tr.].

[35] Xenophanes, frag. 26 [Kathleen Freeman, trans., *Ancilla to the Pre-Socratic Philosophers: A Complete Translation of the Fragments in Diels "Fragmente der Vorsokratiker"* (Oxford: Basil Blackwell, 1962), p. 23].

[36] Xenophanes, cited in Aristotle *Rhetoric* 1399b.

[37] Frag. 14 [*Ancilla*, p. 22].   [38] *Phaedrus* 97c. 98b, s.

[39] *Phaedrus* 65a–67b; *Sophist* 232e ff.

particular, can be conceived only with great difficulty, and inadequately at that.[40] Plato himself later coined the famous formula that the Good "transcends essence."[41] Nevertheless, the expanded view of the intellectuality of the deity involves a weakening of his otherness. Thus, Aristotle could find nothing in the rational nature of the divine[42] that would prevent him from classifying God as an essence belonging in the category of substance.[43] Even the transcendence of the divine over the cosmos was by no means guaranteed by the predicate of intellectuality. The Stoics understood the deity as mind, as logos, but in such a way that together with the world it formed a single living being.

Philosophical insight into the otherness of the divine could not come to rest with the adoption of the idea of his intellectuality as mind. The idea of the simplicity of God provided a motive which pushed beyond this. Perhaps Anaxagoras has already understood the true deity as simple. In any event, Plato did.[44] Everything composite can also be divided again, and consequently is mutable, as Plato in *Timaeus* allows the Demiurge to say to the gods brought forth by him.[45] The meaning of the simplicity of God in Plato can be understood from this standpoint. Everything composite necessarily has a ground of its composition outside itself, and therefore cannot be the ultimate origin. This origin must therefore be simple. Aristotle also shared this conviction.[46] Now Aristotle asserted that all things are composed of different, complementary determinations, and

---

[40] *Republic* 505a, 517b.

[41] *Republic* 509b [*epekeina tēs ousias*; translation from *The Republic*, 2 vols., Loeb Classical Library (Cambridge and London: Harvard University Press and W. A. Heinemann, 1935), 2:107].

[42] *Metaphysics* 1074b–1075a.   [43] *Nicomachean Ethics* 1096a23f.

[44] *Republic* B. 382e. Anaxagoras speaks about spirit ruling all things by its being "unmixed" with anything else (frag. 12) [*Ancilla*, pp. 84ff.].

[45] *Timaeus* 41a, b.

[46] *Metaphysics* 1074a33–38. The first mind [*nous*], in its imperishable immovableness, cannot possess any matter and must therefore be utterly simple. The simplicity of God (his unity, according to reason) thereby furnishes the basis for his singularity (his unity, according to number). Cf. *ibid.*, 1071b20f., and 1072a32f.; 1072b5–13; and also 1015b11f.

that our knowledge has these composite beings for its object, and itself proceeds by composition, by combining different determinations. But in that case must not our knowledge be inadequate in relation to the simplicity of the divine?[47] Aristotle himself did not yet draw this conclusion. It is first encountered among those Platonists of late antiquity who took over the Aristotelian logic and doctrine of categories. Here, in Middle Platonism,[48] we do find it first explicitly laid down that the simplicity of God excludes from him not only composition of accidents (and, therewith, mutability), but also composition out of genus and specific difference,[49] so that he cannot be defined and consequently cannot be conceived. But even the Middle Platonic thinkers still maintained that God is mind [*nous*][50] and

[47] The question of the knowability of the simple had already occupied Plato in *Theatetus* (201e ff.) where he debated with the thesis of Antisthenes that the simple cannot be grasped by means of a logos but can only be named. However, it is not the simplicity of the deity that is being treated here but the simple elements of which things are composed. Therefore Plato can answer here that an unknowability in relation to the simple elements of things would also entail as a consequence the unknowability of the things composed by them (*ibid.*, 202d ff.). The problem presents itself differently in relation to the simplicity of God, of course, since God does not belong to the elements out of which things are composed. Here, Plato's answer does not yet suffice. But *Theatetus* 201e ff. does however make it possible to understand the fact that Plato was not led by his concept of the simplicity of God immediately to arrive at the consequence of a radical agnosticism.

[48] Not yet in Philo. Wolfson, who supposes he finds in Philo the idea that God is beyond genus and specific difference, can only "logically" infer it from him (*Philo*, 2:108). His sole argument for this is that Philo intends the absence of qualities in God in the sense of the Stoic category of quality. But a passage like *Legum Allegoria* 3. 2. 36 shows that the expression, God is without qualities, only excludes composition of accidents from him, and not expressly that of genus and specific difference; for the error that God has qualitative attributes is here paralleled by the error that he is corruptible. If, however, God's freedom from a composition out of genus and difference was not of concern to Philo, one will also be unable to follow Wolfson in the further conclusion that Philo's statements about the incomprehensibility and unknowability of God are grounded in this.

[49] Albinus *Didaskalikos* 165. 5ff.; Celsus, in Origen *Against Celsus* 7. 42 (*MPG* 11, 1481c–1484a) [*ANF* 4, p. 628]; Clement of Alexandria *Stromata* 5. 12 (*MPG* 9, 121a) [*ANF* 2, p. 463].

[50] Albinus *Didaskalikos* 165. 4. On this point see H. Dörrie, "Zum Ursprung der neuplatonischen Hypostasenlehre," *Hermes* 82 (1954): 339f.

thus also knowable to the human mind in one way or another. Thus, on the one hand, they asserted the unknowability of God, and, on the other hand, that he could be known only by the human mind.[51] Plotinus was the first to see that the ultimate origin could not be mind because a plurality of knower and known, subject and object, is always posited in mind, so that the mind cannot be the First, the strictly simple One.[52] Thus, the ultimate origin, the One, must be sought beyond mind. Therefore it is unattainable by our mind, inaccessible to our knowledge, and is to be experienced only in ecstasy. This conclusion of Plotinus's is no merely accidental assertion. It draws its weight from the fact that it is consistent with the initial tendency of the philosophical question about the form of the divine.

We have brought to light something of the inner unity of the philosophical concept of God, regardless of all the variations in its formation. This inner consistency of the philosophical idea of God derives from the original formulation of the question underlying it. The question about the origin [*archē*] of known reality is the guiding notion even of such ideas as the intellectuality, unity, simplicity, and incomprehensibility of the primal origin. We saw, however, that the construction of the nature of the divine by inference back from normal reality was possible only on the soil of a particular religion, viz., in the atmosphere of the Olympian gods who themselves belonged to

---

[51] This remarkable fact has been strikingly emphasized by H. Koch, *Pronoia und Paideusis*, p. 257n.

[52] *Enneads* 6. 9. 2; cf. 3. 8. 9; 5. 1. 4. Aristotle had also noticed the duality in the mind of the act of knowing and the object known, and was convinced that the mind is not strictly one so long as subject and object are distinct – as in the case of knowledge bound to material reality (*Metaphysics* 1074b36f.) But the immaterial, divine mind has no object distinct from itself. It is pure consciousness of its thought [*noēsis noēseōs*], and in this case, Aristotle believed, subject and object are identical (*ibid.*, 1075a3f.) and – on account of being immaterial – also simple (*ibid.*, 1075a5ff.). Plotinus, on the other hand, recognizes (*Enneads* 6. 9. 2) that the act of knowing [*noein*] always contains some multiplicity, at least – as in the case of the *noēsis noēseōs* – a "logical" multiplicity. Even in pure self-consciousness, subject and object remain formally distinct, even if in a certain way the knower is one with the known.

the cosmic order. Thus, the understanding of God in Greek religion lived on in philosophy. It remained alive even in Scholastic and modern philosophy to the extent that the procedure of causal inference remained standard for the philosophical doctrine of God, whether as an inference from the structure of the cosmos to its "first cause," or from the structure of subjectivity to its own inevitably presupposed ground, as in modern philosophy.[53] Even here the inferential procedure of the understanding of God in Olympian religion was still influential. How does this inferentially attainable concept of God relate to the biblical traditions' testimony to God, however?

II. THE TASK AND DANGER IN THEOLOGICAL LINKAGE WITH THE PHILOSOPHICAL IDEA OF GOD

For Judaism, and then also for Christianity, connecting the biblical idea of God with the philosophical concept of God was not simply the result of the external situation, the fact that philosophy was the spiritual power of the Hellenistic age, which one joined for the sake of tactical advantage. This conception, which was widespread in the older research in the history of dogma, explains the process too much in terms of externals. The debate with the philosophical question about the true form of the divine was indeed occasioned by encounter with the Hellenistic intellectual world, but it is also grounded in the biblical witness to God as the universal God, pertinent not only to Israel but to all peoples.

This universal claim does not seem always to have been native to faith in Yahweh. Israel for a long time reckoned not only with the existence of other gods but also with the idea that the other nations belonged to these other gods and not to Yahweh.[54] For Israel itself, the worship of Yahweh in accord with the first

[53] On the latter, cf. W. Schulz, *Der Gott der neuzeitlichen Metaphysik* (Pfüllingen, 1957).

[54] Thus, according to the message of Jephthah to the king of the Ammonites: "Will you not possess what Chemosh your god gives you to possess? And all that the Lord our God has dispossessed before us, we will possess" (Judg. 11:24; cf. 2 Kings 3:27).

commandment was probably well established from the beginning. But this monolatry attained a more monotheistic character, in the sense of a consciousness that Yahweh alone was God,[55] only in the course of history. For all this, however, Yahwistic faith acquired a universal tendency from very early on. This came about by the union of the God of Israel with the Canaanitic heavenly Creator God, El. This fusion obviously has already taken place by the time the gods of the fathers became resident in the cultivated areas. In any case, the Yahwistic historical writing presupposes them.[56] Furthermore, the universality of Yahweh's deity came to the fore in the cultic traditions of Jerusalem, too, in which the ancient Near Eastern divine-kingship ideology was influential.[57] Only a universal god can give his earthly representative "the ends of the earth (as) your possession" (Ps. 2:8) and make him the ruler of the world. Isaiah looked for the historical realization of this universal rule of Yahweh in the form of all nations streaming to Zion in order to serve Yahweh (Is. 2:2ff.). But already in the present, the world power Assyria follows the commands of Yahweh (Isa. 7:18ff.). Jeremiah calls Nebuchadnezzar Yahweh's servant (Jer. 27:6), and, for Deutero-Isaiah, Cyrus is Yahweh's anointed (Isa. 45:1). Deutero-Isaiah now explicitly states: "Besides me there is no god" (Isa. 44:6). For Judaism, this universal claim of Yahweh's is taken for granted, just as in primitive Christianity. The Father of Jesus Christ alone is the true God (John 17:3). He is the God not only of the Jews but of the Gentiles, too (Rom. 3:29).

How is this universal claim of the Judaeo-Christian God[58] to

[55] Cf. Gerhard von Rad, *Old Testament Theology*, trans. D. M. G. Stalker (Edinburgh: Oliver and Boyd and New York: Harper and Row, 1962), 1:210f. and the literature cited there.

[56] On this point, see Otto Eissfeldt, "El and Jahwe," *Journal of Semitic Studies* 1 (1956): 25–37.

[57] On this limitation of its influence, cf. Rolf Rendtorff, "Der Kultus im alten Israel," in *Jahrbuch für Liturgik und Hymnologie* (Kassel, 1956), vol. 2, esp. pp. 15ff.

[58] In opposition to Aulen, *Das christliche Gottesbild*, pp. 20ff., I would not want to speak of a radical break between Judaism and the New Testament with regard to their pictures of God. The "religiosity of the legal order"

receive a correspondingly universal recognition? The Jews were obligated to him by their national identity. But how could non-Jews be brought to the insight that the God of Israel is the absolute God? The universal claim of the God of Israel first acquired compelling validity for all men by virtue of the fact that first the Jewish and then the Christian mission presented the God of Israel as the true God sought by philosophy. Thus, the claim of the God of Israel to be alone the God to whom all men belong provides the *theological* basis for the fact that Christian faith has to become involved in the philosophical question about the true God and has to give an account of its answer right down to the present time.

This fundamental state of affairs is expressed in the fact that Paul, in Galatians 4:8, designates the heathen gods, whom the members of the congregation had previously served, as "by nature no gods."[59] This statement implies that the God Paul preaches is alone God by virtue of his essence. And this assertion basically involves linking up with the philosophical question about that which is divine "by nature." Paul himself effected such a linkage with Stoic natural theology – even if by means of a critical refraction[60] – and assimilated the negative designations of God as invisible and incorruptible (Rom. 1:20ff.).

---

which is set in contrast to the Christian faith presents only a fossilized form of the Jewish understanding of God (exactly that, a *picture* of God!). But the most important point about the God of the Israelites, of Judaism, and of the Christians is to be found not in such a *picture* of God but in the fact that he is the God of history. If one loses sight of this, then the God of the New Testament is only too easily transformed into the personification of the "motif" of love, whereby a Christian *picture* of God would step into his place.

[59] Heinrich Schlier, in *Der Brief an die Galater* (Göttingen, [11]1951), p. 142, writes on this point: "One can almost think of this 'nature' [*physei*] as set in opposition to a 'convention' [*thesei*] in the Stoic sense. But it probably has a blunted and nonexplicit meaning." This restriction is nevertheless given no support whatever.

[60] Rom. 1:19f. Concerning the critical refraction with which the natural theology of Stoicism is here – in a way that is exemplary for all theological appropriation of philosophical concepts – taken up and transformed, cf. Günther Bornkamm, "The Revelation of God's Wrath", in *Early Christian Experience* (London: SCM Press and New York: Harper and Row, 1969), esp. pp. 50ff.

Sympathy with the terminology of philosophical theology is encountered elsewhere in the New Testament, too. Later on, with the apostolic fathers, there was a marked increase of especially the negative predicates applied to God. In all this, Christian theology followed the path the Hellenistic-Jewish mission had already taken.[61] But, whereas in Hellenistic Judaism Philo had already worked over philosophical theology in a comprehensive manner and with an awareness of its inner connections, Christian theology up to the time of the Apologists confined itself to occasional approbations. It was the Apologists who first began to assimilate philosophical theology into Christian theology on a larger scale as the basis of their Logos theories.

The linkage with philosophy was facilitated by the tendency of the philosophical idea of God toward unity. This philosophical "monotheism" was a natural ally for the Jewish as well as for the Christian mission in the struggle against polytheistic popular belief. Even the supraworldly character of the biblical God found a certain correspondence in the Platonic transcendental idea of God. This instigated the heavy dependence of the Christian representation of God upon the Platonic. As was the case with Middle Platonism, too, only the doctrine of providence was accepted from Stoic teaching, whereas its pantheism was strongly rejected. The far-reaching analogy of the Platonic view of God with the biblical view is precisely what brought with it the danger of too carefree a manner of accomplishing the linkage with philosophy. An unbroken, unreserved identification of the biblical with the Platonic idea of God had to be excluded, however. For the philosophical idea of God (including even the Platonic) was shaped differently from the biblical idea because of its origin in Olympian religion, with the specifically immanental character of its deities. The guiding idea of the Greek concept of God was that of the origin of everything presently in existence. Accordingly, philosophy could

[61] Further details may be found in Rudolf Bultmann, *Theology of the New Testament* (New York: Charles Scribner's Sons and London: SCM Press, 1951), 1:65ff., esp. 69ff.

construct its concept of God by inference back from the world. This corresponded to the peculiar character of the ancient Greek understanding of God, but not to the biblical God's essential freedom in relation to the world. "Behold, I am the Lord, the God of all flesh; is anything too hard for me?" (Jer. 32:27). Such freedom on the part of God for ever new, as yet unheard of works in his world was beyond the scope of Greek philosophy. The origin that can be deduced by inference from present reality can never be conceived as the ground of something unheard of in comparison with all present reality. That is simply not forthcoming from the procedure of inference from the known back to the unknown. On the other hand, the biblical God is indeed also the origin of present reality, but the manner and way in which he is this is already decisively determined by the fact that his essence is not exhausted in this function. God, as the origin, is never merely the invisible ground of present reality, but the free, creative source of the ever new and unforeseen. This essential characteristic of the creator and of his historical acts is unambiguously revealed for the first time by the resurrection. He is the God "who gives life to the dead and calls into existence the things that are not" (Rom. 4:17). For this reason, the only bond man has to this God is in faith that "in hope . . . believe(s) against hope" (Rom. 4:18). Because this freedom of God in relation to the world necessarily remains inaccessible to the inferential procedure that is fundamental to philosophical theology, neither could it grasp the fact that a special gift of God to men was necessary for knowledge of God; that knowledge of God occurs as man's being known by God (Gal. 4:9; 1 Cor. 8:2f.); that in the electing gift of God (Rom. 8:29) which is decided in this being known is to be found the condition for genuine knowledge of God. Since the necessity, grounded in the freedom of God, of a special gift of God to men as the presupposition of all fellowship between men and God, including that which occurs in knowledge of God, remained foreign to philosophy, it was also unable to achieve a true understanding of the personal mode in which the living God confronted men, but could instead only construe personal language about God as an anthropomorphic mode of expression.

From all this it becomes evident that Christian theology can link up with the philosophical idea of God only by breaking through it at the same time. On the one hand, it must hold its own on the philosophical question about the true God, and bring this to a genuine fulfillment; for even if the essence of the biblical God is not exhausted in being the origin of present reality and of the repetitive, normal processes, he nevertheless must remain at least conceivable as the origin of present reality, too. The necessity of Christian theology uniting with the philosophical idea of God is disclosed herein. In addition, it is possible here to determine the, to be sure, limited critical right that the philosophical idea of God possesses even in relation to the Christian theological doctrine of God. Philosophical criticism of the theological representation of God can help guarantee that the Christian God remain at least conceivable as the author of present reality, too. On the other hand, Christian theology can effect a link-up with the philosophical concept of God only when it undertakes a penetrating transformation of the philosophical concept right down to its roots. Wherever philosophical concepts are taken over, they must be remolded in the light of the history-shaping freedom of the biblical God. This is not accomplished simply by adding certain revealed truths to the philosophical concept of God. The philosophical concept of God does not tolerate such a supplementation. The philosophical question about the true God aims precisely at that which is essential to the divine, the elements that define its nature. It therefore contradicts the peculiar character of the philosophical idea of God if features that are precisely essential to God are reserved for, say, a revelation. On the other hand, no Christian theology can be satisfied with the idea that the content of the historical revelation of God in Jesus Christ can be presented, say, as a non-essential supplement to or even a mere illustration of the philosophical idea of God. Clearly, every mere combination here must remain superficial. Theology must push on to the basic elements of the philosophical idea of God and transform these elements in the critical light of the biblical idea of God.

The linkage accomplished in the course of this wrestling will not, however, bring any alien content into Christian faith in God. The tendency toward such linkage with the Greek spirit belongs to the historical foundation of primitive Christianity itself. A "hellenization" in the sense of being overcome by foreign interests, e.g., by the philosophical idea of God, does not necessarily appear already where theology undertakes to come to grips with it, but only where theology fails in the midst of this struggle by losing its assimilative, transforming power.

III. THE THEOLOGICAL APPROPRIATION

The appropriation of the philosophers' doctrine of God was by no means formulated programmatically by all the theologians of the second century. It is well known that the Apologists of this epoch set forth their relationship to philosophy in very different ways. Athenagoras somehow found the unity of God expressed in all the philosophers and could therefore without further ado claim the most diverse philosophical systems as witnesses for this truth.[62] Minucius Felix proceeded in a similar fashion.[63] For his rejection of polytheism, Justin appealed to Socrates[64] and asserted that the teachings of Plato and of other philosophers were not exactly equivalent to the Christian but nevertheless akin to them,[65] although on the other hand he was certainly aware of the exaltedness of the Judaeo-Christian understanding of God over the philosophical.[66] Tatian, by contrast, was concerned with demonstrating the uniqueness of Christianity by disparaging the philosophical competition, by casting suspicion upon the ethical conduct of its leading figures,[67] by allusions to the contradictoriness[68] and dependency[69] of its

---

[62] *A Plea for Christians* 5 [*ANF* 2, p. 131].
[63] *Octavius* 19. 3ff. [*ANF* 4, p. 183].
[64] *First Apology* 5. 3 [*ANF* 1, p. 164].
[65] *Second Apology* 13. 2f. [*ANF* 1, p. 193].
[66] *Dialogue with Trypho* 6. 1 [*ANF* 1, p. 198].
[67] *Address to the Greeks* 2 [*ANF* 2, p. 65].
[68] *Ibid,* 25. 5ff. [*ANF* 2, pp. 75f.].
[69] *Ibid.* 1. 6; 26. 1. 6 [*ANF* 2, pp. 65, 76].

thought. The polemical utterances of Theophilus against philosophy and even Plato himself are hardly less pungent than those directed at polytheistic popular belief.[70] From Irenaeus, one hears of "all those who were ignorant of God, and who are termed philosophers."[71] If the philosophers had already known the truth, the coming of the Redeemer would have been superfluous.[72] Thus, Tertullian is not at all alone in his repudiation of philosophy, especially as the negative features of his position should not be overdrawn. Although he, like Irenaeus, supposes that the philosophers are the source of heretical ideas,[73] even Tertullian acknowledges that not everything the philosophers assert is false.[74]

Despite the different positions taken toward philosophy, the influence of the philosophical idea of God is in actuality nevertheless universal. To this extent, the sharp repudiations of philosophy by Tatian, Theophilus, Tertullian, and even Irenaeus easily produce a false picture. This rejection was by no means directed at the procedure of grasping the existence of God and certain properties of his being by inference from the world, apart from historical revelation. On the contrary, even Tatian and Theophilus, like the other Apologists, followed Hellenistic Judaism (e.g., *The Wisdom of Solomon* 13) in emphasizing that God can be known by inference from his works.[75] The critical utterances against philosophy mean, on the one hand, that the

---

[70] *To Autolycus* 2. 4 [*ANF* 2, p. 95] and esp. 3. 5–8 [*ANF* 2, pp. 112f.]. Cf., however, 2. 8 [*ANF* 2, p. 97]. On Tatian's polemic against philosophy, as well as his close substantive kinship with Middle Platonism, cf. now Martin Elze, *Tatian und seine Theologie* (Göttingen, 1960), pp. 13–36, 55f.

[71] *Against the Heresies* 2. 14. 2 [*ANF* 1, p. 376].

[72] *Ibid.* 2. 14. 7 [*ANF* 1, p. 378]. [73] *On the Soul* 3 [*ANF* 3, pp. 183f.].

[74] *Ibid.* 2 [*ANF* 3, p. 182]. A. Labhard, "Tertullien et la philosophie ou la recherche d'une position pure," *Museum Helveticum* 7 (1950): 159–80, enables one to see that Tertullian's judgment upon philosophy does not have only negative elements (*ibid.*, pp. 169ff.).

[75] Tatian *Address* 4. 3 [*ANF* 2, p. 66] (cf., however, 12. 5f. [*ANF* 2, pp. 70f.]); Theophilus *To Autolycus* 1. 5–6, *passim* [*ANF* 2, p. 90]. In 1. 3 [*ANF* 2, pp. 89f.], Theophilus lays it down that we can comprehend God only from his effects, while his form remains inconceivable. This assertion can be combined with the detailed cosmoteleological arguments of 1. 6 in such a way that the creaturely effects point to the existence of precisely an origin that is inconceivable to us.

philosophers have *not* known the truth *in its entirety* – so Irenaeus, but also Justin and Clement of Alexandria – and, on the other hand, that *not all* the different philosophical doctrines correspond to the truth and that the moral conduct of the philosophers was *not in every respect* beyond reproach. For this reason, a broad, common basis did not need to be denied. It would be stressed more by some, less by others. But all were aware of this common possession. That is proved by the general need to explain the agreement with philosophy. Such an explanation was attempted along various lines: in Justin, notoriously, by his theory of the seminal reason [*logos spermatikos*], but otherwise mostly by means of the assumption that philosophy knew and used Old Testament writings, in other words, by the theory of the so-called plagiarism of the Greeks.[76] In substance, the differences between the individual theologians in their attitudes toward philosophy were not deep. Still, several features of the philosophical idea of God were more thoroughly transformed along the more critical line taken by Tatian, Theophilus, Irenaeus, and Tertullian than was the case with the other Apologists of that time.

We will now look more closely, without being able to attempt any sort of comprehensiveness, at how the theological assimilation of the philosophical idea of God succeeded within the positions different theologians took toward its individual elements.

1. Monotheism and Creation

Even at the point at which the proximity of Greek philosophy to the Judaeo-Christian understanding of God is most strikingly evident, namely, in the thesis of the unity of God, there is basically no full agreement. The tendency of Greek philosophy in the direction of affirming the unity of God had a limit which was never broken through: the divine spirit always remained bound to a material principle, whether as the immanent Logos of the cosmos, as in Stoicism, or as something transcending

[76] On this, see Einar Molland, *The Conception of God in the Alexandrian Theology* (Oslo, 1938), pp. 52–67.

formless matter, the form-giving principle of mind that stands opposite it, as in Plato.[77] This limitation belonged to the philosophical question about the divine origin from the very beginning and is essential to it, since the philosophical question always proceeds by way of inference from present reality back to its origin, and thus always presupposes the duality of effect and cause. This duality, once its correlative character is emphasized, can be understood as a dynamic unity, as was already the case in Anaximander and then with Diogenes and in Stoicism. However, it could also become differentiated into an opposition between two principles – a path already taken by Anaxagoras and later by the Socratic-Platonic tradition.[78] The concept of the origin [*archē*], therefore, was not kept reserved for the divine; rather, several kinds of principles were distinguished. Their number depended upon the extent to which the formative principle, opposed to matter, was divided again into a plurality of elements. Thus, as is well known, Aristotle reckoned with four principles. The Platonist Albinus distinguished three principles [*archai*]: matter, the ideas, and God. In any case, the differentiation within the formative principle was already overcome in Middle Platonism by the thought that the ideas do not exist independently but belong to the divine mind.[79] In so doing, the juxtaposition of God and matter in

[77] This "dualism" is not confined to the myth of the Demiurge in the *Timaeus*. It returns again in the didactic writing about the Good as a tension between the principle of the One Good and the undefined duality.

[78] Jaeger describes this development as follows: "The more the dynamic conception of the 'primal ground' . . . disappeared and this approximated a merely abstract matter or 'stuff,' the more, on the other hand, it became an enigma that this blind mass of matter should nevertheless still prove to be of service in so many works of the nature of artful arrangement and purposeful formation. All the greater, therefore, becomes the need for an additional second force as a conscious creator of the world-order, analogous to the human mind, regardless of whether it is to be distinguished sharply from the rest of the corporeal world, as 'the purest and thinnest' body, as in Anaxagoras, or thought of as immanent in the material basic principle itself and identified with it, as in Diogenes" (*Theology of the Early Greek Philosophers*, p. 171 [translation revised in accord with German text cited by the author – Tr.]).

[79] Praechter, *Überwegs Grundriss der Philosophie*, 1:542f.; H. Koch, *Pronoia und Paideusis*, pp. 256f.

the "doctrine of the first principles" [*Ursprüngen*] was thrown into sharp relief.

The almighty freedom of the biblical God was incompatible with such a correlation between material and form-giving principles. The Priestly account of creation, in contrast to the Babylonian epic of creation, had already avoided all suggestion of anything like a stuff of some sort presupposed by Yahweh's creative activity. True, it did not speak expressly of a creation "out of nothing."[80] This concept first appears in Jewish literature in the first century A.D.[81] But one begins to hear sounds of it in Paul, too (Rom. 4:17). *The Wisdom of Solomon* (11:17), in contrast, represents the act of creation as the shaping of formless matter. And Philo at least did not make explicit use of the idea of a creation out of nothing against the postulate of an uncreated matter.[82]

Even in Christian theology the idea of creation out of nothing does not appear to have been taken for granted as an article of faith from the start. The formula indeed already

[80] Von Rad, *Old Testament Theology*, 1:142ff.

[81] 2 Macc. 7:28; cf. *Pirke Rabbi Eliezer* c. 3.

[82] The usual view that even Philo thought of the act of creation as the shaping of an uncreated, formless matter (so Drummond and Brehier) is contradicted by H. A. Wolfson (*Philo*, 1:302ff.). Wolfson wants to prove, by means of a combination of citations from Philo and the conclusions he draws from them, that Philo wanted to assert the creation of matter (in either of its senses). This attempt is unconvincing, however. Philo indeed speaks of a creation of the ideas (e.g., *De Opificio Mundi* 7. 29). Still, there is no mention of a creation of prime matter in this context, which is highly reminiscent of the *Timaeus*. On the other hand, Philo takes an expression that was suitable for this matter [*chōra*] and uses it elsewhere for the passing remark that space [*chōra*] and place [*topos*] were created coincidentally with bodies (*De Confusione Linguarum* 27. 136). And at another place he holds, against Aristotle, that God should not be represented as merely the mover of what is already present, because in that case one would be accepting two original principles instead of only one (*Legum Allegoria* 3. 3. 7) – an argument that might equally well be used against the Platonic postulate of a matter co-original with God and presupposed by the act of creation (and this argument was so used by Tatian in this sense: cf. below, n. 85). Still, it is noteworthy that Philo himself did not utilize this argument against Plato, but repeats his ideas without objection (see above). A systematization of his statements in the direction of the thesis of a creation out of nothing, such as Wolfson has attempted, is therefore impossible without doing violence to the evidence.

appears in the *Shepherd of Hermas*.[83] But Justin manifestly was no threat to the singularity and free lordship of God in the assumption of a formless matter presupposed at the creation. In any case, he never disputed the uncreated character of such a primal matter. On the contrary, a series of his formulations makes it plain that Justin was not aware of any conflict between the Christian faith and the Platonic cosmogony.[84] It was otherwise with Tatian. He stressed the point that matter cannot be without beginning, like God. A matter without beginning must in fact be equal to the divine power of God.[85] For the same reason, Theophilus of Antioch attacked the Platonic thesis of the eternality of matter: were matter without beginning, then it would be immutable like God, and equal to him. God would then no longer be singular and no longer be the creator of all things.[86] For this reason, matter, too, is to be thought of as created by God, but creation is to be understood strictly as creation out of nothing. For Irenaeus, creation out of nothing[87] and the createdness of matter[88] are already taken entirely for granted as matters of faith, just as for Tertullian.[89]

[83] Book Second, Commandments, 1 [*ANF* 2, p. 20].

[84] Justin's relationship to the thesis of creation out of nothing is examined in detail by Pfättisch, *Der Einfluss Platos*, pp. 93–103. Pfättisch (p. 99) points particularly to the fact that in his *First Apology* 1. 59 [*ANF* 1, p. 183] Justin is not aware of any opposition to Plato's teaching. Loofs (*Leitfaden* [⁵1950], 1:89, n. 9), in dependence upon Engelhardt, could still read out of *First Apology* 67. 8 (7?) [*ANF* 1, p. 186] that God had also "changed" matter and so created the cosmos. Andresen, in "Justin und der mittlere Platonismus" (pp. 164ff.), has shown that Justin follows the common doctrine of Middle Platonism on this point.

[85] *Address to the Greeks* 5. 7 [*ANF* 2, p. 67]. On the connection of this assertion with the Platonic idea of creation as the shaping of matter, cf. Elze, *Tatian und seine Theologie*, p. 88.

[86] *To Autolycus* 2. 4 [*ANF* 2, p. 95]; cf. 2. 10 [*ANF* 2, pp. 97ff.], as well as 1. 3 [*ANF* 2, pp. 89f.]. The same argument is submitted later in a much expanded form by Methodius of Olympus *Concerning Free Will* 5f. [*ANF* 6, pp. 358f.]. Cf. G. L. Prestige, *God in Patristic Thought* (London: SPCK, 1956; reissue of 1936 ed.), pp. 28ff.

[87] *Against the Heresies* 2. 10. 2 [*ANF* 1, p. 370].

[88] *Ibid.* 2. 10. 3 [*ANF* 1, p. 360].

[89] *Apology* 17. 1 [*ANF* 3, p. 31]. Cf. also J. Lortz, *Tertullian als Apologet*, 2 vols. (Münster, 1927–28), 1:248ff.

One can see that on this important point, despite initial vacillation, early Christian theology was relatively quick and decisive in breaking through the confines of the philosophical concept of God and creating fitting room for the freedom of the biblical God.[90] Only through the rejection of the idea of matter as eternally coexisting with God did the philosophical concept of God become really exclusively monotheistic.[91] In any case, it is another question whether the procession of all things from God still remained intelligible on philosophical grounds, and thus whether the obligation of a theological doctrine of God to answer the philosophical question adequately could be lived up to. Otherwise the denial of matter as eternally coexistent with God would remain a mere theological postulate, lagging behind the indispensable claim of the theological doctrine of God to possess universal validity. Irenaeus at least had a point of departure for the resolution of this problem in the idea that the contingency of the world's creation goes back to the contingency of the divine willing.[92] Nevertheless, only if the representation

[90] The concept of freedom from want [*anepideēs*], which had been applied to God since as early as Socrates and Euripides and remained usable even in the philosophical schools, offered something of a point of contact here (the evidence for this is furnished by J. Geffcken, *Zwei griechische Apologeten* [Leipzig and Berlin, 1907], p. 38). It was used by Philo (*Legum Allegoria* 2. 1; *De Mutatione Nominum* 1. 582 [cf. Wolfson, *Philo*, 1:172, 203, 249]). Even early Christian theology used it: Aristides *Apology* 13. 4 [*ANF* 9, p. 264]; Justin *First Apology* 10. 13 [*ANF* 1, pp. 165ff.]; Tatian *Address* 4. 5 [*ANF* 2, p. 67]; Theophilus *To Autolycus* 2. 10 [*ANF* 2, pp. 97f.]; Athenagoras *Plea* 16. 2 [*ANF* 2, p. 136]. The concept appears already in *The Preaching of Peter.* Cf. also Irenaeus *Against the Heresies* 2. 2. 4 and 4. 14. 1ff. [*ANF* 1, pp. 361, 478f.]. Aristides *Apology* 1. 4, defines God's perfection in terms of his freedom from want.

[91] On the monotheism of the Apologists, cf. Lortz, *Tertullian*, 2:3ff.

[92] Irenaeus *Against the Heresies* 2. 10. 4 [*ANF* 1, p. 370]. Even though Middle Platonism could also speak of God's willing [*Boulēsis*] as the origin of things, it still did not express the contingency of the act of creation as Irenaeus did. Rather, for Atticus, for example, it was a matter of God's ability (and essential character!) to will the good [*Boulēthēnai ta kala*], in Eusebius *Praeparatio Evangelica* 15. 6. 10ff. (ed. Mras [1956], p. 362, 10). And Plotinus explicitly contrasts the expression of the spiritual essence of the Good by the will (which is identical with it) to a possible contingency of things (*Enneads* 6. 8. 13).

of God as a willing being can be maintained without engendering conflict with his incomprehensibility – a problem which was not taken hold of seriously enough in early Christian theology – can this idea prove satisfactory.

2. *God's Otherness and Spirituality*

Because of its emphasis on the otherness of God in contrast to the world, Platonism had to be especially attractive for Christian as well as Jewish apologetics. Philosophy seemed to come especially close to the biblical witness to God on this point. For Philo, the incomparability of God was expressed above all in Numbers 23:19: "God is not as a man."[93] He finds in the Platonists a similar distinction between God and worldly entities. They are able to distinguish Him Who Is from the form of existence of material things because they reckon with incorporeal, intelligible natures.[94] Philo saw in the philosophical thesis of the incorporeality of God an expression of his biblically attested otherness in relation to the creation. But for Philo, incorporeality was only the negative side of pure spirituality.[95] The Christian Apologists, too, spoke in a similar way of God's spirituality. Even if Justin stressed the incorporeality of God[96] more than its positive correlate, spirituality, it is nevertheless

[93] *Quod Deus Immutabilis Sit* 11. 53f. [translation from *Philo*, Loeb Classical Library (London: William Heinemann, and Nes York: G. P. Putman's Sons, 1929ff.), 3:37]; *De Somniis* 1. 40. 237; *Quaestiones et Solutiones in Genesin* 2. 54. Cf. on this and what follows, Wolfson, *Philo*, 2:94ff. Irenaeus (*Against the Heresies* 2. 13. 3 [*ANF* 1, pp. 373f.]) also cites Num. 23:19 in the same sense as Philo.

[94] *Quod Deus Immutabilis Sit* 11. 55. This reference shows that Philo had connected the Platonic statements about the deity with those about the ideas. This is generally characteristic of Middle Platonism, which understood the ideas as the content of the divine mind (cf. Andresen, *Logos und Nomos*, p. 136 and n. 68).

[95] Cf. the documentation in Wolfson, *Philo*, 1:38–41.

[96] If God were a body he would be burdened with corruptibility and mutability (Justin *Second Apology* 7. 9 [*ANF* 1, p. 91]. This argument belongs to the usual refutation Middle Platonism directed against Stoic theology (on this point, see Andresen, "Justin und der mittlere Platonismus," pp. 169ff. and n. 54).

also in harmony with him when his pupil, Tatian, designates the spirituality of God as the reason that he is not materially extended.[97] Athenagoras likewise designates God's essence not only as inaccessible light, in itself a perfect cosmos, power, and logos, but also as spirit.[98] In this connection, the expression "spirit" [*pneuma*] contains a nuance noticeably different from that in New Testament usage. While Paul understood the divine Spirit as contrasted not only to man's corporeality but to his whole existence including his spiritual dimension,[99] the Apologists saw the spirituality of God as drawn by its relationship to incorporeality into proximity with the spirit-body dualism of Platonic anthropology. In any case, it was at first only hesitatingly that God was designated as mind [*nous*], as in Middle Platonism.[100] In using this expression,[101] Justin offers less his own opinion and more the school doctrine of the Platonists. Aristides, it is true, calls God wisdom [*sapientia*] and understanding [*intellectus*], and Minucius Felix seems to have no difficulty using a similar formulation.[102] Theophilus, nonetheless, calls attention to the inadequacy of this designation, even if only in a purely philosophical sense: we experience only the thoughtful activity of God, and can express by the term "reason" only this, not the form of God's essence.[103] Irenaeus, likewise, was aware of the problem that even such terms as "spirit" and "reason" were still too inferior as designations of God,[104] but he used them anyway as relatively the most appropriate.[105]

[97] Tatian *Address* 7. 1f. [*ANF* 2, p. 66]. On the bodilessness of God, cf. *ibid.* 15. 2 [*ANF* 2, p. 71]; and 25 [*ANF* 2, p. 76].

[98] *Plea* 16. 2 [*ANF* 2, p. 136].

[99] Bultmann, *Theology of the New Testament*, pp. 205ff.

[100] Albinus *Didaskalikos* 164. 26. Middle Platonism took over this designation from Aristotle, according to Hal Koch, *Pronoia und Paideusis*, p. 233.

[101] *Dialogue with Trypho* 4. 2 [*ANF* 1, p. 196].

[102] Aristides *Apology* 1. 5 [*ANF* 9, p. 264]; Minucius Felix *Octavius* 17. 4ff. [*ANF* 4, p. 182], where, analogous to the argument already developed by Diogenes and Xenophon, the spirituality of God is deduced from the order of the cosmos.   [103] *To Autolycus* 1. 3 [*ANF* 2, pp. 89f.].

[104] *Against the Heresies* 2. 13. 4–8 [*ANF* 1, pp. 374f.].

[105] *Ibid.* 2. 13. 8 [*ANF* 1, p. 375]. Athenagoras *Plea* 24. 1 [*ANF* 2, p. 141], on the contrary, uses the title "mind" [*nous*] for the first time when speaking of the Son.

"For with the name of God the following words will harmonize: intelligence, word, life, incorruption, truth, wisdom, goodness and such like."[106] Everywhere the spirituality of God is not distinguished radically enough from that of men. To be sure, it cannot be said that no distinction at all was made. Tatian and, later, Irenaeus[107] gave prominence to the distinction between the pure, divine Spirit and the creaturely, matter-bound spirit. Tatian takes up an idea of Philo's in this connection. Against the Stoics, Philo once grounded the self-sufficiency of the divine world-spirit by arguing that one may not conclude from the fact that the human spirit is bound to a body to an analogous substrate belonging to the divine Spirit (viz., the cosmos). The human spirit is bound to the body because it did not create its own body and is not joined to it by its own will; instead, it was brought forth along with its body and bound to it by the will of someone else. The divine Spirit, in contrast, created the universe and precisely for this reason is not bound to any material substrate. The material universe is instead his freely willed creature.[108] Tatian appears to express the same thought when he says that the divine Spirit has no material extension but is *instead* the Author of material forms and also of matter-bound spirits.[109] Precisely because God is the creator of matter and of the spirits that are bound to it he is himself bodiless, immaterial.

The distinguishing of the divine spirit from the human spirit, then, pertains only to the relationship to a material substrate. The idea of God as possessing a pure spirituality certainly made it easier to hold the line against Stoicism's pantheism. But this distinction between the divine and the human spirit needs to

---

[106] Irenaeus *Against the Heresies* 2. 19. 9 [*ANF* 1, p. 375]; cf. 1. 12. 2 [*ANF* 1, p. 333].

[107] Irenaeus explicitly says (*Against the Heresies* 2. 13. 4 [*ANF* 1, p. 374]) that the divine reason is not like the human. Perhaps considerations similar to those of Philo and Tatian stand in the background of this sentence.

[108] Philo *De Migratione Abrahami* 35. 193. Wolfson, *Philo*, 2:78ff. comments on the whole line of thought of which this argument forms the conclusion.

[109] Tatian *Address* 4. 2 [*ANF* 2, p. 66]. On this, see Elze, *Tatian und seine Theologie*, pp. 69ff.

be applied to the essential structure of human reason itself. Precisely the transcendence of God, which the reference to God's pure spirituality was supposed to protect in the debate with the Stoic idea of God, was exposed to a new threat by the Platonic schema of spirit-body dualism. On the other hand, the otherness of God was given radical expression by means of the idea of his incomprehensibility.

3. God's Otherness as Incomprehensibility and Ineffability

That God is ineffable and that his essence cannot be adequately designated by any name was among the convictions that were in general circulation in Middle Platonism.[110] The statements of the Christian Apologists on the ineffability of God are nevertheless not always to be connected with the philosophical doctrine of God. This applies especially to the predicate of the namelessness of God. In Aristides one might still suspect a philosophical source when he explains the namelessness of God with the remark that only created beings have names.[111] The similar basis given by Justin — God is nameless because unbegotten[112] — nevertheless allows us to recognize the non-philosophical meaning of his thought. Justin continues: If anyone has a name, then the giver of the name is older than him. Thus, being born and receiving a name are interrelated, and therefore, for Justin, the unbegotten God has no name but only designations based on his works. Even when at baptism the name of God is explained over the baptizand, it is a matter of a human designation of God, and not of the proper name of God's essence. To desire in a genuine sense to give a name to the nameless God would be nonsensical.[113] For this reason, even in the revelation of the divine name to Moses described in Exodus 3:14 it was not the invisible God himself who ap-

[110] Andresen, "Justin und der mittlere Platonismus," p. 167, n. 39, points to Celsus, frag. 6. 65; Albinus *Didaskalikos* 10. 164; 7. 28; Apuleius *De Platone* 1. 5; Maximus of Tyre *Or.* 2. 10a; 11. 9d.

[111] *Apology* 1. 5 [*ANF* 9, p. 264].

[112] *Second Apology* 6. 1 [*ANF* 1, p. 190].

[113] *First Apology* 61. 10f. [*ANF* 1, p. 183].

peared,[114] as the Jews suppose, but the Revealer, the Son.[115] Because of its connection with the concept of unbegottenness, Justin's whole conception of the namelessness of God cannot be traced directly to Plato, but instead points back to Philo.[116] What is at stake there is more a Gnostic than a philosophically compelling line of argument. Irenaeus comes much closer to the philosophical meaning of the namelessness of God. For him, as Theophilus earlier, the ineffability of the divine essence is bound up with the fact that God is exalted beyond all human knowing because of his immensity.[117] Irenaeus finds this exaltedness of God beyond all human knowing chiefly in God's simplicity, in comparison with which our inevitably piecemeal statements remain inadequate.[118] Clement of Alexandria then provides a strict formulation, in keeping with the philosophy of the time, of the consequences of the simplicity of God for human knowledge of God: God cannot be comprehended by any category.[119] In contrast to the Gnostic view, the philosophical way of thinking that was at work in Irenaeus and Clement led back from namelessness and ineffability to incomprehensibility and unknowableness. This is the fundamental state of the matter, from a philosophical standpoint.

The other Apologists mention the incomprehensibility of God in a more incidental manner.[120] It is noteworthy that

---

[114] *Ibid.* 63. 1 [*ANF* 1, p. 184].   [115] *Ibid.* 63. 13 [*ANF* 1, p. 184].

[116] E. R. Goodenough (*The Theology of Justin Martyr* [Jena, 1923], p. 130, with reference to Philo *De Mutatione Nominum* 13ff.) proved this likely, against Pfättisch and other authors. Philo does in fact provide the closest parallels on this point, although Goodenough's endeavor to construe Justin wholly from the side of Philo (cf. p. 124) does not do justice to the latter's direct contact with Platonism.

[117] On this point, see N. Bonwetsch, *Die Theologie des Irenäus* (Gütersloh, 1925), p. 52, on *Adversus Haereses* 2. 13. 3 [*ANF* 2, pp. 373f.]; 4. 6. 3 [*ANF* 2, p. 48]; 4. 19. 2f. [*ANF* 2, p. 497]; 4. 20. 5f. [*ANF* 2, pp. 488f.]; 5. 11 [*ANF* 2, pp. 536f.]; and Theophilus *Ad Autolycus* 1. 3 [*ANF* 2, pp. 89f.]. Even Tertullian says that God, because of his immeasurable magnitude, is known only to himself; *Apologeticus* 17. 3 [*ANF* 3, p. 32].

[118] *Against the Heresies* 2. 13. 4, and 8f. [*ANF* 1, pp. 374f.].

[119] *Stromata* 5. 11 [*ANF* 2, p. 461].

[120] *The Preaching of Peter* 2 [an English translation of this work may be found in *The Apocryphal New Testament*, trans. M. R. James (Oxford:

Athenagoras, like Middle Platonism, affirms the unknowability of God and also, in the same breath, his knowability by means of the mind alone.[121] Justin, on the other hand, does not want to concede without qualification the mind's ability to obtain knowledge of God. The kinship with God requisite to knowledge of God does not belong to the mind as such, but comes to it only through prudence and righteousness,[122] in other words – to use the formulation of his Jewish conversant – when it is adorned by the Holy Spirit.[123] Plato's famous formulation of his concept of knowledge, set forth in his seventh Letter, according to which a "sudden" illumination of the truth comes to worthy spirits, is used in Justin's *Dialogue with Trypho* as a "bridge to the truth of the prophets." The spiritual vision that even Plato had already said was not simply identical with the natural mind could be "proclaimed as the Holy Spirit."[124] Christian teaching about the knowledge of God persisted in this finding of Justin's. Patristic theology for the most part also maintained that man cannot know God by his own efforts but only by means of a divine illumination. This idea is encountered, for example, in Origen's debate with Celsus. However, Origen no longer wants to link it to a philosophical concept of knowledge for apologetic purposes, as Justin did, but hopes only to defend a specifically Christian thesis against Celsus's principle of analogy.[125]

Clarendon Press, 1924), pp. 16ff.]; Aristides *Apology* 1. 2 [*ANF* 9, p. 264] names the incomprehensibility of God alongside his perfection, as later Tatian similarly connects namelessness and perfection (*Address* 4. 2, 5 [*ANF* 2, p. 66]). According to Justin, man associates the word "God" only with an innate idea of an unknowable being (*Second Apology* 6. 3 [*ANF* 1, p. 190]; "a thing that can hardly be explained" [*pragmatos dusexēgētou*]).

[121] *Plea* 10 [*ANF* 2, p. 133].

[122] *Dialogue with Trypho* 4. 2 [*ANF* 1, p. 196].

[123] *Ibid.* 4. 1 [*ANF* 1, p. 196].

[124] W. Schmid, "Frühe Apologetik und Platonismus: Ein Beitrag zur Interpretation des proems von Justins Dialogus," in *Hermeneia: Festschrift for Otto Regenbogen zum 60. Geburtstag* (Heidelberg, 1952), pp. 163–82, citation from p. 181. Cf. Andresen, "Justin und der Mittlere Platonismus," pp. 165f., on the connection with Plato *Epistle VII* 341 C and D.

[125] Origen *Against Celsus* 7. 42 [*ANF* 4, p. 628 = *MPG* 11, col. 1481]. Origen recognizes that the Platonic doctrine of illumination presupposes divine assistance for knowledge of God (*ibid.* 6, 5 [*ANF* 4, p. 575 = *MPG* 11,

The incomprehensibility of God acquired special theological significance in the thought of Irenaeus and Clement of Alexandria. At one place, after he had stressed the dependency of the Gnostic doctrine of emanation upon Neo-Pythagoreanism,[126] Irenaeus raises the question whether the philosophers had known the truth. He answers this question, not, for instance, by critically examining the emanation schema once again, but by remarking: "If they knew it, then the descent of the Savior into this world was superfluous. For why [in that case] did he descend? Was it that he might bring that truth which was [already] known to the knowledge of those who knew it?"[127] Irenaeus shared with his Gnostic opponents the view that the Redeemer came in order to impart a new, unheard of knowledge [*gnosis*], and he attacks the doctrine of emanation on the basis of just this presupposition. For him, the incomprehensibility of God became a presupposition and thereby a point of contact for the Christian message of revelation. This explains why Irenaeus emphasizes the incomprehensibility of God over and over again. It is noteworthy that Clement of Alexandria can speak in a similar fashion. According to Clement, if the natural, innate knowledge of God were perfect, then God's commandments and the Incarnation had been superfluous.[128] But the natural knowledge of God is insufficient. Even the Greeks knew God only "in an indirect manner" [*kata periphrasin*], not "by positive knowledge" [*kat' epignōsin*].[129]

---

col. 1296]). Nevertheless, he comments on Plato's *Epistle VII* 341 C and D that the doctrine of illumination had already been stated beforehand by Hosea and afterwards by John.

[126] *Against the Heresies* 2. 14. 6 [*ANF* 1, p. 377].

[127] *Ibid.* 2. 14. 7 [*ANF* 1, p. 378].

[128] *Stromata* 5. 1 [*ANF* 2, p. 444]. On this point, see Molland, *Conception of the Gospel in the Alexandrian Theology*, pp. 35f. [Here, and in other references to *Stromata*, the chapter numbers given in the text are those of the *ANF* edition. These differ from the numbers given in the original text, which follows Klotz's division of the work into paragraphs instead of chapters. The sub-paragraph numbers in the original are from the German translation by Stählin in *Bibliothek der Kirchenväter*, Second series, – Tr.]

[129] *Stromata* 6. 5 [*ANF* 2, p. 489]; 5. 14 [*ANF* 2, p. 474]; 1. 19 [*ANF* 2, pp. 321, 322]. In his exposition of this matter, Molland rightly asserts that

Catholic studies have contested this stress upon the transcendence of God and the incomprehensibility connected with it. Justin is supposed to have distorted the Christian idea of God by a Platonizing, "exaggerated emphasis on the transcendence of God."[130] In response to this it must be said that it was precisely in calling attention to the otherness of God in comparison with everything non-divine, as was most radically expressed in the statements about the incomprehensibility of God, that the philosophical idea of God came closest to the Judaeo-Christian view.

For Israel's faith, God is essentially hidden. This is not because he stays away from men, so to speak. On the contrary, God is hidden precisely in his historical acts (Isa. 45:15), and his history-governing wisdom is inscrutable (Isa. 40:28). According to the testimony of the Deuteronomist (Deut. 4:12ff.), precisely in Yahweh's act of revelation, the Israelites saw no form. "Holiness" is the Old Testament's word for God's otherness. Yahweh's holiness prohibits not only his representation in a cult-image, but absolutely every attempt to compare him with something else.[131] When Philo grounded the unnameability of God in the second commandment, he did not grasp its historical meaning, to be sure, but perhaps he was nevertheless not very far from the spirit of the Old Testament. In every act of naming there is an element of seizing possession (Gen. 2:19), which was supposed to be guarded against in relation to God by the prohibition against misusing his name just as much as by the prohibition against images.[132] Nor was knowledge of the holy otherness and incomprehensibility of God lost in primitive Christianity. It underlies the whole primitive Christian procla-

---

there is some vacillation in Clement's conception of the range of natural knowledge of God.

[130] Pfättisch, *Der Einfluss Platos*, pp. 35f. (cf. pp. 19ff.).

[131] Isa. 40:25: "To whom then will you compare me, that I should be like him? says the Holy One." I am grateful to Klaus Koch for pointing out that Deutero-Isaiah provides a comprehensive basis for the prohibition against images in this repudiation of all comparisons.

[132] Cf. von Rad, *Old Testament Theology*, 1:217, and *ibid.*, n. 67 on K. H. Bernhardt, *Gott und Bild* (Berlin, 1956), pp. 153f.

mation even if it is seldom its object. Nevertheless, Paul not only spoke of the unsearchability of the ways of God (Rom. 11:33) and of his invisibility to mortal eyes (Rom. 1:20), but appears also to have presupposed the unknowability of the genuine essence of God for human comprehension.[133]

Thus, the fact that early Christian theology linked up with the philosophical assertions of precisely the otherness, transcendence, and incomprehensibility of God is surely no reason for reproaching it. The manner in which theology since Irenaeus and Clement made use of the philosophical establishment of the incomprehensibility of God is indeed attractive, but suspect nevertheless. The philosophical thesis about the unknowability of God is not like some kind of vacuum that could be filled up by any sort of revelatory contents whatever. This point cannot be construed as simply a provisional ignorance that could be set aside by revelation. For it means precisely that God is and remains *essentially* incomprehensible to man. From this standpoint, every claim of a revelation to impart knowledge of God in spite of this will be judged as either illusory or, at best, a symbol of something basically inexpressible. Thereupon theology itself, with the Alexandrians and especially with the Areopagite, under the influence of Neoplatonism, took a symbolical view of its positive statements about God. The autonomy of the theological doctrine of God was lost in consequence of this development. It could only provide symbolic illustrations of the philosophical concept of God. But is a genuine or even the sole alternative to this wrong track to be found along the lines of a substantive addition to the philosophical doctrine of God and thus of combining heterogeneous elements with it in an external way? In that case would it not be necessary to put to philosophy the question of whether it was serious about the incomprehensibility and otherness of God? Could not the

[133] The formulation "what can be known about God" (Rom. 1:19) sets limits upon understanding and, as Max Pohlenz ("Paulus und die Stoa," *Zeitschrift für Neutestamentliche Wissenschaft* 42 [1949]: 71f.) was able to show, is reminiscent of the Hellenistic-Jewish and especially the Philonic exegesis of Exod. 33. It implies, as follows from the comparison, that God's real essence remains unknowable nevertheless.

"new" in the Christian message with regard to the knowledge of God have been seen in the fact that only in view of God's presence in the destiny of Jesus can man endure the incomprehensibility of God and thus even in the face of the truth of God be truly man? Christian theology did not take this way of linking critically with the philosophical thesis about the incomprehensibility of God. The beautiful saying of Tertullian that one comprehends God precisely in knowing him as incomprehensible[134] was without consequence for his understanding of the revelation of God in Jesus Christ. Revelation was understood not as revelation of the incomprehensible God but as providing a positive complement to his incomprehensibility. The thesis of Irenaeus, used repeatedly in ever new ways, that God is indeed unknown to us in his magnitude but has made himself knowable to us by his love in Jesus Christ,[135] could even give rise to the impression that through the revelation in Christ man was carried beyond the point where he had to remain content with the incomprehensibility of God. That, however, would be a misconception. Irenaeus here expressly distinguishes between the knowledge of God disclosed by his loving condescension and a knowledge that would comprehend God in his entire magnitude. Even someone who believes in Christ still sees himself confronted by the incomprehensible God. Nevertheless, Irenaeus does not say that it is the believer in Christ who first becomes at all aware of the incomprehensible God, and that the loving condescension of God to man discloses this existence in the unconcealed presence of the incomprehensible God, and that it has its revelatory character precisely in this. Irenaeus, who could so effectively introduce the incomprehensibility of God into the battle against Gnostic speculations,[136] could also have utilized it against philosophical theology, to wit, that on its presuppositions it is unable to do justice to the full

---

[134] *Apology* 17. 3 [*ANF* 3, p. 32].

[135] Irenaeus *Against the Heresies* 2. 24. 2 [*ANF* 1, p. 458]; cf. 4. 20. 1 [*ANF* 1, p. 487] and *passim*. The possibility of assigning terms to him — even if inadequately — rests upon the loving condescension of God (2. 13 [*ANF* 1, p. 374]).

[136] *Against the Heresies* 2. 13. 4 [*ANF* 1, p. 374].

scope of the postulated incomprehensibility of God, and that it inevitably violates this concept in its projected concept of God. Irenaeus could then have found the novel element in the revelation of God in Christ in precisely the disclosure of God's incomprehensibility. Since he did not undertake this usurpation of the philosophical concept of God – to which his critical discussions did not even apply, in the first instance – and instead posited the content of the revelation of God's love as something secondary alongside the incomprehensibility of God, he took a fateful step in the direction of a compromise which was actually impossible from the standpoint of philosophy as well as from that of theology. He took the path of a two-level structure setting revelational, theological elements in the concept of God on top of the philosophical elements, in other words, the path whose classical shape was to be given it much later by the work of Latin Scholasticism.

4. *The Consequences of the Method of Causal Inference: Unchangeability, Simplicity, Absence of Properties*

In taking over the proofs for the existence of God,[137] early Christian theology adopted the method of reasoning *a posteriori* from the world to its presupposed origin.[138] It did so in the first instance to make the natural man cognizant of the existence

[137] In addition to Tatian and Theophilus, who were referred to above in n. 5, cf. Aristides *Apology* 13. 7 and 1. 1–2 [*ANF* 9, pp. 274f., 263f.]; Athenagoras *Plea* 13. 1f.; 16. 2f. [*ANF* 2, pp. 134f., 136]; Minucius Felix *Octavius* 17f. [*ANF* 4, pp. 181f.]; Irenaeus, *Against the Heresies* 2. 9. 1, and esp. 2. 25. 2 [*ANF* 1, p. 369, and esp. p. 396]. Justin (*Second Apology* 6. 3 [*ANF* 1, p. 190]) speaks of an innate knowledge of an incomprehensible divine being, but, as the passage just cited shows, thinks of this natural knowledge of God more as a purely intellectual vision than as an inference based on the order of the world (cf. Schmid, "Frühe Apologetik und Platonismus," p. 176, on Justin *Dialogue with Trypho* 4. 1 [*ANF* 1, p. 196]).

[138] The word "origin" [*archē*] itself is seldom applied to God in early Christian theology, e.g., Tatian *Address* 4. 3 [*ANF* 2, p. 66]; more frequently in Irenaeus (*Against the Heresies* 2. 1. 1; 2. 3 and passim [*ANF* 1, pp. 359, 361, and *passim*]). The primary reason for this might be that this expression was not reserved for the divine in the philosophy of that period (cf. above, pp. 142ff.).

of God – of the existence of the One God whose revelation was
attested by the proclamation. This approach is not unbiblical
since even Paul laid great stress upon the fact that no man can
excuse himself for not knowing God. To be sure, Paul spoke of
this knowledge as something posited by God as a reality from
which men cannot escape and which burdens them with God's
judgment.[139] The reference here was to a manifestation from
the side of God, not a possibility on man's side for obtaining
knowledge of God by means of a causal inference (Rom. 1:19).
Man's contribution in this is more that of perverting the divine
truth (Rom. 1:21f.). Paul had in view, as an example of such
a perversion, polytheistic popular religion, first of all, but it was
undoubtedly in harmony with Paul's intention to uncover this
perversion in the philosophical approach, too (Rom. 3:9ff.).
Since the Pauline refraction of the philosophical question of God
was neglected by early Christian theology in that in the process
of appropriating the method of causal inference it failed to
subject this to criticism but adopted it as a valid possibility of
knowledge, it carried over even the prejudgments about the
essence of God which were inherent in the philosophical question about God. The original function of the philosophical
method of inference from the known to its unknown ground
was by no means simply that of proving the existence of the
divine – this was really already presupposed – but rather that
of disclosing the essential character of the deity. Thus, even in
early Christian theology, this inferential procedure operated as
a set of prior decisions about specific essential features of the
concept of God which consequently appeared to be knowable
independently of historical revelation and not in need of any
critical refraction. Obviously, it was not seen that a constriction
of the biblical idea of God, an abridgment of his transcendent
freedom and omnipotence, would necessarily be involved in
thec onsistent working out of the philosophical formulation of the

[139] So, Bornkamm, "The Revelation of God's Wrath," pp. 55ff. Rom.
1:29 "points to the freedom and majesty of God. Thus a description of the
nature of God, in which an ascending wisdom issues from a viewing of the
world by 'comparison' or 'negation', is not to be found in Paul."

question about God. If this abridgment was not forthcoming all along the line but only at a series of points of which the two most important will be treated in the discussion that follows; and if, on the contrary, the ideas of God's omnipotence and freedom were explicitly defended; that happened in contradiction to the fundamental, inherent tendencies of the inferential procedure.

(*a*) As we saw, the predicate of immutability belongs essentially to the concept of God that grew out of the question about the ground of the universe. This concept was appropriated as early as Aristides.[140] Justin fought against Stoicism's pantheism with the Platonic argument that on their grounds God must change along with the world.[141] Against this, he asserted the indestructibility of God in the sense of immutability.[142] The Apologists thought of the immutability of God in close connection with his eternity and unoriginateness. Justin could set immutability and eternity in apposition.[143] Aristides saw in God's being unoriginate the presupposition of his immutability.[144] And Athenagoras perceived in unoriginateness the fundamental condition of eternity so that "only the God who is without beginning is eternal."[145] Manifestly, fundamental

---

[140] *Apology* 4. 1 [*ANF* 9, p. 266]: "who is indestructible and immutable" [*Aphthartos te kai analloiōtos*]. The predicate of indestructibility stands in the foreground in this instance (*ibid.* 1. 4; 4. 3; 7. 1 [*ANF* 9, pp. 264, 266, 268]). In *The Preaching of Peter* this predicate still stands alone at the place which it later shared with the substantively related but more abstract and also more precise concept of immutability. On indestructibility [*aphthartos*], cf. also Rom. 1:23 and 1 Tim. 1:17. These two concepts differ fundamentally in their respective impacts. The concept of indestructibility does not compel the weighty consequences that the concept of immutability brings with it: even a living, self-altering being can be indestructible.

[141] *Second Apology* 7. 9 [*ANF* 1, pp. 190f.].

[142] *First Apology* 20. 2 [*ANF* 1, p. 169].

[143] *First Apology* 13. 4 [*ANF* 1, p. 167].

[144] *Apology* 1. 4 [*ANF* 9, p. 264]: "And when I say that he is 'without beginning' [= 'unoriginate' – Tr.], this means that everything which has a beginning has also an end, and that which has an end may be brought to an end" [*Et quod eum sine initio esse dico significat omnia quae initium habeant finem quoque habere, et quod fineam habeat, dissolubile esse*].

[145] *Plea* 4. 1; 8. 3 [*ANF* 2, pp. 131, 132]. According to the better reading, Athenagoras writes "unoriginate" [*agenētos*] not "unbegotten" [*agennētos*].

importance is assigned here to unoriginateness. It constitutes the basis for eternity as well as for immutability: God is "immutable because without beginning."[146] According to Athenagoras, unoriginateness (or being without becoming) is for its part grounded in the fact that becoming occurs only in the realm of entities that do not (fully) possess being, while (true) being is exalted beyond becoming.[147] Tatian's formula, God is the unoriginate origin of all things,[148] tersely expresses the fact that the idea of unoriginateness is always implicitly included in the idea of a primal origin [*archē*], as Anaximander had already recognized.

The close relationship between immutability and unoriginateness is expressed by Theophilus through the parallelization of both predicates.[149] Here, Theophilus connects immutability with immortality, and thereby brings to light the redemptive significance this predicate had for the theology of the primitive church: imitative participation in the divine immutability also guarantees man immortality.[150] According to Tatian, this participation is realized through knowledge of God coupled with righteous conduct.[151] Justin explicitly says: virtue bestows incorruptibility.[152] The immutability of God was therefore not only an abstract theorem but a pointer to the way of salvation insofar as by means of virtue one attains constancy and consequently immortality, and thus also godlikeness.

The difference between these two words is not in itself very important since, as Prestige has shown (*God in Patristic Thought*, pp. 37–54), these two words were used promiscuously.

[146] Theophilus *To Autolycus* 2. 4 [*ANF* 2, p. 95]. Immutability is simply "the inevitable consequence of the Platonic concept of eternity," as Werner Elert has it (*Der Ausgang der altkirchlichen Christologie* [Berlin, 1957], p. 43). Historically and substantively its original context is much more the question about the origin [*archē*].

[147] *Plea* 4. 2 [*ANF* 2, p. 131]: "for that which is does not come to be, but that which is not" [*hoti to ou ginetai, alla to mē on*]. That God did not come to be, a point repeatedly stressed by Athenagoras, can be viewed as equivalent to the term "unoriginate". Cf. Minucius Felix *Octavius* 18. 7 [*ANF* 4, p. 183].

[148] *Address* 4. 3 [*ANF* 2, p. 66].   [149] *To Autolycus* 1. 4 [*ANF* 2, p. 90].

[150] Tatian *Address* 7. 1 [*ANF* 1, p. 67].

[151] On this, see Elze, *Tatian und seine Theologie*, pp. 98ff.

[152] *Second Apology* 9 [*ANF* 1, p. 192].

It hardly needs proof that this pathway to salvation by becoming assimilated to God did not correspond to what was meant by saving faith in primitive Christianity. It is possible here only to mention the fact that this difference is related to a difference in the understanding of God (with regard to God's freedom!). The difference in the understanding of God is expressed at this point in the fact that the representation of God as immutable is not only unknown in the biblical witnesses but also inappropriate if applied to them without qualification. To be sure, Paul says: "the gifts and the call of God are irrevocable" (Rom. 11:29).[153] The many assurances that God does not change his decisions or "repent" seem to have a similar intention: "(he) will not lie or repent; for he is not a man, that he should repent" (1 Sam. 15:29). Even Hebrews 6:17f. grounds the trustworthiness of the divine promise in this way: it is impossible that God should have lied. Such sayings nevertheless differ profoundly from philosophical ideas of an immovable ground of the universe. Yet the concept of immutability rightly says that God is no originated and transitory thing. Insofar as mutability is known to us only in connection with the process of coming into being and passing away, the author of the world cannot in fact be mutable if he is to be the basis of the endurance of all things. But immutability says too little, since God not only immovably establishes and maintains present reality in its lawful course, but has within himself an infinite plenitude of ever new possibilities in the realization of which he manifests the freedom of his invisible essence. For this reason, while he is unoriginate and indestructible, God is nevertheless not immobile, but rather, in this inner plenitude, the living God. Therefore, it can also be said of him, apparently in contradiction to 1 Samuel 15:29 and the other passages mentioned above, that he allows himself to repent of some things (Jer. 18:8, 10; Gen. 6:6). The durability of the world indeed does depend upon the fact that God does not jump from one possibility to another but abides by his creative decisions, "not changing" them or

[153] [The German text cited by the author uses a term meaning "unchangeable" where the RSV, cited above, has "irrevocable". – Tr.]

simply dropping them. But the fact that God does not change in his acts is an expression not of an immobility constitutive of his essence but rather of his free, momentary, humanly un-anticipatable decision, just as much as is his creative activity. It is identical with the faithfulness of God. In his faithfulness, God does not simply allow his previous deeds to fall to the ground for the sake of the new possibilities of his freedom, but instead includes the prior ones in the new. This is what first makes possible duration and continuity in created being. To this extent, it is not only the indestructibility of God himself but also the constancy and continuity of his activity that is the presupposition of the world's stability. But the enabling of a specific order and duration is only a partial aspect of the activity of the living God. The philosophical thesis of the immutability of the primal ground of being at once isolates this partial aspect and raises it to a total view. In so doing, the philosophical idea of God neglects the element of freedom in the constancy of God's acts and thereby at the same time loses sight of the contingency of world-reality. But the constancy of God is realized as free act precisely in his contingent, historical action. In contrast to this, the concept of a God who is by nature immutable necessarily obstructs the theological understanding of his historical action, and it has done so to an extent that can hardly be exaggerated. It indeed constitutes the background for the idea of the im-passibility of God which so fatefully determined the Christology of the early church right down to the theopaschitic controversy.[154] Above all, however, the concept of the immutability of God necessarily leads to the consequence that the transition to every innovation in the relationship between God and man has to be sought as much as possible on the side of man. Thus, the idea of God becoming man has to recede into the background behind that of God assuming human nature.[155] In addition to this, the concept of God's immutability pressed in the direction of con-ceiving this "assumption" of a man by God in terms of the schema of assimilation to God, and thus finding this realized

[154] On this, see Elert, *Ausgang der altkirchlichen Christologie*, pp. 71ff., 121f.
[155] *Ibid.*, p. 43.

in the ethical striving of Jesus, a tendency which is traceable from Origen and Paul of Samosata right on into the later Antiochene Christology.[156] These christological consequences are perhaps profoundly related to the fact that even Pelagian views inevitably find a foothold in the concept of the immutability of God. If God is immutable, then surely every change in man's situation in relation to salvation must be initiated by a change from man's side. One still remains close to this fundamental viewpoint even if the saving reversal from wrath to grace brought about by Christ is traced to the meritorious, free volition of the man Jesus, in keeping with a heightened diothelitism, as happened in the case of Anselm of Canterbury.[157] Finally, the so-called conversion argument, which was the point of departure for the rise of the doctrine of created grace in twelfth-century Scholasticism, runs along the same lines: the fact that a man who belongs among those damned by God becomes one who is loved by God cannot, on account of the immutability of God, be explained on the basis of a divine gift but only by means of a change on the side of man. To be sure, this change may not be within the natural powers of man – that would be Pelagian – but even as a supernatural embellishment, it must nevertheless be a component of man as a creature

---

[156] Cf. Aloys Grillmeier, "Die theologische und sprachliche Vorbereitung der christologischen Formel von Chalkedon," in *Das Konzil von Chalkedon*, 3 vols. (Würzburg, 1953), pp. 64ff. (Origen); p. 127 (an utterance of Eustathius of Antioch [frag. 15 = *De Anima et Adv. Arianos*] on the intention of the Arians); pp. 147f. (Theodore of Mopsuestia *Catechetical Homily* 5. 11. 14).

[157] This view is expressed with particular clarity in Anselm's eleventh meditation, *Concerning Human Redemption* [*De redemptione humana*]: "Thus the human nature in that man gave what he was to God freely and not out of debt in order to redeem himself (!) in the remainder of what was due, to give back not what he was obliged to . . . not what human nature in that man suffered by any sort of necessity, but solely by free will" [*Dedit itaque humana natura Deo in illo homine sponte et non ex debito quod suum erat ut redimeret se (!) in aliis, in quibus quod ex debito exigebatur, reddere non habebat . . . Nec humana natura in illo homine passa est aliquid ulla necessitate, sed sola libera voluntate* (MPL 158, col. 765c)]. Cf. *Cur Deus Homo* 1. 8; 2. 11 [in Eugene Fairweather ed., *A Scholastic Miscellany*, Library of Christian Classics 10 (Philadelphia: Westminster Press, 1956), pp. 110ff., 158ff.].

distinct from God in order to motivate a new judgment upon this man by the immutable God.[158] The range of impact of the concept of the immutability of God can be gauged by these examples. The difficulty of combining any sort of spontaneous act of God with the metaphysical concept of essential immutability is indeed also completely intelligible. It is well known that the Epicureans denied any intervention of the gods in the changing world and in human destiny just because of the immutability of the divine.[159] When in opposition to this view the Stoics and, following them, also Middle Platonism and early Christian theology emphasized, on the basis of the omnipresence of God,[160] the providential guidance of the world in all the details of every event,[161] this still did not arrive at an understanding of reality marked by the contingency of the divine

---

[158] On this, see J. Auer, *Die Entwicklung der Gnadenlehre in der Hochscholastik: I. Das Wesen der Gnade* (Freiburg in Breisgau, 1942).

[159] Cf. Praechter, *Überwegs Grundriss der Philosophie*, 1:451.

[160] The omnipresence of God was expressed by early Christian theology in ways that had strong spatial overtones. Thus, Aristides stated: "(God) is not limited by anything, but all things receive their bounds from him" [*(Deum) ab nullo comprehensum esse, sed ipsum omnia comprehendere (Apology* 1. 4); translation mine – Tr.; but cf. *ANF* 9, p. 264]. Cf. the similar utterances of Philo cited by Wolfson, *Philo*, 1:274ff., as well as *Bereshit Rabbah*, chap. 68 (cited by Goodenough, *Theology of Justin Martyr*, p. 126, on Justin *Dialogue with Trypho* 127. 1-2 [*ANF* 1, p. 263]). Theophilus formulates the matter even more tangibly: God's breath contains everything like the pomegranate its cells and seeds (*To Autolycus* 1. 5 [*ANF* 2, p. 90]). In Christian literature, the *Shepherd of Hermas* (Commandments, 1 [*ANF* 2, p. 20]) had already stated that God contains all things but is himself incapable of being contained in anything. Irenaeus grounds the assertion that God is not enclosed by anything with the argument that otherwise he would not be God because whatever encloses something is larger than what is enclosed (*Against the Heresies* 2. 1. 2; cf. 2. 30. 9; 4. 20. 2 [*ANF* 1, p. 359; cf. pp. 406, 488]). Since God, who surrounds all things, is not enclosed by anything, Theophilus ([*To Autolycus* 2. 10 [*ANF* 2, p. 98]) can say with Philo (*Legum Allegoria* 1. 44) that God is his own place.

[161] *I Clem.* 20 [*ANF* 1, p. 10] had already developed the idea of providence in detail (for the concept itself, see 24:5 [*ANF* 1, p. 12]). Justin *First Apology* 28 [*ANF* 1, p. 172]) attacked the Epicurean denial of providence. On the other hand, however, he defended the freedom of man (*ibid.* 43 [*ANF* 1, p. 177]) in order to preserve human responsibility against the fatalism of the Stoic doctrine of fate [*heimarmenē*] (cf. also Tatian *Address* 8. 1ff. [*ANF* 2, p. 68]).

action because God's providence, as a divine plan for the world, still remained a rational law of the world's becoming. This was shown with particular clarity by the failure of the repeated attempts to unite providence and contingency (especially in the case of human freedom). Certainly the metaphysics of providence, as Hal Koch has shown, could be fitted into the framework of a comprehensive, systematically executed project, as the Alexandrians did in treating the whole tradition of redemptive history under the theme of the education of the human race. But even in the metaphysics of providence, the divine ground of the world was understood not as acting contingently but rather as the law of the world. Thus, the concept of providence – aside from the fact that the concept of God as a conscious being, which it presupposes, is incompatible with his transcendence – did more to conceal rather than genuinely to resolve the contradiction between the immutable ground of the world and the God who acts in history.

(*b*) The immutability of the first cause leads to the thought of its simplicity. We saw that according to Plato everything composite is divisible and consequently mutable. Thus, only a completely simple being can be immutable. This postulate, too, which results from the initial tendency of the inferential question about the ultimate origin, was taken over by Philo[162] and early Christian theology.[163] Aristides calls attention to the simplicity of God by referring to the fact that composition is a mark of creatureliness.[164] Probably the speech of the Demiurge to the gods in Plato's *Timaeus* was in mind here. The argument suggested by Aristides is even more clearly formulated by Athenagoras: as unoriginate and impassible, God is

---

[162] On this, see Wolfson, *Philo*, 2:98ff. (cf., however, above, n. 48).

[163] Because of the documentation that is shortly to be mentioned, it is impossible to to treat simplicity as something specific to the Western Doctrine of God, as W. Philipp does ("Eigenschaften Gottes," in *RGG*[3], vol. 2, col. 358).

[164] *Apology* 1. 5 [*ANF* 9, p. 264]: "Form he has none, not yet any union of members; for whatsoever possesses these is kindred to things fashioned" [*forma ei non est, nec constitutio membrorum; cui enim haec sint, socius rerum creatarum est*].

indivisible.[165] Thus, simplicity is a consequence of immutability. Even Tatian mentions the simplicity of God several times.[166] In Justin's dialogue, the Platonist uses the undifferentiatedness of the unoriginate as an argument for the idea that there can be only one God.[167]

The simplicity of God plays an especially important role in Irenaeus. He blames the Gnostics for violating the simplicity of God with their doctrine of emanation. "He, therefore, who speaks of the mind of God, and ascribes to it a special origin of its own, declares Him a compound being, as if God were one thing, and the original mind another."[168] The Gnostics unwittingly transfer to God the multiplicity of spiritual elements that proceed independently of each other, such as those occurring in man as a composite being, and thereby deny his simplicity, which is what distinguishes him from creatures:

> He is a simple, uncompounded being, without diverse members, and altogether like, and equal to himself, since he is wholly understanding, and wholly spirit, and wholly thought, and wholly reason, and wholly hearing, and wholly seeing, and wholly light, and wholly the source of all that is good.[169]

What the Gnostics distinguish as emanations are all one in God and are distinct only in our designation of them.[170]

[165] *Plea* 8. 2 [*ANF* 2, p. 132].

[166] *Address* 5. 2; 15. 2 [*ANF* 2, pp. 67, 71] (for a detailed discussion of the latter citation, cf. Elze, *Tatian und seine Theologie*, pp. 66ff.).

[167] *Dialogue with Trypho* 5. 5f.; cf. 114. 3 [*ANF* 1, p. 197; cf. p. 256]; and Goodenough, *Theology of Justin Martyr*, pp. 127f., where the position of Justin on the question of a "form" of God is also treated.

[168] *Against the Heresies* 2. 28. 5; cf. 13. 5 [*ANF* 1, p. 400; cf. p. 374].

[169] *Ibid.* 2. 13. 3 [*ANF* 1, p. 374] (... *et simplex et non compositus et similimembrius et totus ipse sibimetipsi similis et aequalis est, totus cum sit sensus, et totus spiritus, et totus sensuabilitas, et totus ennoea et totus ratio et totus auditus et totus oculus et totus lumen et totus fons omnium bonorum*).

[170] In relation to this idea of the simplicity of God, only the anti-Gnostic point is original with Irenaeus; the substance of the idea stems from the philosophical tradition. One cannot speak of a "simplicity of God in the sense of a *living personality*," as Bonwetsch has it (*Die Theologie des Irenäus*, p. 54). These two concepts have nothing to do with each other. The emphasis on the element of will in Irenaeus' doctrine of God does indeed have strongly personalistic features. But this stands rather in tension with the idea of simplicity since simplicity has the tendency of transcending every concept of a determinate attribute.

For Irenaeus, the concept of God's simplicity means that the fullness of all perfections and properties is realized in him in the mode of unity. At the same time, however, this means that strictly speaking *none* of these attributions of properties is really suitable for God insofar as every attribute is what it is only in distinction from another. The absolutely simple essence of God is therefore to be characterized not only as that which sums up all perfections, but also, with at least equal legitimacy, as propertyless and without qualities – a consequence that was very far from Irenaeus's mind, to be sure. That the first cause is without qualities [*apoios*] on account of its simplicity is a matter which in substance goes back to Plato.[171] Philo repeatedly mentions the propertylessness of God in the sense that there are no substance-inhering accidents in God.[172] According to Philo, the propertylessness of God also includes an absence of every form [*morphē*].[173] The term *apoios*, is at first not to be found in early Christian theology.[174] But the saying of Aristides that God has neither color nor form[175] resembles Philo's thesis about the formlessness of God. It comes even closer to Plato, *Phaedrus* 247c. Andresen has shown that the description given here of the intelligible world was everywhere employed in Middle Platonism to characterize the deity, as for example in Plutarch and Celsus.[176] Even in Justin's dialogue, the Platonist uses the argument that God is without color or form.[177] This is

---

[171] *Republic* 6. 509f. Plato does not use the term *apoios* here, but the famous "transcends essence" [*epekeina tēs ousias*], includes being without determinations. Cf. *Phaedrus* 247c.

[172] Wolfson, *Philo*, 2:104ff.

[173] *Ibid.*, p. 105, on *Quod Deus Immutabilis Sit* 2. 55–6.

[174] According to Elert (*Ausgang altkirchlichen Christologie*, p. 74), the concept of apathy (since Ignatius *Ephesians* 7. 2 [*ANF* 1, p. 52]; *Polycarp* 3. 2 [*ANF* 1, p. 94]) still retains the meaning of inability to suffer in Irenaeus and Tertullian, and does not have the broader sense of absence of qualities.

[175] *Apology* 1. 5 [not in English translation – Tr.]. Only the Armenian text says that God has no color, hence no sensible qualities. The Syrian text limits itself to saying that God has no "form" (Hennecke suggests *schēma* as the Greek equivalent).

[176] Andresen, "Justin und der mittlere Platonismus," p. 166. Cf. Plutarch *De Iside et Osiride* 76; Celsus frag. 6. 64 (Bader).

[177] *Dialogue with Trypho* 4. 1 [*ANF* 1, p. 196]. On the structure of the text

supposed to establish that God is to be thought of as free from
sensible qualities. At this same place Justin continues that there
also cannot be any quantitative determinations [*megethos*] in
God. That Justin himself shared these Platonic convictions can
be seen from his polemics against idols, whose sensible form he
regards as inappropriate for the deity.[178] However, in rejecting
a form like that of sense objects, Justin does not deny the deity
every form whatever. Rather, his complaint against the idols is
that they do "not (possess) the form of God."[179] And Theophilus
is outspoken about an inexpressible, indescribable "form" of
God, which is invisible to physical eyes.[180] Thus, the statements
of the Apologists about God possessing no color or (sensible)
form express only the immateriality of God and not[181] an entire
absence of qualities. The Apologists have not yet drawn out the
full consequences of simplicity in the direction of a complete
absence of properties in the divine being, although Justin once
cites the "transcends essence" [*epekeina ousias*] phrase.[182] Even
Origen, as much as he especially also kept all sensible determinations, "color and form,"[183] away from the concept of God,

---

of this sentence, cf. Schmid, "Frühe Apologetik und Platonismus," pp. 176f.
It is unlikely that this sentence is to be explained as an abbreviation of
Symposium 210e–12, because of the partial verbal dependence upon *Phaedrus*
247c (which, moreover, also makes it superfluous to refer to *Phaedrus* 65e).
Schmid also points to Maximus of Tyre *Or.* 11. 11 as a parallel.

[178] *First Apology* 9 [*ANF* 1, p. 165]. Cf. Philo *Legum Allegoria* 1. 15. 51,
and 3. 11. 36 where the expression *apoias* is used in order to describe the same
state of the matter.

[179] *First Apology* 9. 1 [*ANF* 1, p. 165].

[180] *To Autolycus* 1. 3 [*ANF* 2, pp. 89f. The English translation has "appearance" instead of "form." – Tr.].

[181] It is scarcely possible to affirm a different result in the case of Philo.
The documentation given by Wolfson, *Philo*, 2:104ff., collectively speaks of
sensible accidents as not being ascribable to God. Wolfson's attempt (pp.
106f.) to prove that an understanding of the category of quality in line with
its Stoic sense (thus, as an expression for every form whatever) is to be found
in Philo, remains a hypothesis. The agreements with Stoic categorial terms
found in *Legum Allegoria* 2. 73. 206 do not amount to an exact coincidence,
as Wolfson admits, and even if that were the case it would hardly be possible
to draw far-reaching conclusions on the basis of such an isolated finding.

[182] *Dialogue with Trypho* 4. 1 [*ANF* 1, p. 196].

[183] *De Principiis* 1. 1 [*ANF* 4, pp. 242ff.].

spoke emphatically about the peculiar qualities [*idia poiotēs*] of God. Like Justin, he had in mind particularly the goodness of God.[184] In the meantime, however, Albinus had already taken the road of a radical negation of all intellectual distinctions in the knowledge of God. Albinus explicitly declared (something one searches in vain for in Philo) that God contains neither genus [*genos*] nor idea [*eidos*] nor difference [*diaphora*], and carried the transcendence of God beyond all opposites to such an extreme that he wished even to avoid designating God as good or bad.[185] The reserve of Christian theology on this point becomes intelligible in the light of this development. But this consequence of the commonly accepted idea of the simplicity of God was inescapable on the assumption of a realistic view of universals. If the description of an object by means of different assertions presupposes a real composition in this object, then the simplicity of God requires that he be conceived as property-less.[186]

Awareness of the otherness of God apparently reaches its highest pinnacle with the drawing of this conclusion. But this sort of otherness does not express his unforeseeable action: it is not the otherness of his freedom. Whereas the latter, because it is manifested in his acts, always retains a connection with the reality of human life, the God of propertyless simplicity appears to be withdrawn into that distant, abstract transcendence which has been assailed by the critics of the concept of God developed in Hellenism and the early church.[187]

But this critique, aimed at the "distance" from man of the "abstract" picture of God, is couched in such general terms that it will not stand up. As the invisible ground of present reality,

[184] Cf. H. Koch, *Pronoia und Paideusis*, pp. 257, 23; Justin *Dialogue with Trypho* 4. 1 [*ANF* 1, p. 196].   [185] *Didaskalikos* 10. 165. 5ff.

[186] Clement of Alexandria has already drawn this conclusion and has characterized God as wholly without determinations (*Stromata* 2. 2 [*ANF* 2, p. 348]) and as standing outside all categories (*ibid.* 5. 12 [*ANF* 2, pp. 463f.]). That God is to be conceived as not only beyond being but even beyond unity itself (*The Instructor* 1. 8 [*ANF* 2, p. 227]) was something Philo could already say (*Legum Allegoria* 2. 3) without explicitly drawing the conclusion that God is free from all distinctions, even purely logical ones.

[187] So, for example, Aulen, *Das christliche Gottesbild*, pp. 78f.

the propertyless God can be very near. He is beyond comprehension, to be sure, but present as animating all things.[188]

One could further criticize the idea of propertylessness as a
threat to the connection between God's essence and his action.[189]
An act or operation without properties is in fact inconceivable.[190]
That God's activities are characterized by specific, differenti-
able properties was never questioned – not even by Philo. But
Philo did not unite these properties directly to the divine essence
but rather to divine "powers" that were still distinct from God's
essence.[191] One finds something similar in Christian theology
as early as Theophilus, who in principle reduces every statement we can make about God to his activities, the essence of
God (his "form"), which is situated behind these, remaining
incomprehensible.[192] And yet that does not mean any separation
of the essence from the activities and the properties connected

---

[188] Cf., for instance, Plotinus, *Enneads* 3. 8. 9, 22f., 32f. (ed. P. Henry, and
H. R. Schwyzer, Museum Lessianum, Series Philosophica [Paris, 1951ff.],
vol. 1, p. 407).

[189] This is manifestly the sense of Karl Barth's contention that the concept
of simplicity has been elevated to an "idol" that "swallows everything concrete" and reduces the multiplicity of attributes to inauthenticity (*CD* 2/1,
p. 329). Cf. *ibid.*, p. 325, where it becomes clear that Barth means the connection of the divine essence not with his activity generally but with his
revelatory acts. Insofar as the contingency of the divine action has been
taken into consideration in this criticism, we will adopt it in what follows.

[190] Cremer, *Die christliche Lehre von der Eigenschaften Gottes*, pp. 16f.

[191] Wolfson (*Philo*, 2:126ff. and esp. 134ff.) thinks otherwise. Although
the properties of God are connected with his essence – by means of the
essential power of the divine activity – Philo nevertheless does not say (as
Wolfson interprets him on p. 138) that they are identical with the divine
essence. The distinction between the powers that are proper to God's essence
and those that are subsequently ordered to it (on this, see Wolfson, 1:219ff.)
is drawn far less sharply by Philo than it is by Wolfson (e.g., 1:221; 2:138).
Wolfson himself makes allowance for the fact that the distinction is fluid,
but nevertheless uses this consideration in order to place all "powers" on
the side of the divine essence. "But even the powers as a property of the
ideas, since they have been bestowed upon the ideas by God, may be considered as only an extension of the powers as a property of God and may
therefore be treated as a part of the eternal powers of God" (1:221). In
view of *Quod Deus Immutabilis Sit* 77–81 (cf. Goodenough, *By Light, Light*,
p. 32) one would nevertheless sooner speak of a mediatory position of the
"powers" between God and creation rather than call them "identical with
his essence" (so Wolfson, 1:220).   [192] *To Autolycus* 1. 3 [*ANF* 2, p. 89].

with them. Rather, the essence manifests itself through its powers and effects even if not in such a way as to express it perfectly. For this reason, the essence cannot be adequately comprehended on the basis of the effects and their properties, but can only be surmized as their imperceptible ground. Nevertheless, even if the similarity between the effects and their cause is imperfect, it is enough to permit the properties of the former to be transferred to the latter in a superlative mode.[193] It is true, by this reflection upon the similarity between cause and effect, the otherness of God was reduced and robbed of its radicality.

Now reflection upon the similarity of an effect with its cause is appropriate only where it is a matter of a cause that operates because of a necessity of its essence. In view of the fact that the essence of the world-ground is exhaustively occupied in discharging the world from itself, one can presuppose a similarity between the effects and that imperceptible ground which they only approximately represent. If, on the other hand, an effect is not grounded in a necessity in the essence of the cause, but follows from it contingently, then one cannot without further ado draw conclusions from the effect about the nature of the cause. Thus, if God operates contingently, acts freely, and if the properties of his effects are different from his essence, then the properties of the divine operation, because of its contingency, permit no reflection upon a similarity of the effects with the essence of God, and thus do not allow any statement that would transfer a creaturely perfection to God in a superlative sense. Therefore, the otherness of God in contrast to creatures is radically protected on the presupposition of the contingency of the divine operation. On the other hand, a causally grounded, analogical connection of the operation of God with his essence can be maintained only on the presupposition of the Greek understanding of God as the necessarily operative ground of the world. This presupposition is required even where the essence of God is thought of as in itself without properties, for the relationship of similarity

193 Cf. Origen *De Principiis* 1. 1. 5 [*ANF* 4, p. 243]; *Against Celsus* 7. 38 [*ANF* 4, p. 626].

between effect and cause remains intact even if in such a way that the mode in which this similarity is realized in the divine essence is inscrutable.

That is not to say that God's contingent action had nothing to do with his essence. But the connection is of a different sort than in the case of a cause that operates out of necessity. In a contingent effect, it is not a matter of an indeterminate, underlying cause *expressing* its essence by imparting itself, but rather of the agent *producing* properties for himself. He chooses himself as the one who so acts in that he "decides" for such an effect rather than for another. Thus, the one who acts contingently, completely differently from a necessarily operative cause, is himself present in his effects. The world-ground that operates and imparts itself out of necessity appears in its effects only in a fragmentary way – to the extent that despite the participation of its effects in its being, it itself remains "at a distance" behind them. The contingently operative biblical God is present in his effects not by means of the participation of these effects in their origin, but in a "personal mode," i.e. by the choice of his acts he decides about the properties to which he binds himself precisely by this choice. The same contrast can be formulated in another way looking at the relationship of the individual effect to its origin: the universal world-ground cannot be one with its individual effects, but appears in a fragmented way in their multiplicity. The one who acts contingently, however, produces a property for himself in that he chooses "this" specific act in its particularity and makes it his own, so that now it really is a property of his eternal essence. It is *in that way* that the contingently acting God of the Bible demonstrates his essence in his act, and for this reason his essence is not to be sought behind his acts as a propertyless entity.

Simplicity is not necessarily thereby excluded. Composition does in fact imply destructibility and is therefore inconceivable of the author of the world. But that simplicity entails propertylessness is valid only for an understanding of the relationship of our knowledge to reality which takes a realistic view of universals. If, on the other hand, knowledge, in that it combines different kinds of elements, does not copy the structure of an object but only puts forth a model which represents this object to our consciousness in its relationship with others, then even a thoroughly composite concept can stand for a simple object. With the fundamental distinction between the synthesizing procedure of our knowledge and the constitution of the object, which is presupposed in this conception, the otherness of God in comparison with creatures is no longer adequately expressed in the concept of simplicity, but only in the insight that there is no adequate cognitive model of God, without detriment to the fact that every contingent effect of God occasions assertions about specific properties.

These considerations show how closely the elements of the metaphysical concept of God are related to ideas about the structure of inner-wordly being and of human cognition. Thus, there arises at the periphery of our discussion a question which cannot be followed up here, viz., whether the neglect of contingency which was characteristic of the Greek understanding of God similarly characterized the alternatives between a realistic conception of universals and a nominalistic skepticism; and whether the conceptualistic projections of Ockham and, in his own way, of Cusa, which broke through these alternatives, are not bound up with an understanding of reality stamped by contingency.

5. Transformation and Affirmation of the Biblical Witness to God

Those elements of the philosophical concept of God which were not critically mastered could not remain without influence upon the understanding of the biblical witness to God. Specific nuances necessarily stand to be displaced here.

Thus, the philosophical concept of eternity as separation from everything temporal was intruded into the biblical idea of the eternity of God as powerful presence to every time. Ignatius already designated God as timeless [*achronos*].[194] Timelessness is

[194] *Polycarp* 3. 2 [*ANF* 1, p. 94].

closely related to immutability: for that which remains ever the same,[195] the flow of time is meaningless. Thus, Justin could combine the predicates immutable and eternal in a hendiadys.[196] But the eternity of the God who acts in history cannot consist in timelessness like that of the distant ground of the world, but can be understood only as powerful simultaneity with every time. The eternity of God is thereby closely related to his omnipresence. Even the latter is to be understood from the standpoint of God's powerful freedom, not as a static extension throughout the universe but as a powerful lordship over space, being everywhere he wills [*Ubivoliquität*]. Just as early Christian theology allowed static extension in space to preponderate too one-sidedly in connection with omnipresence, so it also retained a peculiar vacillation between the biblical and *Platonic* meanings of eternity.

Even the idea of the righteousness of God acquired a new look under the influence of the philosophical concept of God. The biblical connection between the righteousness of God and his faithfulness to his promises and to his covenant receded from sight. In the foreground stands the Greek notion of distributive justice. Tendencies in this direction were already visible in Justin and Athenagoras in the description of the way in which God as judge deals with everyone according to his merits.[197] Pursued along these lines, the concept of the right-

---

[195] Justin Martyr *Dialogue with Trypho* 4. 1 [*ANF* 1, p. 196], according to the striking conjecture of Schmid, "Frühe Apologetik und Platonismus," pp. 176f., who by replacing a *tau* by an *eta* emends the expression *alla ti on* [that very being] to *all 'aei on* [that which always is].

[196] *First Apology* 13. 4 [*ANF* 1, p. 166].

[197] Justin Martyr *First Apology* 17 [*ANF* 1, p. 168]; Athenagoras *On the Resurrection* 22 [*ANF* 2, p. 161]. The use here of less emphasized uses of the concept of analogy, instead of the simple "according to" [*kata*] of Prov. 24:12, frequently cited in the New Testament (cf. Matt. 16:27; Rom. 2:6; 2 Tim. 4:14; Rev. 2:23, 20:12f.), and of other passages, points back to the Platonic and Aristotelian definition of righteousness (Plato *Laws* 757b ff.; Aristotle *Nicomachean Ethics* 1311b1of.; 1132a29f.). The cosmological use of this idea, already found in the pseudo-Platonic *Epinomis* (990e), which played an important role in Philo's interpretation of the order of creation (*Quis Rerum Divinarum Heres* 145–60), is first encountered in Christian theology after Clement of Alexandria *Stromata* 6. 10 [*ANF* 2, pp. 498f.]. It

eousness of God would be ever more decisively orientated to a timeless concept of order (proportionality) instead of to the history of the life-creating acts of God in relation to the world.

The danger of surrendering the historicness of the reality shaped ever anew by God's creative activity for a world picture of a cosmic order grounded in a necessity of its timeless origin, inevitably reaches a critical point when it comes to understanding the motivation for the act of creation. When Justin mentions the goodness of God as the motive for the creation of the world,[198] one may ask whether he is thinking here of the free, living gift of the God who acts in history, or of an essential necessity of the Platonic idea of the Good, which gives itself like the sun.[199] Some of the formulations of *1 Clement* completely indulge in the Stoic terminology of the deity's beneficent care for the cosmos.[200] The Good's unavoidable freedom from envy in this conception corresponds to the idea that the divine benefactor is "free of anger" towards the cosmos.[201] Nevertheless, early Christian theology finally offered staunch resistance on this point. Irenaeus, it is true, has likewise, and with explicit reference to Plato, discerned the motive for creation in the goodness of God,[202] but he nevertheless also emphasized, as Theophilus had done before him,[203] the utter freedom of the divine goodness.[204] God is completely free in his decisions and subject to no necessity.[205] Later, Clement provided an even more precise formulation, saying that God created the world by his free volition and not out of any internal necessity.[206]

The earlier Apologists still lacked such formulations. But the freedom of God's active omnipotence, which is highlighted in

---

gives the concept of righteousness an ultimately cosmological instead of a redemptive-historical background.

[198] *First Apology* 10 [*ANF* 1, p. 165].   [199] Plato *Timaeus* 29e.

[200] *1 Clem.* 20:11, 23:1 [*ANF* 1, p. 10, 11f.].

[201] *Ibid.* 19:3 [*ANF* 1, p. 10]; cf. Aristides *Apology* 1. 6 [*ANF* 9, pp. 267f.].

[202] *Against the Heresies* 2. 25. 5 [*ANF* 1, p. 459].

[203] *To Autolycus* 2. 13 [*ANF* 2, p. 99].

[204] Irenaeus *Against the Heresies* 2. 1. 1 [*ANF* 1, p. 359].

[205] *Ibid.* 2. 5. 4; cf. 4. 14. 1 and 4. 20. 1 [*ANF* 1, p. 365; cf. pp. 478, 487].

[206] *Stromata* 7. 7 [*ANF* 2, p. 534].

the Roman confession, was also described in *1 Clement*.[207] Aristides[208] and Tatian[209] at least mentioned it. Justin appealed to belief in the resurrection of the flesh in order to affirm that "with God nothing is impossible,"[210] and pointed to the words of Jesus: "What is impossible with men is possible with God."[211] Theophilus saw proof of the almightiness of God particularly in the act of creation out of nothing.[212] In Irenaeus's view, everything real is filled out by the almighty will of God since he named the essence [*substantia*] of every entity.[213] Such conviction about the almightiness of God could lead to significant incursions into the philsophical concept of God, such as Gregory Thaumaturgus's placing of the free will of God above his 'nature" and the axiom of impassibility grounded in that.[214]

The Cappadocians Basil, Gregory of Nazianzus, and Gregory of Nyssa must have arrived at a similar conviction about the freedom of the divine power of being since they introduced a concept of infinity, transformed in a positive sense, as a term for the divine essence. Origen had still regarded God's power as limited, since otherwise it would be unknown to him.[215] This position was in keeping with the spirit of classical Greek metaphysics, which had viewed infinity as formlessness, chaotic indeterminateness, and as by no means genuine being. Plotinus had already effected a positive transvaluation of this concept. According to him, the One must be conceived as infinite because its dynamism is incomprehensible.[216] But Plotinus would

[207] 27:4f. [*ANF* 1, p. 12].

[208] *Apology* 13 ("the Almighty" [*Pantokrator*]) [*ANF* 9, p. 274]. H. Hommel, *Schöpfer und Erhalter* (Berlin, 1956), pp. 112f., speaks of a "two-facedness" of this title insofar as in addition to the Old Testament element of "almightiness" it also contains the Stoic sense of "all-preserving."

[209] Cf. Wilibald Steuer, *Die Gottes- und Logoslehre des Tatians* (Leipzig, 1893), p. 29.

[210] *First Apology* 18. 6 [*ANF* 1, p. 169].

[211] *Ibid.* 19. 6 [*ANF* 1, p. 169]; cf. Matt. 19:26.

[212] *To Autolycus* 2. 4 [*ANF* 2, p. 95].

[213] *Against the Heresies* 2. 30. 9 [*ANF* 1, p. 406].

[214] On this, see Elert, *Ausgang altkirchlichen Christologie*, pp. 76f.

[215] *De Principiis* 2. 9. 1 [*ANF* 4, p. 289].

[216] *Enneads* 6. 9. 6; cf. 2. 7. 5. On this, see Jonas Cohn, *Geschichte des Unendlichkeitsproblem in abendländischen Denken bis Kant* (Hildesheim, 1960;

hardly have joined the Cappadocians in employing the infinity of God against Eunomius's argument that the ingeneracy [*agennēsia*] of God compels acceptance of the idea that everything that has proceeded from God is not God because it is no longer ingenerate but a creature distinct from him. On the grounds of the method of causal inference belonging to the Greek doctrine of God, this argument was unanswerable. The deity of the Son, at any rate, could not be on the same level with that of the Father. With Plotinus, the infinity of God could only be understood as an attribute of the unoriginate One. He could hardly have used it against the consequences that flowed from the fundamental concept of ingeneracy. That the Cappadocians were able to do this[217] shows that for them the infinity of God included within it the free divine power of being. By means of this idea of the infinity of God, the Cappadocians called into question philosophical theology's method of causal inference which Eunomius had employed against the consubstantiality of the Son with the Father.

Let us now look back in order to summarize. How did early Christian theology discharge the task of assimilating the philosophical concept of God? Obviously it is inappropriate to speak of such a complex matter as a "hellenization" in the sense of a coming under foreign control, a supplanting of the Christian idea of God by a "deistic" one, as Harnack did in dependence

---

reprint of 1896 ed.], pp. 59f., as well as Heinz Heimsoeth, *Die sechs grossen Themen der abendländischen Metaphysik*, 3d ed. (Berlin-Steglitz, 1934), pp. 61 ff. There is no terminological justification for finding the infinity of God already expressed by Philo, as Heimsoeth does (p. 66).

[217] Gregory of Nazianzus, *Oration 38* 7 [*NPNF*, Second Series, 7, p. 346], speaks of God as an "infinite sea of Being"; Gregory of Nyssa, *Answer to Eunomius Second Book* [*NPNF*, Second Series, 5, p. 257 (= *MPG* 45, col. 933A)] calls infinity the measure of the divine essence (in opposition to unoriginateness) [the translation in *NPNF* is very loose here and does not bring out the precise meaning of the Greek text. – Tr.]. Infinity is identical with the perfection of God (*MPL* 44, 873d) [not available in English translation – Tr.]. Cf. Elert, *Ausgang altkirchlichen Christologie*, pp. 67ff., 45ff., who rightly emphasizes that this concept of infinity, in contrast to so many other concepts in the early Christian doctrine of God, has a specifically Christian character (p. 68).

upon Ritschl. Not only must the linkage with the philosophical concept of God which was effected by the Apologists be recognized as a legitimate task from the standpoint of the universal claim of the Judaeo-Christian God, but even with regard to the way in which this task was carried out in early Christian theology a more differentiated judgment is necessary. On the whole, one ought not to speak of an uncritical acceptance of the philosophical idea of God: certainly not on the part of Tatian, Theophilus, and Irenaeus, at any rate; but not even, without qualification, by Justin, either. The personal character of the idea of God precisely in Justin's theology has rightly been defended against all contrary interpretations.[218] It was true that the almighty freedom of the biblical God was not taken into account to the same extent by all early Christian theologians, but it was nevertheless effectively applied in various ways, such as in defense of belief in the resurrection and especially in establishing the formula of creation *ex nihilo*. They did not link up with the variously styled philosophical doctrines of God without examining them, but with well-aimed judgment, chose the form of doctrine that came closest to the Christian message. This is shown by Justin's appropriation and transformation of the Platonic concept of knowledge. It is shown to an even greater extent by the combination of Platonic transcendence and Stoic omnipresence. More profound critical concerns are indicated in Tatian's distancing of God's spirituality from that of man. The work of Irenaeus offers a broadly sketched attempt to develop a historical understanding of the totality of reality from the standpoint of the freely acting God of the Bible, while appropriating the philosophical concepts of simplicity and incomprehensibility. Although the goal of a theological-philosophical synthesis was not the foremost aim of his endeavors, Irenaeus achieved such a synthesis by means of his view, taken over from Justin, of the history of redemption as a sequence of dispensations of the incomprehensible God. In many respects it was more impressive than what Alexandrian theology was able to develop despite its much more deliberate striving for such a synthesis.

[218] Goodenough, *Theology of Justin Martyr*, pp. 136f., against Engelhardt.

The biblical idea of God in his irrational freedom was unquestionably more powerfully expressed in Irenaeus's total conception
than in the Alexandrian construction of the history of redemption as a process of providence and education. The latter
attained the greater systematic cohesiveness but not without
damaging the substance of the biblical witness to God. And yet,
both lines of development were fundamentally subordinated to
the metaphysics of the history of revelation, as the development
of Trinitarian theology and incarnational Christology shows.
The contribution of the early church's theology can be correctly
judged only in comparison with Hellenistic religious philo-
phy and Hellenistic Judaism. While Plutarch, for instance, related the different religious traditions as symbols of the same
metaphysical truth and thus "syncretistically" equated them;
while Philo, although in contrast to Plutarch, strove to prove
the exclusive significance of a particular religious tradition,
namely, the Jewish, and construed the biblical accounts as nothing but the most excellent, most appropriate symbolism for the
unique metaphysical truths they contained; Christian theology
set the freedom of God above his "nature" (in the constricted
sense of the philosophical method of causal inference), and thus,
at least in principle, subordinated metaphysics to redemptive
history.[219]

To be sure, neither Irenaeus nor Alexandrian theology nor
early Christian theology as a whole succeeded in carrying out a
definitive critical revision in the encounter of the Judaeo-
Christian testimony to God with philosophy. The negative
judgment of Harnack retains a limited justification to this
extent. Critical penetration and refinement of the philosophical
concept of God in the fires of the history-empowering freedom of
God did not progress beyond some significant rudiments in
this period. The ideas of God as a world principle and as the
free Lord of history remained for the most part inharmoniously
alongside each other. Therefore the different lineages of the

---

[219] Goodenough, *By Light, Light*, p. 47, compared Philo with Plutarch, on
the one hand, and with early Christian theology, on the other, in a way that
agrees with what is presented above.

elements of the early church's concept of God remained obtrusively visible. The large, encompassing conceptions only superficially linked the heterogeneous elements. The possibility of the Irenaean vision of history as a sequence of divine dispensations remained unintelligible from the standpoint of the transcendence of God in the Platonic view. And the Alexandrian connection of creation and redemption by means of the concept of providence was itself too heavily burdened with the idea of God as origin [*archē*] to be able to provide sufficient room for the free livingness of the biblical God. The mere juxtaposition of heterogeneous elements had to prove unbearable, however, from the standpoint of the biblical as well as of the philosophical concepts of God. As self-enclosed wholes, neither permits of being treated as a mutually complementary part. Therefore those elements of the philosophical concept of God which were not completely blended in had to act as obstacles to the understanding of the historical activity of God. Immutability and timelessness, simplicity, propertylessness, and namelessness have repeatedly forced the concept of God into an unbridgeable distance from the contingent changes of historical reality in which the salvation of men is decided, and the assertions of faith regrading God's historical acts of salvation were purchased only at the expense of violating the strict sense of these attributes.

The complete, critical assimilation of the philosophical concept of God would have presupposed that the world-ground would have to be understood in every detail as the one who out of his otherness effects the new and contingent, and is thus the personal Lord. From here, the concept of immutability would have to be deepened to that of the free, firmly resolved character of the faithfulness of God. Timelessness would have to be reshaped into lordship over time, in the sense of almighty simultaneity to every time. That the otherness of God prevents understanding him as mind was something even philosophy could arrive at, as Plotinus shortly proved. Philosophy surpassed the second-century Christian understanding of God in this regard, and it does not redound to the glory of later theology.

especially in the West, that it has largely lagged behind philosophy on this matter by persisting in representing God as a supradimensional conscious being. This was certainly the basis of the theological conception of providence. If theology had been prepared to give up this conception, it would have been able to understand the otherness of God more radically than philosophy as not only the incomprehensibility of the world-ground but as the otherness of the freedom of God precisely in in his acts, which cut across and surpass all expectations and planning. The incomprehensibility of the world-ground always means no more than that the structures of the known world can only be inexactly traced to their distant origin and can no longer be *completely* comprehended. The direction in which this origin is to be imagined cannot be in doubt, however, and for this reason, despite all its incomprehensibility, it can at least be symbolically represented. The otherness of the author of the world is radically exhibited only where the expectations and world pictures are overturned by concrete, contingent events. It is just this radical otherness that is first demonstrated in an act of God that no longer leads to the consequence of an abstract propertylessness, such as befits the world-ground in its distant generality. Rather, as the otherness of God is demonstrated in specific, contingent events with a concrete meaning for the men participating in it, so God assumes properties into his eternal essence through such deeds in that he chooses these and no other events as the form of his contingent operation. Precisely the God who acts in a personal manner in such deeds is the one who because of his freedom is "wholly other."

Overhauling the philosophical thesis of the incomprehensibility of God in such a way would – if thought through from all angles – perhaps be able to spare the Christian doctrine of God from the gap between the incomprehensible *essence* and the historical *action* of God, by virtue of which each threatens to make the other impossible. If one had discovered the incomprehensibility of God first of all in precisely his action, as the revelation of the divine essence found for the first time in Jesus Christ, then it would not have been necessary to have to lose the ground of

historical revelation from under one's feet in order to recognize
the unity of Jesus Christ and the Spirit conjoined to him with
God himself. One would not have had to first construct a cosmic triad out of the concept of the world-ground by Neopy-
thagorean and Neoplatonic means which, as a triad of equal
divine dignity, must then run into contradiction with the philosophical concept of God as the incomprehensible, unoriginate
origin and finally compromisingly come to rest alongside this
concept of the "essence" of God as a second, supplementary
definition of the divine essence.[220] It remains a task for the
Christian doctrine of God to show that the otherness of God as
well as his unity cannot really be conceived within the philosophical formulation of the question, but can be comprehended
only as the unity of the Father with the Son and the Spirit, so
that the revelation of the triune God is what brings the philosophical question to a genuine fulfillment for the first time.

This task of a critical recasting of the philosophical idea of God
was not posed in a fundamental way nor comprehensively carried through in early Christian theology. Perhaps the reason for
this was that the formulation of the question that underlay the
philosophical idea of God was so much taken for granted by the
men of this Hellenistic period that they were not at all in a
position to elucidate critically the presuppositions inherent in
it. Perhaps it was the crisis of the metaphysical consciousness in
the modern age that first made it possible take a critical look at
the self-evidencies of the philosophical method of causal inference. Today, at any rate, it has become impossible to escape
the insight that in the recasting of the philosophical concept of
God by early Christian theology considerable remnants were
left out, which have become a burden in the history of Christian
thought. For this reason, it is now necessary to avoid the mistake
of demanding that metaphysical elements in the Christian
doctrine of God simply be done away with, for that would compel theology to give up the universal claim of God upon all

[220] On the unsatisfactoriness of a distinction between the doctrine of
God's essence and the doctrine of the Trinity, cf. E. Schlink, article on
"Gott, VI: dogmatisch," in *RGG*³ vol. 2, cols. 1732–41.

men.[221] It remains the task of theology, however, to rework every remnant that has not been recast. This is indispensable just in order to preserve continuity with the early church's theology, its doctrine of God in particular. Continuity with the work of the early church's theology is expressed by affirming the task of critically receiving the philosophical concept of God. But only by posing the critical side of this task more radically, and by working it out to its very end in a more thoroughgoing fashion than was possible then, might it be possible to maintain continuity with the theology of the early church even in the face of the modern crisis of metaphysics, and perhaps even to contribute to the overcoming of this crisis to the extent that it pertains to the idea of God. It could indeed turn out that theology might in our time have to cosuperintend the heritage of metaphysics in the form of a critical examination of the doctrine of God that has been handed down in its own tradition.

[221] For this reason, Adolf Schlatter attacked the constriction of the idea of God involved in Albrecht Ritschl's hostility toward metaphysics. Cf. Adolf Schlatter, *Das Christliche Dogma* (Stuttgart, [2]1923), pp. 26, 29; and on this point, H. Beintker, *Die Christenheit und das Recht bei A. Schlatter* (Berlin, 1957), pp. 30, 31f.

6

TYPES OF ATHEISM AND THEIR
THEOLOGICAL SIGNIFICANCE

This essay was originally delivered at a recess for the dozents of the Hamburg theological faculty on December 3, 1960, and before the Berlin Society for Evangelical Theology on November 24, 1961. First published in *Zeitwende* 34 (1965): 597–808.

THE EMERGENCE of atheistic thought is not something bound to a particular period of history. But the phenomenon of atheism indeed does not have the same character in every age. Contemporary atheism, in particular, is probably closely connected with the previously unheard-of peculiarities of modern Western thought. My discussion will be limited to this *modern* form of atheism and its inner structure. The fact that the inquiry will search for *types* should not be understood as meaning that different positions will be lined up alongside each other without any inner relationship between them. Rather, it will seek to describe some of the features that are typical for the specific structure of modern atheism. One or another of the three essential features to be discussed appears with special prominence in certain individual thinkers. Nevertheless, these features are intimately related to each other.

I. MECHANISTIC PHYSICS AND PSYCHOLOGICAL METAPHYSICS

The presupposition of contemporary Western atheism lies in the development of modern natural science and its mechanistic picture of the world, especially in eighteenth-century France. Laplace's success in developing a mechanistic system of finite causes as a self-sufficient process covering even the problems of cosmogony meant the final dissolution of the bond between physics and philosophical theology developed in the Aristotelian school philosophy that had been regarded as valid until then. If at one time Averroes had assigned the proofs for God's existence to physics and not, for instance, to metaphysics, which should already presuppose it; and if this conception was still influential with Newton; now, in the eighteenth century, the new physics not only declared its incompetence with respect to proofs for the existence of God, but also made it possible to provide a new atheistic metaphysics as a substructure for its self-enclosed picture of the world as an infinity of finite things and processes. To this extent, the mechanistic world picture of classical physics, perfected in the eighteenth century, which no longer needed the hypothesis of a creator, is the presupposition of modern atheism. But it is also no more than that. For in order to establish an atheistic metaphysic, not only was it necessary to prove that the world and even human existence could be understood purely from within themselves, without God, but in addition to this it had to be shown that there is no truth in religious assertions about the existence of divine beings. But this can be achieved only by a genetic explanation of the religions which contradicts their own assertions and pretends to uncover the "real" origin of religious ideas. Without the completion of this second task, the first would not be completely mastered either. If not the world, then at least man and the history of the human race are not yet completely explained from within themselves until someone succeeds in proving that the religions and the very idea of God are not original phenomena but derivative, products of man, *of* man who is previously to be described as essentially a part of nature without recourse to a god. The significance of Ludwig Feuerbach for this history of modern atheism becomes apparent when viewed in the light of these considerations. Until Feuerbach, atheism appeared to be really only an assertion.[1] Feuerbach, however, through his genetic

---

[1] As with Lalande, in 1805, who did not believe in a God because one "can explain everything without him," although he himself could "not prove" this.

theory of religion, handed over to atheism the proof it sought. The natural scientific picture of the world, with its self-contained finitude – which, from the standpoint of faith, stood for the infinity of the world – was only the presupposition for this. That one can explain without God, as Lalande said, demands that one explain religion itself without recourse to God. Only when that has been done has the atheistic position been brought to completion.

II. THE ATHEISM OF THE SCIENTIFIC STUDY OF RELIGION

Thus, the first form of mature atheism is the atheism of Feuerbach's science of religion. His theory of religion in its original form is summed up in this pregnant sentence: "Religion is the disuniting of man from himself; he sets God before him as the antithesis of himself."[2] This statement contains two elements: the idealistic or, more precisely, young-Hegelian concept of the infinity of the human essence, and *Hegel's* concept of estrangement or alienation.

The essence of man is infinite, according to Feuerbach. This is expressed in the essential powers of man – reason, will, and love. These powers belong to man's essence insofar as through them the essence of man holds sway over the individuals, and drives them beyond their finitude: reason drives toward the unending progress of reflection; the ethical will is absolutely unconditioned; the power of feeling breaks through all limits, and in the act of loving surrender the individual gives up his finitude. Through these powers, which drive the individual beyond himself, the infinite essence of man, manhood as "species,"[3] realizes itself in man's life.

Only the means of the idea of the infinity of man's essence is Feuerbach able to link the essence of man and the essence of religion, for "religion . . . is consciousness of the infinite; thus it

[2] Ludwig Feuerbach, *The Essence of Christianity*, trans. George Eliot (New York: Harper Torchbooks, 1957), p. 33.
[3] *Ibid.*, pp. 2f.

is and can be nothing else than the consciousness which man has of his own that is not finite and limited, but infinite nature."[4]

But how does man come to distinguish that which comprises his own essence as another essence, as a God? It is at this point that the second of the above-mentioned elements intervenes, the idea that man is conscious of himself, or his own essence, so that he can make his essence an object of his consciousness.[5] A distinction between the ego and its object already exists in being conscious of an object,[6] and this formal distinction combines with the substantive one that the finite, individual man can have his infinite essence as the object of his consciousness. Thus, in comparison with his own finitude, he regards this other essence of which he is conscious as other than his own essence, as "God". This illusion is related to the fact that the individual, because of his "sloth, vanity and egoism,"[7] regards the limitations of his own finite being as limitations of the human species, of the human essence as such. Consequently he sees this infinite essence as something suprahuman or divine: "The divine being is nothing else than the human being, or, rather, the human nature purified, freed from the limits of the individual man, i.e. real, bodily man, made objective – i.e., contemplated and revered as another, a distinct being."[8] The antihuman tendency of religion, the alienating character in it against which Feuerbach fought, is closely connected with this point. "To enrich God, man must become poor; that God may be all, man must be nothing."[9]

Feuerbach maintained these basic ideas even in the later form of his philosophy of religion. He only transposed them into a more universally intelligible form of expression by utilizing the strict terminology of the Hegelian system. This nevertheless had the effect of obscuring the systematic inner connections of his own ideas.

It is true that Feuerbach broadened his position in his work *The Essence of Religion* (1845), in which he conceded to his critics that man, since he is the creator of God, is nevertheless

---

[4] *Ibid.*, p. 2.   [5] *Ibid.*, p. 4.   [6] *Ibid.*, p. 6.
[7] *Ibid.*, p. 7.   [8] *Ibid.*, p. 14.   [9] *Ibid.*, p. 26.

not a completely self-sufficient, independent being. Man indeed presupposes an "essence" upon which he is dependent, but this is not God but nature.[10] The power man experiences in the primitive stages of religion is the power of nature,[11] and he knows himself to be dependent upon this negatively, through fear,[12] and positively, through enchantment, joy, love, and gratitude.[13] But the power of nature is revered as divine only because it is transformed by the imagination into figures of gods; because man sees his own nature in this power. "Thus man's only way of deifying nature is to humanize it; he deifies himself by deifying nature," he writes in the 1848 *Lectures on the Essence of Religion*.[14] For this reason he still allows the idea to stand that everywhere the one real God is "simply the personified unity and equality of the human race, the generic concept in which all differences between men are annulled and effaced," but which is "viewed as an independent being."[15]

III. THE THEOLOGICAL RESPONSE TO FEUERBACH

What is the significance of Feuerbach's theory of religion[16] for theology — assuming that theology does not accept it as its ultimate refutation? Two paths have been taken in attempting to meet Feuerbach's critique of religion: either one disputes his analysis of religion, or, on the contrary, emphasizes its truth

[10] Three years later, in his *Lectures on the Essence of Religion* (1848; Eng. trans. by Ralph Manheim [New York: Harper & Row, 1967]), Feuerbach explicitly said that he had thereby filled "the gap left in *The Essence of Christianity*" [translation mine – Tr.; cf. *Lectures*, trans. Manheim, p. 19].

[11] *Ibid.*, p. 20.   [12] *Ibid.*, pp. 26ff.

[13] *Ibid.*, pp. 29ff. (These characteristics are precisely the ones found in Hegel's philosophy of religion, particularly in the analysis of feeling as the lowest grade of the religious consciousness.)

[14] *Ibid.*, p. 190.

[15] *Ibid.*, p. 273. Insofar as man, in fabricating gods, projects images of his own essence, God is now also called "a being who fulfills man's *desires* [*Wünsche*]" (italics by the author).

[16] The Marxist theory of religion, as is well known, is very much akin to Feuerbach's. Its distinctiveness consists in its completion of the Feuerbachian conception, namely, in the sociological explanation of religious self-alienation through the social dislocation of man.

while at the same time giving assurances that the Christian faith and sound Christian theology have nothing to do with that sort of religion.

The latter is characteristic of the manner and way in which Protestant theology confronted Feuerbach in the last decade. Karl Barth's judgment regarding Feuerbach is, of course, representative of this tendency. In his *Geschichte der Protestantische Theologie im 19 Jahrhundert*, Barth states that Feuerbach only wanted "to turn theology, which seemed itself half-inclined towards the same goal, completely and finally into anthropology."[17] For Barth, Feuerbach merely drew out the consequences of the anthropological approach that dominated the whole of nineteenth-century theology insofar as the various shades of theology always tried to move from man to God instead of the other way around. Against this, Barth proclaimed a radical turnabout, the restoration of the irreversibility of the relationship with God which always had to be conceived as proceeding from above to below, from God to man.[18] The accomplishment of this reversal was the purpose of the whole of Barth's life work in dogmatics.

But is Feuerbach really overcome in this way? Is it not instead merely a case of withdrawing from controversy with Feuerbach and his disciples if theology, unperturbed, begins to speak about God as if nothing had happened; without establishing any basis, or offering any justification for this concept except by referring to the fact that Christian preaching about God actually goes on? Is that not senseless renunciation of all critical discussion, and thus an act of spiritual capitulation to Feuerbach? Theology has to learn that after Feuerbach it can no longer mouth the word "God" without offering any explanation; that it can no longer speak as if the meaning of this word were self-evident; that it cannot pursue theology "from above," as Barth says, if it does not want to fall into the hopeless and, what is more, self-inflicted isolation of a higher glossolalia, and

---

[17] *Protestant Thought: From Rousseau to Ritschl*, trans. Brian Cozens (London: SCM Press and New York: Harper & Brothers, 1959), p. 355 [a partial translation of the German work whose title is given above – Tr.].

[18] *Ibid.*, pp. 358ff.

lead the whole church into this blind alley. The situation certainly cannot be so simple that Christian theology can afford to surrender the whole field of the religions to the Feuerbachian critique without endangering the truth of the Christian faith itself and its speech about God. The struggle over the concept of God has to be conducted indeed in the fields of philosophy, the sciences of religion, and anthropology. If Feuerbach should prove right in these fields, then the proof of atheism for which he strove would in fact be accomplished.

The other approach to the debate with Feuerbach was taken by Ernst Troeltsch, to name one example. In his essay "The Independence of Religion" ["Die Selbständigkeit der Religion" (1895)], Troeltsch tried to answer the question about the truth of religious experience from the standpoint of religious psychology. There is a "deeper core" in the religious conception of God, namely, the presentiment or the definite declaration of something infinite and unconditioned, or, as it has also been called, something absolute. This presentiment is not "something we learned from reality and bestowed our wishes upon by imagination, but rather a non-arbitrary, *original datum of consciousness* coposited in every religious feeling. . . ."[19] But reference to the non-arbitrariness of religious experiences can neither neutralize Feuerbach's reproach that such experiences rest upon an illusion, nor prove that an "ideal perception" of something "infinite"[20] is presented here. There are also non-arbitrary illusions, and Feuerbach's theory refers to just such a thing. Absolutely no purely psychological argument can settle the question of the *truth* or religious experiences. A philosophical anthropology worked out within the framework of a general ontology is needed for this purpose. Later on, Troeltsch himself realized this. Therefore he endeavored after 1904 to develop a transcendental philosophical foundation for religious experience with his – unfortunate, to be sure — theory of a "religious *a priori.*"[21]

---

[19] *Zeitschrift für Theologie und Kirche* 5 (1895): 406.   [20] *Ibid.*, p. 413.
[21] Ernst Troeltsch, *Psychologie und Erkenntnistheorie in der Religionswissenschaft* (Tübingen, 1905), esp. pp. 18ff. The Ritschlian "theology of value

A much more penetrating approach to a philosophical discussion with Feuerbach would be to operate, at least for a while, with the concepts Feuerbach borrowed from Hegel in constructing his theory and upon which it remains completely dependent. Hegel, too, was able to designate God as the "essence" of man.[22] But Hegel did not mean by this mankind's immanent essence, which is what Feuerbach meant. Rather, for Hegel essence meant precisely that which transcends appearance. God is the "essence" of man as his *transcendent destination*.[23] The destination of man aims at going beyond his finitude, sacrificing it, and surrendering it to the infinite in devotion.[24] But from man's side, from within his finitude, man can achieve unity with the infinite only through conversion: "The finite which exalts itself to the infinite, is mere abstract identity, inherently empty, the supreme form of untruth, falsehood, and evil."[25] The fact that human subjectivity in its infinite self-transcendence, which modern anthropology somewhat misleadingly designates as "openness to the world" [*Weltoffenheit*] or "ec-centricity" [*Exzentrizität*], always presupposes an infinity transcending itself which is to be described not as a mere psychological datum, as in Troeltsch, but as an ontological structure of man's being. This brings out the point that – as Walter Schulz has shown – the modern metaphysics of man's subjectivity is conceivable only on the presupposition of a God.

Against Feuerbach, this means that man is essentially referred to infinity, but is never already infinite in himself. Theology

judgments," which "in relation to religion constantly stresses only the practical indispensability of the values it lays claim to, loses the necessity of the object in which these values inhere, and pulls (them) into the abyss of the theology of wishes and illusions" (*ibid.*, p. 28).

[22] G. W. F. Hegel, *Lectures on the Philosophy of Religion*, trans. from the 2d Ger. ed. by E. B. Spiers and J. Burdon Sanderson, 3 vols. (London: Kegan Paul, Trench, Trübner and Co., 1895), 1:274; *Vorlesungen über die Philosophie der Religion*, ed. Georg Lasson, Philosophische Bibliothek 62 (Hamburg, 1966), p. 96: "The natural spirit is essentially that which it should not be and remain."

[23] *Lectures on the Philosophy of Religion*, 1:278f.; also, among others, esp. pp. 111f.

[24] *Ibid.*, pp. 197ff.   [25] *Ibid.*, p. 193.

may not take the religious-psychological atheism of Feuerbach as an occasion to retreat into a supranaturalistic wildlife sanctuary. Rather, what is called for is to carry the struggle about the truth of the idea of God into the area of the understanding of man.

IV. THE ATHEISM OF FREEDOM

In the depth of Feuerbachian atheism, behind all the religious-psychological arguments, lurks a view of man as an absolutely self-empowered being. This view of man, which was for Hegel the highest form of evil, as we saw, leads us to another form of atheism which expresses the heart of Feuerbachian atheism, too, viz., the atheism of human freedom.

This basic feature of modern atheism was set forth by Friedrich Nietzsche, especially by the fact that he transplanted Feuerbach's theory of religion into the ground of his metaphysics of the will to power. Nietzsche's intimate relationship to Feuerbach has been repeatedly pointed out, particularly by Ernst Benz, for instance.[26] Nietzsche's aphorism about "the death of God" in *Joyful Wisdom*[27] "presupposes that God himself is to be understood as only a mythical projection of the human consciousness, whose unreal character has since been recognized by man himself."[28] The proximity to Feuerbach's thought is especially clear in Aphorism 136 of *The Will to Power*:

Man has never dared to credit *himself* with his strong and startling moods . . . insofar as everything great and strong in man was considered *suprahuman* and *foreign*, man belittled himself, – he laid the two sides, the very pitiable and weak side, and the very strong and startling side, apart in two spheres, and called the one "Man" and the other "God".[29]

---

[26] *Nietzsche's Ideen zur Geschichte des Christentums und der Kirche* (Leiden, 1956), pp. 158ff.

[27] *The Complete Works of Friedrich Nietzsche*, ed. Oscar Levy, 18 vols. (New York: Russell & Russell, 1909–11; reissued 1964), 10:275 (Aphorism 343); cf. also Aphorism 125.

[28] Benz, *Nietzsche's Ideen*, p. 168.

[29] *Complete Works*, 14:116. [NOTE: the number of the aphorism cited by the author differs from that given in the German edition used by him. – TR.]

Against this religious "abasement"[30] of man, Nietzsche demands the *"greatest elevation of man's consciousness of strength*, as that which creates superman."[31] Here, atheism has developed from a matter of mere enlightenment – as in Feuerbach – into a matter of the will, of self-affirmation. "Dead are all the gods; now do we desire the superman to live – let this be our final will at the great noontide!" So did Nietzsche conclude the first part of his *Thus Spake Zarathustra* in 1883.[32]

V. THE DEBATE WITH NIETZSCHE

It would be premature to view the atheism of Nietzsche as a matter of mere arbitrariness or, somewhat in the sense of Augustine, as the "hatred of God" [*odium Dei*] which is the extreme consequence of inordinate self-love [*amor sui*]. Not even theology can get away so easily in debate with Nietzsche's atheism – not to mention his acute criticism of the Christianity of his contemporaries.

In his essay on Nietzsche's saying about the death of God, Heidegger has already shown that Nietzsche's metaphysic of the will was the necessary consequence of the initial tendency of the modern metaphysics of subjectivity.[33] This demonstration is pertinent to, if not the whole phenomenon of modern metaphysics – since the idea of God also belongs essentially to it as the presupposition of subjectivity – then at least to one of the powerful fundamental tendencies at work in it. Just as since Descartes metaphysics referred all truth to the self-certainty of the subject, so it is with Nietzsche, who on the basis of subjectivity in the form of will was driven to subject all truth to the valorization [*Wertsetzung*] of the will. This means that within the horizon of his thought God could only appear as a value, and it is already at this point – and not primarily in the atheistic transvaluation of religious values, especially those of the Christian tradition – that the root of Nietzsche's atheism is to be

[30] *Ibid.*   [31] *Ibid.*, 15:425.
[32] *Ibid.*, 2:91; cf. Karl Löwith, *Nietzsche's Philosophie der ewigen Wiederkehr des Gleichen* (Stuttgart, 1956), p. 47.
[33] Martin Heidegger, *Holzwege* (Frankfurt, 1950), pp. 193–247.

seen. God as the *highest value* is already a posit [*Setzung*] of the human will, and a departure from the deity of God.

The strength of Nietzsche's position becomes apparent in comparing it to the contemporaneous Neo-Kantian-based theology of the Ritschlian school. Since in this theology – more so in the case of Wilhelm Herrmann than with Ritschl himself – God was understood as a postulate of the practical reason and the divinity of Christ as a religious value judgemnt, the valuation of the human will was declared to be the native soil of the Christian faith. Nietzsche's program of a transvaluation of all values attained its maximum destructive power in relation to this theology, whose defenselessness against the Feuerbachian diagnosis of religion as illusion had already been pointed out by Troeltsch. This theology was in fact founded upon Nietzsche's presupposition that religious statements are expressions of the judgments of the value-positing will. It differed from Nietzsche simply in its opposite valuations. For Ritschl, God was precisely an exponent of man's self-affirmation. Ritschl could formulate the astonishing sentence: "In every religion what is sought, with the help of the superhuman spiritual power, reverenced by man, is a solution of the contradiction in which man finds himself, as both a part of the world and a spiritual personality claiming to dominate nature."[34] In other words, religion supports man in his striving as an (ethical) spirit for dominance over nature. Was not Nietzsche justified, in comparison with this view, when he understood the idea of the self-affirmation of the will as something directed against the idea of God itself?

In any case, one can see why Nietzsche inevitably became important for Karl Barth in his debates with the heritage of the Ritschlian school, in which he grew up. But even in relation to Nietzsche, the withdrawal of theology into supranaturalism is no way out. For the possibility of its supranaturalistic talk about God, the truth of which it seems to be very sure, ultimately rests upon the decision of faith. For this reason, it is just supranatural-

[34] Albrecht Ritschl, *The Christian Doctrine of Justification and Reconciliation*, 3 vols. (Edinburgh: T. & T. Clark, 1900), 3:199.

istic thought which turns out in the last analysis to have already presupposed Nietzsche's grounding of the truth upon the will.

It is no accident that the supranaturalism of the nineteenth century leaned on the practical philosophy of Kant. A straight line runs from Tholuck's combination of a supranaturalistic pietism and Kantianism – a position in which the reality and revelation of God were certified by the experience of man's conscience – through Ritschl and Herrmann, on the one hand, and Kähler, on the other, to Barth and Bultmann. The common denominator here, implicitly or explicitly, is the practical necessity – or, in modern terms, the "decision" of faith – which motivates the leap into supranatural truth. Nietzsche cannot be overcome along such lines, however, because wherever faith as decision is constitutive of the truth of its contents, one has not yet departed from the basis of Nietzsche's position, his metaphysic of the will. The only way to overcome this position, whose consequence is the atheistic self-affirmation of the will – everything else, judged from this standpoint, being regarded as "disreputable"[35] – is by means of a more radical inquiry into being. On this point, Heidegger is right.[36]

For theology, this means that its concept of God must be thought out in connection with the philosophical question about being if it is to be a match for the atheism of Nietzsche. Naturally this cannot come about by any kind of retreat to a premodern onto-theology, such as that of the Middle Ages, for which God was the exponent of the world order. Any type of speech about God that fails to take into account the subjectivity of modern man, his sovereignty over nature, his self-transcendence (by which he unendingly oversteps every attempt to fit him into some permanently established order), necessarily lacks convincing power today, especially against a form of atheism which on its part is grounded in the subjectivity of modern man. The question about the being of God can only be stated in the form of the question about the being that must always be presupposed by man precisely with respect to his subjectivity; the

[35] Nietzsche, *The Genealogy of Morals*, bk. 3, Aphorism 27, in *Complete Works*, 13: 208.   [36] Heidegger, *Holzwege*, pp. 243ff.

question about the being to which he is referred for the actual ground of the possibility of his freedom in relation to the world.

VI. THE ATHEISM OF EMPTY TRANSCENDENCE

In the process of reflecting upon the impossibility of a re-vitalization of the old, premodern metaphysics of God and the world, we encounter the third basic tendency of modern atheism which likewise has also appeared as an independent type: the *hiddenness of God* or the emergence of transcendence as the cultural-historical destiny of the modern period.

The hiddenness of God, his inaccessibility to human thought and judgment, is not a specifically modern thought, to be sure. On the contrary, modern philosophy seems at first glance to have entirely forgotten the hiddenness of God, and to have dragged him down into immanence, as mind [*Geist*]. The idea of the hiddenness of God is rooted, on the one hand, in the *biblical view* of the hiddenness of God's action in his freedom in relation to the canons of human foresight and judgment.[37] The other root is Neoplatonism, with its thesis about the unknowability, from the standpoint of finite appearances, of the one, absolutely simple world-ground. Both lines come together in, for instance, Luther's concept of the hidden God. The *Neoplatonic* idea of the incomprehensibility and ineffability of the world-ground does not lead to atheistic consequences because the world-ground is conceived as the exponent of the cosmic order which points back to it as its ground. It can be designated, at least symbolically, from the side of the world since the emanation of the world from its ground is thought of as analogous to the relation of an effect to its cause. In the modern metaphysics of subjectivity, for which the edifice of cosmological thought had collapsed, it was inevitable that the hiddenness of God was experienced in a much more unsettling way. For the binding of all the contents of consciousness to the finitude of the consciousness meant not only that one is unable to conceive the infinity of God but also that he can no longer in any way imagine the deity of the

[37] Isa. 45:15 = Rom. 11:33; cf. Matt. 11:25.

infinite. The objective basis for a symbolical theology had in fact collapsed along with the Neoplatonic cosmology. The radical consequence of the reduction of all contents of consciousness to finite subjectivity were first brought to light in 1799 Fichte's "atheistic controversy," when Fichte demonstrated that not even consciousness – self-consciousness – could be ascribed to the infinite. This declaration seals the end of theism and its concept of God as a conscious being who, as self-conscious, was also a person. Even though theism was revived within the nineteenth century, its refutation by Fichte was never surmounted. Even in his later philosophy, Fichte did not return to a theistic position in the sense of an absolute, conscious being distinct from the world, but rather thought of the world-process itself as the process of the consciousness of an absolute ego.

VII. THE OPEN QUESTION TODAY

If thought remained bound to the soil of human subjectivity, this meant the reduction of all contents of consciousness to man, the total hiddenness of God, and even the disappearance of the very word "God." God and the whole world of religion must in that case be understood as mythical projections, self-objectifications of man, as Feuerbach maintained. This also shows that Feuerbach's conception is not simply false. It shares in the truth of the modern metaphysics of subjectivity. It is not without reason that the world of religious representations has again and again, e.g., in Freud, Max Weber, and van der Leeuw, given rise to the kinds of questions Feuerbach raised, viz., whether this might be described as an expression of human experience and behavior. But the question remains whether the religious behavior of man (from which one may not exempt the Christian religion without further explanation) does not rest upon different presuppositions than those described by Feuerbach.

The cultural destiny of the modern metaphysics of subjectivity was recognized by Heidegger in his previously mentioned essay when he saw in it the background of Nietzsche's aphorism about the death of God. When Nietzsche names as "the greatest new event" the fact "that God is dead," that "belief in the the Christian God has become unworthy of belief,"[38] he intends only to tally up the result of a process in Western cultural history that has come to an end. And when the idiot says: "*We have killed him* – you and I! We are all his murderers!"[39] he interprets this event as the result of the anthropocentricity of modern thought.[40] But for Nietzsche this means at the same time that the idiot "cried unceasingly, I seek God!" And Heidegger asks in relation to this: "Did perhaps a thinker really cry 'from the depths' [*de profundis*] there?"[41] That is a question which, in the mouth of Heidegger, is not only pertinent to Nietzsche, but perhaps even overinterprets him. But that makes it all the more indicative of Heidegger's own thought. Heidegger, who in his various developments has been determined by the concern not to think of being from the standpoint of human existence but to do the reverse, thinking of human existence within the horizon of being – Heidegger can no longer bring himself to call this being, which human existence must presuppose, "God." The way in which, for him, being and nothingness coinhere seems to him, even more than it did to Hölderlin and Rilke, to be connected with *modern lyric poetry* and its "empty transcendence," which Hugo Friedrich pointed out in Baudelaire, Rimbaud, and Mallarmé.[42] A similar attitude seems to have been characteristic of that generation of thinkers, to whom Heidegger also belonged, who succeeded in effecting some kind of breakthrough in the period shortly after World War I: among the philosophers, Jaspers and Bloch; among the lyric poets, Benn; among the theologians, Barth and Bultmann – to name only a few. With Jaspers and, more hesitatingly, with Benn, the question of God was raised in view of the fact that man exists with reference

---

[38] *Joyful Wisdom*, Aphorism 343; in *Complete Works*, 10:275.

[39] *Ibid.*, Aphorism 125; *Complete Works*, 10:167.

[40] Heidegger, *Holzwege*, pp. 240ff.

[41] *Ibid.*, p. 246.

[42] Hugo Friedrich, *Die Struktur der modernen Lyrik* (Hamburg, 1956).

to an empty transcendence. But the question remains an open one.

If one should still want to term "atheism" this position of holding the question open, then a different sort of atheism than Nietzsche's is involved, in any case. The triumphal tone is lacking. The death of God is no longer celebrated as the liberation of man. Still, the question remains open, since return to a theistic world view is no longer possible.

Early dialectical theology came very close to this attitude with its emphasis on the non-objectifiability of God, e.g., Bultmann, in his early essay, "What Does It Mean to Speak of God?"[43] The non-objectifiability of God was taken by Bultmann as the deeper reason that theological statements should henceforth be formulated only as statements about man in his relationship to God. Above all, however, the second edition of Barth's *Epistle to the Romans* must be mentioned here, where the modern concept of the non-objectifiability of God was deepened by means of the ideas of crisis and the theology of the cross.

The problem that then necessarily arises for theology out of the idea of the non-objectifiability of God lies in this question: How, in that case, can one still speak of God – utter the word "God" at all? Or, to put it another way, How is revelation possible? Dialectical theology found no genuine solution to this problem. Bultmann retreated into existentialist interpretation, although at a decisive point he still continued to speak in a quasi-mythological way of "God's act." Barth, however, effected a leap into the biblical supranaturalism of *Church Dogmatics*. Nevertheless, the problem of the early dialectical theology still remains. *Theology can meet the atheism* of "empty transcendence," for which the theistic world of thought is no longer negotiable, *only if it thinks through in all its consequences the biblically grounded idea of the hiddenness of God* as hiddenness even in his revelation. To use a sentence from Barth's *Epistle to the Romans*: "God is revealed as the Unknown."

In this last, deepest, and most serious basic tendency of an assertion of transcendence and the simultaneous declaration of

[43] *Faith and Understanding* (see p. 210, n. 37 below), pp. 53ff.

its emptiness, modern atheism has, so to speak, called itself into question. For here it becomes apparent that its negation is directed only against the traditional concept of God. What God might be beyond what this concept portrays remains an open question. Theological controversy with atheism on its own grounds (the understanding of man) cannot go any further than the explication of this question. That this "empty transcendence" is encountered as person, as God, is something that has to be carried out in the field of the history of religions; and the test of its truth is reserved for investigation of the particular form of the individual religions.

7

THE QUESTION OF GOD

This essay was a lecture given before the theological society in Göttingen on July 1, 1964, and was originally published in *EvTh* 25 (1965): 238–62. An English translation by Carl E. Braaten, which was consulted in the preparation of this one, appeared in *Interpretation* 21 (1967): 289–314.

I

ANYONE who tries to speak of God today can no longer count on being immediately understood – at least, not if he has in mind the living God of the Bible as the reality which determines everything, as the creator of the world. Talk about the living God, the creator of the world, is threatening to become hollow today, even on the lips of the Christian. The term "God" seems to be dispensable, if not indeed an interference, in the understanding of the reality of the world in which we exist, determined as it is by science and technology. The everyday life of every person, and the Christian too, is conditioned by a life and thought without God. This lived atheism is today the obvious point of departure for all thoughtful reflection. Even the mere question whether God exists and who he is needs special justification today if such a question is to lay claim to being taken seriously by men generally, at least as a question. The question of God as the ultimate ground of all being has become so fundamentally problematic to philosophical thought in the last 150 years that it causes a sensation when a modern philosopher attempts to revive the ancient theme of a philosophical doctrine of God.[1]

[1] See Wilhelm Weischedel, "Philosophische Theologie im Schatten des Nihilismus," *EvTh* 22 (1962): 233–49.

Ever since Fichte's "atheistic controversy" in 1799 the traditional concepts of God as the highest being and as personal in nature have been regarded as reifications and anthropomorphisms that are incompatible with God's infinity. These concepts have never completely recovered from Fichte's criticism. When idealism replaced them by the notions of the absolute ego or the absolute spirit, this was unmasked by Feuerbach as a fantastic projection of the nature of man into an imaginary heaven. Nietzsche summed up this criticism with his phrase about the death of God. And a few years ago Heidegger characterized the present state of the question in this way: "Whoever has come to know theology from within its development, both that of the Christian faith as well as that of philosophy, prefers to be silent about God today in the realm of thinking."[2]

Secular atheism, that is, life and thought without God, is evidently the given premise on which even the question of God is being debated today. This applies to Christian thought, too, insofar as it cannot simply remain aloof from the assumptions of its own epoch, but is always related to them in some way, even if in the form of contradicting them.

What this situation means for Christian preaching and theology has been a matter of debate up to now, and only in recent years has the inescapability of this problem become generally recognized through Bishop Robinson's book *Honest to God*, and within German theology, through the discussion over Herbert Braun's demythologization of the idea of God.

Karl Barth, however, in the theological breakthrough of his *Epistle to the Romans*, has already accepted the situation of godlessness created, or at least characterized, by Feuerbach's criticism of religion as the situation of the man to whom preaching and theology have to be addressed. H. J. Birkner was able

---

[2] M. Heidegger, *Identität und Differenz* (Pfüllingen, 1960), p. 51. Here Heidegger is not thinking so much of Feuerbach and Nietzsche. The questionable aspect of the ontotheological character of metaphysics is "based not on any kind of atheism" but in consideration of the unclarified nature of this ontotheology, with regard to the ambiguity in the idea of the unifying unity of being which is conceived as, on the one hand, the most universal and, on the other, as the highest being (pp. 58, 67ff.).

to express this in a pregnant formulation, namely, that for Barth's theology Feuerbach's critique of religion has a function similar to the one natural theology had for the dogmatics of Protestant orthodoxy.[3] If the presupposition of Protestant dogmatics was a knowledge of God already established from another quarter, Barth seemed to presuppose that all talk of God outside the Christian proclamation issues in man's self-deification and has nothing whatever to do with the reality of God. Thus it becomes a privilege of Christian proclamation to speak of God. Indeed, what characterizes Barth's thought is this concentration on the self-disclosure of the reality of God, breaking all anthropological "points of contact" and all supports for speech about God which compete with God's own self-manifestation. Yet, we will see that this does not fully describe the view of the early Barth. But what is characteristic of Barth's theological view is undoubtedly his principle that "God can be known through God alone," a principle that deepened Erich Schaeder's turn toward *theocentrism.*

To what extent is this an answer to our spiritual situation, which has been determined by atheism since the end of World War I? From such a perspective, it appears normal that men outside the sphere of Christian proclamation should not know God. The remnants of religious consciousness appear simply to be particular expressions of man's separation from God, of man's rebellion against the true God, who is not the familiar God of religion but the unknown God who is the crisis of all religions and of all human realities generally.

In his recent book *The Existence of God as Confessed by Faith,* Helmut Gollwitzer has once again impressively defended the view that the reality of God becomes manifest only through Christian proclamation, and that for this reason all criticism of the theistic idea of God does not bear upon Christian speech about God at all. For Gollwitzer, Christian speech about God arises "from the concrete and contingent experience of being addressed by God," an event which happens "ever anew"

[3] H. J. Birkner, "Natürliche Theologie und Offenbarungstheologie," *Neue Zeitschrift für Systematische Theologie* 3 (1961): 279–95, esp. 294.

through Christian proclamation with the "power of self-authentication."[4] Through this "happening" of being called, "the God of whom the biblical writers speak is sharply distinguished . . . from any idea of God which is a necessary element of man's self-interpretation."[5] This latter sort of God is "man accessible to himself and nothing else."[6] Thus, it turns out here that this "idea of God is only an auxiliary factor of a mythological kind to serve the self-interpretation of man, and as soon as its intention is seen through it resolves itself into speaking of man and of nothing else but man."[7] If a person asserts this about the Christian idea of God, too, he cannot be refuted." The Christian faith cannot protect itself against the endeavour to give it a purely anthropological interpretation."[8] According to Gollwitzer, the Christian "cannot refute, but only protest and testify."[9] He can "only give the assurance, but cannot prove."[10] On the other hand, Gollwitzer reproaches Herbert Braun for explaining and criticizing the biblical statements about God by analogy with theistic conceptions that can be found elsewhere.

It is significant that Braun . . . does not distinguish between "theism" as a presupposition of understanding [i.e., on our part], which is naturally out of the question, and "theism" as a presupposition on the part of the New Testament writers, which has to be taken into account in understanding them.[11]

But then are we supposed to accept the "theism" of the New Testament writers simply on authority, although, or rather since a theistic presupposition corresponding to theirs is out of the

[4] Helmut Gollwitzer, *The Existence of God as Confessed by Faith*, trans. James W. Leitch (Philadelphia: Westminster Press, 1965), p. 142 [Leitch's translation has been altered slightly in this and other passages, sometimes in preference for Braaten's rendering, and sometimes for the sake of consistency with the rest of my translation. – TR.].   [5] *Ibid.*, p. 140.

[6] *Ibid.*, p. 141.   [7] *Ibid.*   [8] *Ibid.*, p. 102.   [9] *Ibid.*

[10] *Ibid.*, p. 103. With the words quoted here Gollwitzer is drawing a parallel with the attitude of the lover who wants to convince others "that his love . . . is directed to the other himself" (*ibid.*). But the comparison is defective because in the case of the lover it is just himself that he is binding in his assurance, whereas the Christian who speaks of God is not himself God, but with respect to the possibility of speaking about God must be just as vexed as anyone else.   [11] *Ibid.*, p. 38.

question for us? Are conceptions of God that are theistic in form suddenly different from what they would otherwise be the moment they happen to show up in the New Testament or in Christian preaching? Are they *then* no longer, as otherwise, "only an auxiliary factor of a mythological kind to serve the self-interpretation of man,"[12] but now "the happening of God's address"[13] instead? And can theology, merely by protests and assurances, prevent the Christian proclamation from "being confused with a theistic world view?"[14] This would seem to confirm what an atheistic book that just appeared in East Germany had to say about the Christian faith, namely, that it is irrational and "for this reason cannot be binding upon society, but can only be a matter of *private* belief. Genuine certainty is excluded in faith because there can be no objective criteria for the truth of the content of faith."[15]

It can hardly be assumed that Gollwitzer's argumentation will in the future keep Braun from explaining the biblical statements about God by analogy with non-Christian theistic concepts. For to the extent that this analogy actually applies, one can hardly raise any serious objection to such a procedure. If the idea of a personal God is everywhere else judged to be a mythological self-interpretation of man, one would hardly be able to prevent this view from having repercussions on Christian theology and its language about God. Braun is therefore

---

[12] *Ibid.*, p. 142.   [13] *Ibid.*, p. 141.

[14] *Ibid.*, p. 41. Gollwitzer would like to avoid such a confusion and the accompanying danger of a kind of understandability which, according to him, would be "the sharpest argument . . . for Feuerbach's transferring of theology into anthropology" (p. 141), by means of his thesis that in order to reveal himself God enters "into the conditions of statements about particular beings, but not the conditions of knowledge that apply to such" [translation mine – Tr.; cf. *ibid.*, p. 143]. Gollwitzer criticizes me for not having observed this distinction (*ibid.*, pp. 143ff.). But how is it now possible "to speak of God in human language" (p. 148) if God is not also known? And how is it possible for him to be known without entering "into the conditions of knowledge applying to particular beings"? And how do things stand with regard to the incarnation of God if in his revelation he remains outside our cognitive conditions?

[15] *Moderne Naturwissenschaft und Atheismus*, ed. O. Klohr (Berlin, 1964), p. 31.

being consistent when on the basis of this presupposition he tries to demythologize the term "God," indeed, even to get along without it.[16] Of course, one also cannot but agree with Gollwitzer that Braun's dissolution of the divine counterpart into existential relations, consistently thought through to the end, "is then also the end of theology."[17]

The term "God" is in fact superfluous if it is merely a designation for existential relations in the interpersonal realm.[18] The fact that in spite of this Braun still speaks of God indicates, perhaps, that he means something else by it, viz., "that life comes to us ever from beyond, from outside by own self."[19] This expresses something which cannot in any case be reduced to a psychological or sociological description of interpersonal relations. True, it does not yet provide any justification for using the word "God". But the mere postulate of a special status for biblical speech about God in contrast to analogous theistic ideas is even less able to provide the proper justification for speaking of God.

The controversy between Gollwitzer and Braun shows that theology has fallen into a dilemma in the face of the atheistic criticism of theistic conceptions. On the one side, theology claims a special status for Christian speech about God, in spite of the fact that it can be confused with other theistic ideas of God. Nevertheless, as the basis for this claim we heard only the subjective reassurance that here we are dealing with something totally different from anything else, namely, the real God. On the other side, the criticism of theistic conceptions is expanded to cover Christian speech about God, too. But that probably means the end of theology.

Is there a way out of this dilemma? Obviously there is a way only if the claim of Christian proclamation to derive from an

---

[16] Herbert Braun, *Gesammelte Studien zum Neuen Testament und seiner Umwelt* (Tübingen, 1962), pp. 291ff.

[17] Gollwitzer, *Existence of God*, p. 38. Max Horckheimer has expressed himself similarly on Bishop Robinson's book *Honest to God*, in *Zeugnisse: Theodor W. Adorno zum 60. Geburtstag*, ed. M. Horckheimer (Frankfurt, 1963).

[18] *Ibid.*, p. 94.

[19] Braun, *Gesammelte Studien*, p. 296.

experience of God does not remain a mere assertion but is capable of verification. This need not involve a court of appeal *prior* to the biblical revelation of God before which the latter would have to legitimate itself. Such a court of appeal would in fact be incompatible with the majesty of divine revelation.[20] Christian speech about God can be verified only in such a way that it is the revelation of God itself which discloses that about man and his world in relation to which its truth is proved. In this way Christian speech about God would be more than mere assertion. It could lay claim to the existence of man and of the world, in the way they are disclosed in the light of the biblical tradition, but thereafter perceivable as really being so characterized, as witnesses for the reality of the biblical God.

II

A start in such a direction was made in the early period of dialectical theology. The truth-claim of Christian speech about God did not appear as isolated here as with Gollwitzer.

In the second edition of his *Epistle to the Romans* (1922), Barth wrote that God had not abandoned his creation in spite of his opposition to the world of sin. The faithfulness of God remains constant: ". . . there still abides too that profound agreement between the will of God and that which men, longing to be free from themselves, also secretly desire; there is also the divine answer which is given to us when the final human question awakens in us."[21] Barth here speaks of a correspondence indeed of a coincidence of the human question and the divine answer. This idea can be found in a number of places.[22]

---

[20] This is the element of truth in Gollwitzer's statement: "If he (viz., God) entered under the conditions of human knowledge, then he would have lost his divinity with his revelation . . ." (*Existence of God*, p. 147).

[21] Karl Barth, *The Epistle to the Romans*, trans. Edwyn C. Hoskyns (London: Oxford University Press, 1933), p. 41.

[22] E.g., *ibid.*, pp. 80, 271f., 380. Barth also speaks of the coincidence of the divine answer with the question that man is in *The Word of God and the Word of Man*, trans. Douglas Horton (New York: Harper Torchbooks, 1957), p. 191.

The real meaning of the law and of the religions is to keep this question open.[23] Yet the divine is materially prior to the human question. Without the call of the Lord, who in utmost hiddenness is the answer to this question, there would be no laws, no religions, and thus neither would there be that question that manifests itself in them about the most hidden meaning of life. "Men call upon God, *because*, and only *because*, he has answered before they call."[24] Therefore, this answer, which is God himself,[25] is the basis of the question which animates man's existence. We do not ask the question of ourselves, but we do it because God himself through Jesus Christ has placed us in question, because he is the *answer* to the question of our existence.[26]

Similarly, in *Christliche Dogmatik* (1927), it is when man hears God *speaking* that his own existence becomes a question, namely, the question of overcoming the contradiction coming at him from God's side, and of "the realization of his own being,"[27] Man does not merely *think* this question; "he is it."[28] Here, too, Barth places decisive importance on the fact that the questionableness of human existence is disclosed from the side of the *answer* and cannot be established out of itself. The answer is "the meaning and the presupposition of the question."[29] Therefore, man's questioning is not *ended* by the answer, but is instead *awakened* by it.

The question remains as question, if it is the case that it is not sustained by its own weight but by the answer that confronts it and which existed *before* it did. The answer itself would make impossible every attempt to weaken the seriousness of the question. The question would be based on it; the answer would necessarily make the question at every moment as burning and vital as can be imagined.[30]

The question remains, therefore, not "*in spite of* the given *answer*, but *on account of it.*"[31] In this sense Barth could also formulate the dialectically pointed maxim that the question is itself the answer.[32]

---

[23] Barth, *Romans*, p. 254.   [24] *Ibid.*, p. 383.
[25] *Ibid.*, p. 80.   [26] *Ibid.*, p. 282.
[27] Karl Barth, *Christliche Dogmatik im Entwurf* (Munich, 1927), p. 70.
[28] *Ibid.*, p. 71.   [29] *Ibid.*, p. 74.   [30] *Ibid.*
[31] *Ibid.*, p. 78.   [32] Cf. above, n. 22.

In reworking these ideas in his *Church Dogmatics*, Barth avoided using the terminology of "question" and "answer" in order, supposedly, to exclude any idea of a possibility on the side of man by means of which he could attain knowledge of God on his own.[33] To be sure, such a misunderstanding had already been guarded against by his stress on the priority of the answer over the question. On the other hand, in abandoning this terminology Barth at first gave up the possibility of claiming human existence itself a witness for the truth of revelation. The fact that Barth nevertheless clung to this intention or returned to it later, at any rate, is shown by his statements in the last volumes of *Church Dogmatics* concerning the relation of all men and every creature to the revelation of God in Jesus Christ. Even the non-Christian religions are now again, as once before in *Epistle to the Romans*,[34] related to the real God, and are thus not simply, with Feuerbach, unmasked as the ideological self-interpretation of man. The "religious relationship" of man to God is indeed a perversion or "degeneration" of the covenant relationship between the Creator and the creature. "But as such it is a confirmation that that relationship has not been destroyed by God." In his religions man must, even in his conflict against God, seal "the fact that he cannot be without God."[35]

The correspondence between God's revelation as answer and the question of man, which is uncovered as a question by this answer, is further discussed by H. J. Iwand in his posthumously published lectures on faith and knowledge.[36] It is true that

---

[33] *CD* 1/1, pp. 217ff.   [34] P. 383.

[35] *CD* 4/1, pp. 483. On the question of the continuity of Barth's view in spite of a transitional tendency, conditioned by his resistance against "natural theology," toward "a reduction of revelation to Jesus Christ," see the essay by A. Szekeres, "Karl Barth und die natürliche Theologie," *EvTh* 24 (1964): 229–42, esp. 240f.

[36] H. J. Iwand, *Nachgelassene Werke* (Munich, 1962ff.), 1:92ff., 118ff., 155ff. Occasionally there is mention of the fact – of course, not as much as in Barth – that the question itself can be understood only from the standpoint of the answer (pp. 114, 124f.). On the other hand, Iwand acknowledges that the relation to the question of God which the believer has in common

Iwand does not in this context make the point that the very existence of man already has the character of a question, indeed, the question of God.

This theme has been all the more emphatically developed by Rudolf Bultmann. Here this idea is dealt with as profoundly as by the early Barth. Bultmann stated in 1924 that man must raise the question about himself because he *"has been called in question"* by God, who, is at the same time the answer to man's question about himself.[37] In 1934, Bultmann stresses the point that even the natural man in his existence knows about God, since he is a question to himself.[38] In this sense philosophy also knows about faith in that it knows about the freedom of human existence: "just because it knows about the questionableness which is an essential part of this freedom."[39]

Thus Bultmann believes, like Barth, that the question which man himself is can be rightly understood only from the side of God, who is the answer to man's question about his own authenticity. In contrast to Barth, however, he emphasizes that even the natural man and philosophy are already aware of the questionableness of existence. Of course, it still holds that "the *question* is not the *answer*, though the unbelieving existence always yields to the temptation to interpret it as the answer"[40] by seizing upon this questionableness as his freedom in order thereby to ground himself in himself. This is the basic theme that we encounter again in Bultmann's essay "The Question of

with the unbeliever keeps faith from a "retreat into subjectivity" (pp. 112ff., 115f.).

[37] Rudolf Bultmann, "Liberal Theology and the Latest Theological Movement," *Faith and Understanding*, trans. Louise Pettibone Smith (London: SCM Press and New York: Harper and Row, 1969), p. 47: "Man as such, the whole man, is called in question by God. . . . But to know this judgment is also to know it as grace, since it is really liberation. Man then knows that the question is also the answer, for it is only God who can so question him. And he knows that the answer is primary. A question so radical cannot originate from man or from the world. But if the question is asked by God, then it originates from the claim of God upon man. Man is called." Cf. pp. 316f.

[38] Rudolf Bultmann, "The Problem of 'Natural Theology'," *Faith and Understanding*, pp. 316f.

[39] *Ibid.*, pp. 328f.   [40] *Ibid.*, p. 323.

Natural Revelation."[41] Man as such knows about God, which is shown by the fact that he forms the *idea* of God. But "thereby he has reached only the stage of an inquiry about God."[42] The knowledge that is expressed in it is "that of the uncanniness and the enigmatic nature of life — of the mystery and finitude of man. From it arises the inquiry concerning the power which could bring light into the darkness, order into the confusion, and life into death."[43] In this inquiry about God, man expresses the knowledge he has about the demand laid upon him, "with respect to his authenticity, which continually lies before him,"[44] and with respect to his own provisionality. But now it happens that man "neither sees nor maintains the idea of God, which is accessible to him in what he knows about his existence, as an inquiry about God, and that he contorts his negative knowledge into a positive knowledge."[45] And again:

If he would keep this knowledge thoroughly open, and persist in his inquiry about God, then creation would speak as God's Word for him. But, in fact, man does not do this: he twists this negative knowledge into a positive knowledge, and so creation becomes mute for him who holds God's truth a prisoner.[46]

Therefore, God's revelation enters into contradiction with man. However, "the Christian faith criticizes . . . not the non-Christian inquiry about God – it can only penetrate into it and illumine it – but only the answer which the non-Christian inquiry constructs."[47] This is the basis for the "points of contact and conflict" in man's existence for the revelation of God, elaborated by Bultmann in an essay by this title in 1946.[48] The point of contact in man is "the question confronting him about his own authenticity."[49] The Christian proclamation, however, does not simply find this point of contact given *beforehand*, but

[41] In Rudolf Bultmann, *Essays Philosophical and Theological*, trans. James C. G. Grieg (London: SCM Press and New York: Macmillan Co., 1955). This essay first appeared in 1941.   [42] *Ibid.*, p. 94.   [43]*Ibid.*, p. 95.
[44] *Ibid.* [My translation – Tr.]
[45] *Ibid.*, p. 113.   [46] *Ibid.*, pp. 114f.
[47] *Ibid.*, p. 98. [Translation slightly revised – Tr.]
[48] In *Essays Philosophical and Theological*, pp. 133–50.
[49] Bultmann, *Glauben und Verstehen*, 2:120. [My translation – Tr., cf. *Essays*, p. 136.]

in the very conflict of God with the sinner this point of contact is "uncovered."[50] Thus Bultmann firmly maintains the priority of the divine answer for the knowledge of man's question about God. Only in the light of the answer is the question revealed as a "point of contact." This stands in a certain tension with Bultmann's view that man as such already knows about the questionableness of his existence and that philosophy is able to elaborate this knowledge. In fact, this is the basis for Bultmann's close alliance with existentialist philosophy, and it explains his difference from Barth. On the one hand, the natural man and philosophy already know about the *questionableness* of human existence; on the other hand, man's questionableness is first fully disclosed by the Christian message, because man of himself always "twists" the question into the answer.

The problem facing us here can be seen still more clearly in the thought of Paul Tillich. From the standpoint of our inquiry, his "method of correlation" comes astonishingly close to Barth and Bultmann. Tillich's systematic theology is so constructed that in each part of the system the Christian "answer" is correlated with an "existential question,"[51] namely, the question that man himself is,[52] the "question implied in man's finitude and finitude generally."[53] Tillich differs from Bultmann in that for him the answer of revelation is correlated not only with the question of *human existence* (in the sense of an existentialist interpretation), but also with the finitude disclosed "in everything that exists" whatsoever.

On the whole, Tillich, too, emphasizes that the content of the answer cannot be derived from the question.[54] "Man is the question, not the answer."[55] However, he also states, conversely,

[50] *Ibid.* [My translation – Tr.] Herein lies the difference between Bultmann's position and Emil Brunner's talk about the personality of man as a point of contact for the Christian message.

[51] Tillich also says: "Man is the question he asks about himself, before any question has been formulated" (*Systematic Theology* [Chicago: University of Chicago Press and Welwyn: James Nisbet, 1951], 1:62). Cf. *ibid.*, 1:66; 2:13.

[52] *Ibid.*, p. 64.   [53] *Ibid.*   [54] *Ibid.*, p. 65.

[55] *Ibid.*, 2:13. For Tillich, God himself is "the answer to the question implied in man's finitude" (*ibid.*, 1:66).

that it is "equally wrong to derive the question implied in human existence from the revelatory answer."[56] If the answer is not in response to a previously posed question, "the revelatory answer is meaningless." Thus, Tillich makes it even clearer than Bultmann that what is at stake in the effort to interpret the Christian revelation as the answer to the question of human existence and of finitude generally is the ability of theological statements to compel conviction; or, to use Tillich's words, the *expression* of the "truth of the Christian message . . . must be adequate to every new generation" in order to be "received" as the truth.[57]

In a similar fashion, Gerhard Ebeling has designated the questionableness not only of man himself[58] but "of the reality that encounters me" as the "reason why it can be claimed that what is said of God concerns every man and therefore, can also in principle be intelligible to every man."[59] Thus, theology establishes the possibility of its talk about God having the power to compel conviction by explaining it as an answer to the questionableness of human existence and of reality generally as it confronts man.[60]

---

[56] *Ibid.*, 2:13.   [57] *Ibid.*, 1:3.

[58] Cf. Ebeling's statement in "Theological Reflexions on Conscience," in *Word and Faith*, trans. James W. Leitch (Philadelphia: Fortress Press, 1963), p. 417. "Man experiences himself as one who is not identical with himself, but whose essence it is to be questioned about his identity with himself. Only in being thus questioned is his identity given." In his essay, "Rudimentary Reflexions on Speaking Responsibly of God," it is similarly stated of the conscience that it is "man himself under the aspect of his involvement in radical questionableness" (*ibid.*, p. 349).

[59] *Ibid.*, p. 347.

[60] Ebeling attributes this experience of universal questionableness especially to the conscience. In the conscience "the fact of man's identity being open to question opens also the question of God" (*ibid.*, p. 419). For conscience is concerned "with the whole, because it is concerned with the question of the finally valid" and therefore with the question of the wholeness of the world as well as of God as the "first and the last" in relation to this wholeness of the world (p. 412). In the conscience "man can find himself asking how in spite of his constant non-identity with himself he yet remains upheld in that identity, in remaining questioned about it and summoned to it" (p. 419).

These fine statements of Ebeling's take on a problematic aspect only

This should make explicit what certainly in the case of Bultmann and probably also in Barth the actual function of relating Christian speech about God to the questionableness of human existence really is. Reflection upon this relationship would be superfluous if it did not exhibit the binding force of speech about God.

The problem here is only whether the questionableness of existence is disclosed exclusively in the light of the answer contained in God's revelation, or whether it is universally accessible. Not only Bultmann but also Tillich and Ebeling wish to maintain that aspect which is decisive for Barth, namely, that the questionableness of human existence and of all finite reality can only be understood in its true meaning from the perspective of the divine answer. Hence Tillich speaks of a "dependence of the question on the answer."[61] The *formulation* of the existential question in the individual parts of his systematic theology is itself already a matter for the *theologian*.[62] He does not find

---

when Ebeling makes a sharp distinction between conscience as he describes it and reason. He states: "The responsibility to which man as such is summoned is *not* fulfilled in thought *but* only in the word-event that has grown out of the questionableness confronting him in the conscience" (*RGG*³, vol. 6, col. 822; italics mine). Is this *alternative* correct? Is reason only to be characterized as controlling knowledge? According to Ebeling, man must "think of himself as sovereign" in this realm (*ibid.*). But is not rational thought concerned with the "apprehension" [*Vernehmen*] of something, even if this apprehension falls short of allowing it to be characterized as a photographic copying [*Aufnehmen*] of things, but is more a process in which thought is dependent upon notions that reach out beyond everything presently existing and precisely in so doing brings out their essence? Above all, however, it must be said that the experience of questionableness, which Ebeling ascribes to the conscience, is precisely the essence of reason itself in its process of reflection which is always questioning beyond what has already been thought and reaching further with its projections. It is not accidental that the themes named by Ebeling – the wholeness of the world, the foundational ultimate reality of God, and the identity of man with himself – have been the three basic themes of metaphysics in the past (world, God, and soul). This is not to dispute the fact that these questions concern the conscience. But should one juxtapose conscience, so understood, and reason? Does this not abridge the phenomenon of reason? Is the conscience anything else than the existential relevance of reason itself?

[61] Tillich, *Systematic Theology*, 2:14.   [62] *Ibid.*, p. 15.

the question ready-made so that all he would have to do would be to formulate the suitable answer. Even the formulation of the question and the "choice of the material" is the task of the theologian. In this way the dependence of the question upon the answer becomes effective. Correspondingly, Ebeling emphasizes that the experience of the questionableness of existence is not to be characterized purely and simply "as a quest for God that is native to man as man."[63]

This observation rightly tells us that the "object" [*das "Wonach"*] of the question can be definitively determined only from the answer.[64] Nevertheless, the answer, viz., God's revelation and the theological talk about God which it occasions, is related to a universal experience of questionableness as "the common ground of every man's experience."[65] Similarly, Tillich emphasizes that despite the dependence of the question upon the answer, there is also an inverse dependence of the question upon the answer.[66] But what is the precise relationship of this questionability to the answer? The mere reference to a correlation between question and answer leaves something to be desired. On the one hand, it leaves undecided the extent to which our knowledge of the human question is in fact irreversibly dependent upon the divine answer. And on the other hand, it does not tell us to what extent the questionableness of existence really has something to do with the God of whom the Christian proclamation speaks.

---

[63] Ebeling, "Rudimentary Reflexions," in *Word and Faith*, p. 348.

[64] To be sure, Ebeling does not go further into the questions that arise here. Isn't a question always a question *about* something? The aim of a question would therefore have to be corrigible from the side of the answer, even though it already anticipates the answer to a certain extent (as Ebeling observes when he says that "the quest for God already presupposes some kind of knowledge of what it seeks" [*Word and Faith*, p. 348]).

[65] *Ibid.*

[66] Tillich, *Systematic Theology*, 2:15. Tillich says that the influence on the theological answer of the question implied in the structure of finitude is of a *formal* kind (*ibid.*, 1:4), whereas the *content* of the Christian answers are independent of the question. But is it possible to separate form and content so simply? Isn't there a problem in this distinction that requires further clarification?

III

The formula of the questionableness of existence is suitable as a comprehensive expression of our contemporary knowledge about man. This is true not only in the negative sense that Albert Camus makes prominent when he speaks of the "hopeless gap between the question of man and the silence of the universe."[67] The questionableness of man has just as much the positive meaning that man is a being who inquires beyond himself. Since Max Scheler, anthropology has spoken of this basic phenomenon as man's openness to the world. Today this is brought out especially by Adolf Portmann, Arnold Gehlen, and Michael Landmann. In contrast to animals, which are bound by their instincts, man is able to go beyond every situation and can change his environment. Helmut Plessner makes the same point when he calls man the "eccentric" being by virtue of his ability to take up a position in relation to himself and thereby transcend himself. Ernst Bloch has described man as the being who reaches beyond everything that has happened by means of his anticipations, wishes, and hopes. In a similar vein, Jean-Paul Sartre says that man's reality is "a perpetual surpassing toward coincidence with itself, which is never given."[68] "The being-for-itself is the being who is itself its own lack of being."[69] Therefore this being projects itself upon a being-in-itself: ". . . man is basically the desire to be God."[70]

The designation of this basic structure of man's being as a question which drives toward an answer is not a mere metaphor. For the ability to transcend one's own situation, which characterizes man, is realized in the process of an inquiry, which is also something that underlies every human projection. Every projection is an anticipation of an answer to a question that underlies it. The inquiry is directed toward what is not yet

[67] Albert Camus, *The Rebel*, trans. Anthony Bower (New York: Vintage Books, 1956), p. 6. [Translation revised to German translation cited by the author – Tr.].

[68] Jean-Paul Sartre, *Being and Nothingness*, trans. Hazel E. Barnes (New York: Philosophical Library, 1956), p. 89.

[69] *Ibid.*, p. 617f.   [70] *Ibid.*, p. 626.

known. Through it man proceeds beyond the realm of the known and thus beyond his own situation. His openness to the world is expressed by the very fact that he is able to make an inquiry and that his life is a process of inquiry that continually drives him on into the open. In questioning the reality he encounters and going beyond its currently given aspects to its very essence through this inquiry, thus disclosing *its* questionableness, man is in the last analysis asking about himself, about his own destination. Thus it makes good sense to describe man as a question that continually pushes him further into the open.

But what does this question have to do with God? Is it perhaps the case that man's questioning nature is so fashioned that it does not aim toward an ultimate answer? Is it not characteristic of the modern experience of nihilism that the inquiry pulls everything into its vortex, so that now absolutely everything has become questionable and no answer can any longer be regarded as unsurpassable? In this sense Wilhelm Weischedel has made the modern experience of radical questionableness as groundlessness the point of departure for his reflections on a "Philosophical Theology in the Shadow of Nihilism."[71] In contrast to the way in which theology from Barth to Tillich and Ebeling has spoken of the question-character of human existence, the questionableness of nihilism described by Weischedel has nothing to do with a question that is oriented upon an answer, but only with the calling of everything into question in the sense of a doubting that has itself become a position. Now Weischedel thinks that this entire questionableness must itself once more be called into question.

If the self-certainty of radical inquiry is itself placed in question, then, in his view, we have taken a step beyond nihilism. That would be the "moment of metamorphosis of the now really absolute collapse into an utterly new birth."[72] And God would again become thinkable as the "whence of the challenge to inquiry"[73] once inquiry has lost its self-evidence and itself has come to stand in need of a foundation.

[71] Wilhelm Weischedel, "Philosophische Theologie im Schatten des Nihilismus," *EvTh* 22 (1962): 233–49.   [72] *Ibid.*, p. 247.   [73] *Ibid.*, p. 248.

It seems to me that the legitimacy of this last step has rightly been contested.[74] The transition from the total questionableness of nihilism to the idea that inquiry points to some "whence" has a different structure from that of nihilistic inquiry itself, and for this reason it cannot be conclusively demonstrated to be a consequence of the nihilistic sort of inquiry. The nihilistic questioning of all assumed certainties is characterized by an attitude of pure detachment, by an empty negation. The question concerning the ground and source of something is a question "about something" and seeks a possible answer. These two types of question are repeatedly confused by Weischedel. The philosophical inquiry is sometimes characterized as intending a possible answer, and at other times as one which calls into question of all assumed certainties.

Weischedel at first characterizes philosophical inquiry as an inquiry aiming at an answer. He tell us that the philosopher would not be a "serious inquirer if he were not out for an answer."[75] Now Weischedel is certainly right in maintaining that every answer that is attained can be surpassed. The philosopher must "ever again call (such answers) into question," in order "to draw them back out of every solidification of thought into the process of inquiry."[76] In so doing, the inquiry will still have the meaning of intending new answers. The "relentlessness of the inquiry" need by no means result in "rendering (everything) questionable."[77] The fact that every answer that is attained can

---

[74] Wolfgang Müller-Lauter, "Zarathustras Schatten hat lange Beine," *EvTh* 23 (1963): 113–31, esp. 128f. Müller-Lauter is justified in saying that inquiry into the origin of the nihilistic kind of questionableness within the history of thought can be meaningfully made only "within the framework of a presentation of the inner dialectic of nihilism" (p. 129). His essay deals with a few essential stages along its way. Of course, it also seems to Müller-Lauter that the "negative dialectic" which prevails in the history of nihilism must be regarded as inevitable because it is nothing else than the course of the very process rendering things questionable (p. 130). This stems from the fact that Müller-Lauter does not distinguish between inquiry in the sense of making things questionable and the original meaning of inquiry, which aims at a possible answer.

[75] Weischedel, "Philosophische Theologie," p. 236.
[76] *Ibid.*, p. 237.   [77] *Ibid.*

be surpassed does not rule out the possibility that the inquiry be directed toward a new answer. But when it is maintained that philosophical inquiry "in its radicality cannot cease until its ultimate goal (i.e., the idea of God as its primal ground or origin) has been made questionable,"[78] then such a process of rendering things questionable has the sense of empty doubt, which is just what Weischedel had previously denied the honour of the name philosophy.[79]

The assertion that the nihilistic way of making everything questionable is the necessary result of radical inquiry, such as it is claimed philosophy carries out, must therefore be contested. Even if the inquiry which aims at an *answer* must once again raise questions beyond every answer it *achieves*, still such a process of questioning does not for this reason eventuate in the nihilistic consciousness of questionableness which is no longer concerned about finding answers. Indeed, the possibility of even the nihilistic kind of doubt is rooted in the nature of inquiry generally,[80] insofar as it belongs to human inquiry to be able to press beyond every answer it arrives at. This negative element in inquiry has become absolutized in modern cultural history. This turn of events is nevertheless not to be taken as a necessary outcome of the very nature of inquiry, but is rather to be explained as the result of special historical circumstances, probably above all that of the striving for emancipation from the Christian heritage.

The weakness of the nihilistic mode of questioning consists in its being so abstract, an empty distancing of itself from present assertions. Both this nihilism and the opposed views that

---

[78] *Ibid.*

[79] *Ibid.*, p. 236. Here Weischedel says that ". . . the skeptical game of 'art for art's sake' is not philosophy."

[80] Müller-Lauter rightly contests the idea that inquiry arises out of a transitory experience of questioning (in the specifically nihilistic sense) and asserts on the contrary that it is the inquiry which first produces the total questioning ("Zarathustras Schatten," p. 128). But even so, this result is by no means necessary, but arises only if a partial element of inquiry, viz., going beyond existing answers, is taken in abstraction by itself so that the inquiry only remains in an attitude of detachment from all asserted certainties and no longer contains any intentions about answers.

confront its negation with mere affirmation, bespeak a spiritual indolence. Concrete, critical reflection upon the tradition and on the situation of current experience does not reach the point of nihilistic dissolution because, although it makes use of the same negative dialectic, it does not do so in abstract isolation, as nihilism does, but as an element of its inquiry into the *essential content* about which it is reflecting. Solely for the sake of this essential content must all previously given answers be superseded. In this attitude, critical inquiry remains directed toward the content that will appear in the form of a new answer.

Thus, we may leave the nihilistic form of questionableness aside. The primary form of inquiry is always expecting an answer. Only so long as an answer is regarded as possible does it remain meaningful to inquire. To this extent, the "challenge to inquiry" does indeed arise from the object of the inquiry insofar as it may possibly afford an answer to the question. Only as the answer coming to meet the question of man's existence would God be at once the one from whom the "challenge to inquiry" proceeds, and thus the "origin of human freedom."[81]

The question that intends an answer manifests itself as referred to such in that an answer *occurs* to it with respect to the matter in question. Does this hold true for the question structure of human existence as well? Precisely in this regard the phenomenon of inquiry appears to be an excellent example of the structure of human existence. For in his openness to the world man is not only creatively free to shape and produce things ever anew,[82] but is also thrown back upon a ground supporting both himself and his world, and which indeed supports him in

---

[81] Weischedel, "Philosophische Theologie," p. 248.

[82] Arnold Gehlen so characterizes man, with respect to his "openness to the world" one-sidedly as "an acting being" who "must create his own chances in life by his own doing" (*Der Mensch: Seine Natur und seine Stellung in der Welt* [Berlin, ⁶1950], pp. 24, 66; cf. pp. 33, 56 *passim*). Hardly once does he mention the presuppositions that man is thrown back upon to be able to engage in such independent activity. That man is open to the future is for Gehlen unqualifiedly identical with the fact that man lives actively (p. 326). With Nietzsche's metaphysic of the will, he sees in volition "the primal phenomenon of man himself" (pp. 394ff.).

such a way that it can not be identified with anything that shows up in the world.[83]

Whether this characteristic openness of human behavior presupposes such a supporting ground, different from the entire realm of existing beings (that is to say, from the world) precisely because what is being inquired into is man's openness to inquire beyond everything in existence; or whether this openness is only an expression of the self-creative power of man as an "acting being," is probably the central problem inherent in the modern idea of man's "openness to the world" or self-transcendence — an idea about which there is such remarkable agreement among the most diverse trends of modern thought. The problem is especially clear in Sartre, because he sees that the openness of man is determined by a fundamental element of *lack*.[84]

He takes human reality as characterized simply by "its own lack,"[85] that is, in view of "the particular totality which it is lacking."[86] Herein Sartre indeed explicitly sees the truth of second Cartesian proof of the existence of God: "the being which is the foundation only of its nothingness surpasses itself toward the being which is the foundation of its being."[87] And yet he goes on to say that this being toward which the human reality strives to surpass itself is "not a transcendent God."[88] For such a totality cannot exist, "since it would combine in itself the incompatible characteristics of the in-itself and the for-itself."[89] As much as we have to pay attention to its suggestion, this explanation of Sartre's, that the idea of an objectively existing God would be self-contradictory, ignores his own starting point, that is, his insight into the element of lack in the being-for-itself. If, as Sartre himself says, the lack is "a phenomenon on the basis of a totality,"[90] then the existence of man at least

[83] In implicit debate with Gehlen, I have already called attention to the element in man's openness to the world of being referred back to a ground. See my *Was ist der Mensch?* (Göttingen, 1962), pp. 10f.

[84] Sartre, *Being and Nothingness*, pp. 84ff., 617ff.   [85] *Ibid.*, p. 88.

[86] *Ibid.*, p. 89.   [87] *Ibid.*   [88] *Ibid.*   [89] *Ibid.*, p. 90.

[90] *Ibid.*, p. 88. Sartre says rightly that for the phenomenon of lack and the totality presupposed in it, ". . . it matters little whether this totality has

presupposes the *possibiltity* of that totality. And insofar as it is
the case that the ground that makes it possible can lie neither
in man himself nor in the extant world, it is always previously
presupposed in the existence of man and his world as the
reality that supports them. This reality is therefore not simply
"hypostatized"[91] as transcendence beyond the world, nor is it
only the "ideal" that man projects in his desire for self-realization,[92] since he is instead already dependent for all self-realization upon that supporting reality, which is antecedent to all
such projections as the ground of their possibility.

Now is this dependence of man upon a ground[93] which transcends everything in existence and supports him from out of the
depth of reality in the openness of his existence to be described
as dependence upon *God*, as a question about *God*? Let us first
of all make clear what it is to which this dependence is directly
related. The question of man's existence does not refer directly

---

been originally given and is now broken (e.g., 'The arms of Venus di Milo
are now *lacking*') or whether it has never yet been realized (e.g., 'He lacks
courage')" (p. 88). In either case what is lacked is presupposed as *possible*,
and in the first case even as once having been real.

[91] *Ibid.*, p. 90.

[92] Similarly, for Ernst Bloch, God appears as "a hypostatized ideal of the
as yet unrealized essence of man" (*Das Prinzip Hoffnung*, 2 vols. [Frankfurt,
[2]1959], 2:1523). The "vacuum left behind by the removal of the God-
hypostasis" (p. 1529) still remains intact, even if not "in the sense of something actually present – just as that intended totality does for Sartre
(besides, Bloch also uses the term "the good whole" [p. 1530] for the as
yet unrevealed goal on the "path" of human life). The vacuum is described
as "a space held open for coming possibilities, for the yet undecided reality
in this vacuum" (p. 1530), corresponding to Sartre's formula about man's
desire to become God. Just like Sartre, Bloch fails to appreciate the fact that
because man's self-transcendence is an expression not of an abundance
driving toward self-unfolding but of a lack which cannot be overcome by
himself, man must presuppose the reality that makes it possible to overcome
this lack, provided that the basic transcending movement of his existence
is to have some kind of meaning.

[93] Herbert Braun also points out, when he speaks of experience that I am
grasped and borne from outside myself (and thereby also from beyond
everything we meet in the world, everything manipulable), "that life always
comes to me from beyond myself" (*Gesammelte Studien*, p. 282). I do not
really understand how Gollwitzer can dismiss this statement as an inconsequential "general truth" (*Existence of God*, p. 90).

to a person, and therefore not directly to God. Rather, at first it shows man as dependent upon being encountered by something that functions as a supportive ground for the existence of man in its transcending movement into openness, as well as for the totality of all extant reality, the world. Only if man gains access to such a ground can he base his own behavior on a solid footing instead of on an illusory foundation that in truth lacks any basis. Only the ground of all reality, or, better, the power over all reality, is able to guarantee a security that cannot be destroyed by any other power. Therefore, man inquires after a ground which can support himself and all reality, which as the power over all reality is also able to carry him beyond the limits of his own present existence, and which therefore supports him precisely in the openness of his freedom. But this question does not aim directly at a person.

This question does have reference to something, however. In every question there is always an anticipatory projection of a possible answer. This why is the attempt has repeatedly been made to deduce the answer from the question of human existence or from the questionableness of the finite world discovered thereby. It has justly been said that this inferential method of natural theology and its proofs for the existence of God do not so much prove the reality of God as the finitude of man and the world.[94] The so-called proofs for the existence of God show only that man must inquire beyond the world and himself if he is to find a ground capable of supporting the being and meaning of his existence. The proofs of God constitute the theoretical formulation for the sort of rising above everything finite to the idea of an infinite reality that goes on in such inquiry. They retain their significance as elaborations of the questionableness of finite being which drive man beyond the whole compass of

---

[94] So Tillich, *Systematic Theology*, 1:65, 204ff., esp. 205, 209f. Similarly, Ebeling, *Word and Faith*, pp. 348f. Hence, H. G. Geyer is only partly right when he says of metaphysics that "its real and true subject is and remains finite being" ("Theologie des Nihilismus," *EvTh* 23 [1963]: 99), for finite being is the subject of metaphysics only to the extent that it drives thought to inquire beyond its own orbit.

finite reality. But they do not provide the answer to this question.

Still, in the history of thought, the arguments for the existence of God have again and again been understood as ways to answer the question of finitude, instead of mere elaborations of the question itself. The confusion of the question with the answer described by Bultmann has repeatedly been characteristic of philosophical theology.[95] Of course, one should not be content merely to criticize this confusion. The investigation leads further into its causes. Then it becomes evident that to conclude the answer from the question is possible only because the question is always framed in relation to a projection of its answer. Insofar as a question is a genuine question and asks about something, it already anticipates a possible answer. To be sure, as a question it is also always open to the reality it seeks as something different from itself and before which it stands to be tested. This openness, the angle of opening, as it were, of a question with respect to the reality it seeks, can be of very different breadth. The more indefinite the question is, the more it permits of different answers, and thus the greater is its angle of opening. The more definite the question, the narrower becomes the field of possible answers, to the point that eventually there is only room for a *yes* or a *no*. In this case the entire content of the answer is already anticipated in the question.

In all important spheres of life men shape their existence on the basis of a projected answer to a powerful inner urge, even if such an answer, which orients the urge and raises it to a need, can also be recognized as only provisionally viable. The projection is maintained, so long as it is verified to some extent, until a better one takes its place. To live in the attitude of radically open inquiry without any anticipation of a possible

[95] This holds also for Weischedel's demand that honest philosophizing base itself "exclusively upon itself, and that means, upon the radicality of its own inquiry" ("Philosophische Theologie," p. 246), for this is the point of departure for his inference of God as "the source of the questionableness" (p. 248). (Here we are disregarding the viewpoint discussed earlier that this statement would be meaningful only in relation to a substantively oriented inquiry, and not with reference to the total questionableness of nihilism.)

answer is possible under normal conditions probably only with regard to questions which for the people involved in the inquiry are not – or no longer – concerned with the central issues of life. Otherwise there is as a rule an envisaged answer. If no answer appears at this point, that signifies a threat to the very possibility of living, which cannot be endured for very long.

From whence come the projections of answers which are always in the intention of the questions man asks? Are they the creations of the questioner? This is certainly always also the case. But the matter has still another side to it. It would be an abstraction to imagine the questioner as still prior to all contact with the reality he is inquiring about. Rather, the question is always framed only in association with the reality in question. This is particularly true of the question which man not only asks but actually is. In that man's existence is animated by the question about his destination and fulfilment, he is already borne by the reality at which such inquiry is directed. He always already stands in the experience of the reality about which he is concerned in his question – the experience of a non-objective depth of reality, which underlies all extant objects and supports his own life. His projected answers are put to the test in the course of such experience. Inadequate answers and too narrowly formulated questions are shattered by it. The power over *all* reality, which is also able to bring man's existence into its wholeness, appears particularly in events that disclose the coherence, the wholeness, of a wide range of experience. The answer that arises out of such occurrences to the question of existence corrects the way the question was previously formulated. Often the questionableness of existence, lurking beneath projected answers that seem satisfying on the surface, is first set free again only by such happenings. Of course, the new answer included in such a happening can again only be comprehended as a corrective of the previously projected answer and thus as a new project of understanding.

Thus, the experience of the power man seeks to lift him beyond his finitude, and the projecting of possible answers by the seeker himself, interlock to a great extent. But, in any case, all projecting of possible answers is always mediated by an experience of the reality about which the question asks, even where projected answers arise as counter-images to a no longer convincing tradition or to a contemporary situation one is rejecting. For this reason, a philosophical doctrine of God that concludes from the questionableness of human existence and of finitude generally to the answer intended in such questionableness, always discovers only those answers that have emerged out of historical experience of the reality with which the question of human existence is concerned. That is to say, it discovers the religious answers which always precede philosophical reflection and which are the first to reveal to it a specifically new understanding of the question of existence. For the religions have to do with the current experience of the power that supports all reality, toward which the question of man's existence is directed. To this extent we must agree with Barth's thesis that the human question is first disclosed from the side of the answer. That applies also to the pre- and non-Christian religions, too, however. They are not merely the expression of an isolated human question and its accompanying projected answer. It is not only in Christian faith that the human question lives from the happening of a divine answer. All religions stem from particular happenings of the reality inquired after in the question of human existence. From the standpoint of the Christian faith, in any case, it can be said that the non-Christian religions are based on unclear provisional forms of the true answer to mankind that has happened in the history of Jesus. Of course, the happening on which these religions are based is itself distorted by the fact that the powers they accept as the ground of all reality still belong to the realm of finitude.

I am coming to the conclusion. Bound up with the occurrence of the power that sustains all reality and lifts it above its finitude, to which man is referred in his being and about which he therefore cannot help but ask, is the conviction shared by most religions of the personal character of this power.[96] This

[96] See the discussions by G. van der Leeuw, *Religion in Essence and Manifestation*, 2 vols. (New York: Harper Torchbooks, 1963), 1:83ff., 155ff.,

point first makes it possible to understand and characterize the question of human existence as the question about *God*, not in the sense that it is universally experienced as such but because this brings out its real meaning.

In that we call the power that determines all reality God, we are already thinking of it as personal. But what does this mean? Obviously, the word "person" automatically brings to the fore an understanding whose combination with the idea of an all-determining power has become unbelievable for us. If I see the matter correctly, the crisis of the idea of God since the eighteenth century is connected chiefly with the problem of how the power that determines all reality can be thought of as a person. Usually a concept of personality developed with regard to man has been transferred to God. Nevertheless, all such attempts, from Anaxagoras's idea of the divine reason to Max Scheler's concept of a personal God, are subject to Fichte's criticism – which goes back to Spinoza – of the idea of God inaugurated by Leibnitz, which N. Hartmann has revived in modern times against Scheler. According to it, every concept of "person" conceived in this way includes within itself the finitude of man as a constitutive element, and therefore is unfit as a designation of the infinite power that determines all reality.[97]

---

dealing with the will and form of the divine power, as well as with its connection with the phenomenon of the proper name of the divine power. Although van der Leeuw himself does not understand these phenomena as personal, we may still ask whether the root of the personal as such is to be found in them, so that in relation to them our ordinary concept of person, which is oriented toward the human ego, is to be regarded as a derivative concept.

[97] J. G. Fichte wrote, in his article "On the Basis of Our Belief in a Divine World Government" ["Über den Grund unseres Glaubens an eine göttliche Weltregierung"] (1798), which touched off the atheistic controversy: "What then do you call personality and consciousness? Is it not something you have found within yourself, which you have come to know in yourself and have designated by this name? The fact that you do not at all think of this without limitation and finitude, nor could do so, you can learn from the most cursory attention to the way you have constructed this concept. You make this being, accordingly, by attributing this predicate to a finite being, to a being like yourself, and you have not, as you intended,

The only thing that can lead us beyond this critical dissolution of the concept of the personality of God and therewith of the idea of God as such is the observation that the personal character of man is itself by no means self-evident. What our humanistic tradition designates as the inviolable dignity of man as a person is obviously not so fashioned that it is beyond the possibility of being dismissed. The individual can also be treated as a thing. Does not his dignity as a person have more the character of an article of faith than a demonstrable element singled out from experienced anthropological realities? Are not the anthropological evidence for human personality and its precise definition subject to the same sorts of difficulties as the character of man's openness to the world as openness to God – similar also in the fact that in both cases it is a question of the wholeness of man's being? Is, then, the idea of the personal attained primarily with reference to man? Should we not perhaps look for the origin of the idea of person precisely in the phenomenology of religious experience, to the extent that in so

---

conceived God, but only reduplicated yourself in thought" ("Philosophisches Journal," 8 [1798]: 16, in *Die Schriften zu J. G. Fichtes Atheismusstreit*, ed. H. Lindau, Bibliothek der Philosophen 4 [Munich, 1912], p. 34; cf. also Fichte's "Gerichtlichen Verantwortungschriften" [1799], *ibid.*, pp. 225ff.). Fichte's argumentation has not become obsolete in every respect, either by his own later doctrine of God as absolute ego, or by Hegel's related concept of God as absolute subject, and certainly not by the theistic philosophy and theology of the nineteenth century. On the other hand, Feuerbach's theory of projection is already clearly prefigured in it. On the history of the problem see David Friedrich Strauss, *Die christliche Glaubenslehre* 2 vols. (Tübingen, 1840–41), 1:502–24 ("On the Personality of God"), esp. pp. 504f. One will have to find here a decisive motive for the pantheistic interpretation of Hegel, harking back to Spinoza, by the young Hegelians.

On Scheler's argument for the personality of God see his *Der Formalismus in der Ethik und die materiale Wertethik* (*Gesammelte Werke* 2; Bern and Munich, ⁴1954), pp. 116, 240f., 302f., 403ff., 503; in addition, *On the Eternal in Man*, trans. Bernard Noble (New York: Harper & Row, 1960), pp. 150ff., 253ff. and esp. the preface to the 2d ed., pp. 24ff., 26ff. For Nicolai Hartmann's criticism of this, see his *Ethics*, trans. Stanton Coit, 3 vols. (London: G. Allen & Unwin, 1932), 1:319f., 324f. Scheler himself later drew back from his idea of a transcendent personal God after his lecture "Die Formen des Wissens und der Bildung" (1925). Cf. also the preface to the 3d ed. of his *Formalismus* (1926), pp. 17f., as well as *Man's Place in Nature*, p. 92.

doing one takes note of the happening that asserts itself in it? Was not the personality of man originally thought of as a participation in the inviolable majesty of God, just as the ancient commandment against murder in Israel was motivated by man's being in the image of God (Gen. 9:6)? Do we not have in the idea of the image of God in man the Old Testament expression for what we call personality? In any case, this idea is the nearest thing to our concept of personality that we find among the anthropological concepts in the Old Testament. The fact that the modern concept of the personal has arisen out of Christian theology, and indeed from the problems of Christology and the doctrine of the Trinity,[98] points in the same direction. But even the idea, stemming from ancient Greece, of the person as an intellectual individual seems to derive its peculiar pathos from the religious motif of man as a being that participates in the divine world reason by virtue of his intellectual essence.

Such considerations suggest that in dealing with personality we are treating a category that originates in the phenomenology of religion. As such it characterizes the *non-manipulatableness* [*Unverfügbarkeit*] of this power, which at the same time, however, makes a concrete *claim* upon man in that happening which is constitutive of religious experience. This combination of concretely experienced claim and non-manipulatableness, and therefore also the impenetrability of the power making the claim, appears to be characteristic also of the tendency of children to "personify" things in their environment. The adult in our culture, who knows about the manipulability – at least in principle even if not always in fact – of these things and thereby knows them as *mere things*, no longer personifies them. But only from the vantage point of this adult consciousness is the child's (or the primitive man's) conduct appropriately described as a personification of that which in and of itself is not personal. Talk about personification, therefore, cannot explain what originally constituted the personal character of the power encountered in religious happenings; for such a characterization already proceeds from a separation of the spheres of reality which the child

[98] See my article, "Person," in *RGG*³ 5, cols. 230-35.

and the primitive man experience in their original unity, as indicated by their "personifying." But even after this separation has been made we are not deprived of the possibility of understanding as personal the power determining all reality, which is at work in the depths of the appearances that to a superficial view seem objectified and at our disposal. In any event, that can only depend on religious experience itself; for it cannot be concluded by means of analogical reasoning from the objectification of the world of finite things that the infinite (i.e. not finite) power that determines all reality must likewise be conceived as impersonal. If personality is originally encountered in the concrete claim made by a power that remains beyond our disposal,[99] then it may rather be supposed that its reality is distorted by transposing in terms of the objectifying interpretation of finite entities.

If the concept of the personal is originally based on a religiously determined experience of reality, or of the powers governing it, then it is not inherently anthropomorphic to experience and describe a concrete occurrence of being laid claim to by a reality beyond our control in personal terms.

---

[99] It is in this that I see the element of truth in the efforts of modern personalism – from F. Ebner and M. Buber to F. Gogarten and E. Brunner, among others – to understand personality from the side of the claim of the Thou, and to understand the primary Thou that makes claims upon man as the Thou of God. In fact, what has been set forth above can also be formulated by saying that man is awakened to personality by the Divine Thou, and in this way first learns to respect the thou of the fellowman as a person. But the personalistic thinkers were unable in the development of their thought to avoid giving the impression that what was involved here was nevertheless only an analogical transference of the I–Thou relationship between fellow humans to the relationship between man and God. In such a way only something like a myth of the personal could arise. The priority of the relation to God for the phenomenon of the personal remains a mere assertion so long as we do not reflect on the origin of personality in the phenomenology of religion, in contrast to a purely anthropological founding of personality. In order to maintain this distinction, however, it is essential not to explain the talk about the divine Thou directly and entirely by means of analogy with the human Thou, but to establish it independently on the basis of the character of the divine power as happening. The personality of man needs to be clarified in the light of the peculiar character of the divine personality, provided that it does have its origin in this.

Even gods shaped like animals could be experienced as realities having personal character. But, on the other hand, the possibility of anthropomorphic speaking about the reality constitutive of religious experience could be grounded in the fact that man participates in the personal character of the divine power or has received this already from his creation.

Fichte's criticism of the idea of God as person – and therewith of the possibility of understanding the power determining all reality as "God" at all – can be met only if this power does not receive its personal character, by means of which it appears as God, through a transference from man's experience of himself, but the other way around: by the fact that all talk about personality has its origin in the realm of religious experience. Understood in this way, the idea of the personality of God would precisely not entail limits that would contradict the idea of an all-determining power, but would instead express just its non-manipulatableness, its holiness. At the same time it would be fundamentally distinguishable from all anthropomorphic modes of representation, but suited to render the meaning of the anthropomorphic speech encountered in religious language more intelligible.

A personal conception of the divine reality on the sense described above is unquestionably common to wide areas of the history of religions. It is not in every sense something specific to the biblical understanding of God. On the other hand, there seem to be great differences among the different religions and even between the different deities of one and the same religion with respect to the peculiar manner and significance of their personal character. Thus the personal element in the conception of God in the Olympian religion of the Greeks seems to have been from the first far less important than in the ancient Near East, and here the leading deities of the Tigris-Euphrates valley seem to have had more sharply drawn personalitites than those of Egypt. In comparison with them, the personality of the biblical God exhibits still other specific features. This God is characterized by a freedom of action that, together with the exclusivity of his claim upon those in covenant with him, sets the God of Israel off from the other divine figures with whom the people of the ancient Near East otherwise associated. This freedom gives an unmistakable character even to Yahweh's faithfulness, which together with freedom defines the historical action of this God. The historical experience of reality, that is, experience of it as a history of ever new events, was gained from the freedom and free faithfulness of the divine activity. From here, too, the historicness of man was discovered, namely, his freedom over the presently given aspects of his situation for a future which has not yet appeared. To this extent, as Jürgen Moltmann has rightly stressed,[100] the experience of the questionableness of man was released by the biblical understanding of God as a challenge to a *quest* for God which will issue in a conclusive finding only in the eschatological future of God's public reign.

The definitive answer to the question of human existence is thus God himself in the future of his *reign*, which will be the definitive revelation of his deity insofar as it sets the history of the world in the light of its end; definitively decides and reveals the essence of every one of its individual trends, figures, and events; and thereby demonstrates the coming God as the Lord of all things. This future has already become determinative of the present since the appearance of Jesus. In virtue of the public ministry and destiny of Jesus it has become possible to live one's present existence in its current, concrete configuration in the way it appears in the light of God's future and thus in his ultimate truth.

The future of God will bring the answer to the questionableness of every phenomenon in the world of nature and of mankind that still remains open in the flow of history. And thus, from the side of God's future, decisive light is shed upon the pre- and non-Israelitic history of man's religions, as well as

---

[100] J. Moltmann, "Anfrage und Kritik: Zu G. Ebeling's 'Theologie und Verkundigung,'" *EvTh* 24 (1964): 25ff., esp. 31f. Moltmann refers to Augustine in particular as the one who mediated to Western theology and philosophy as a fundamental theme of anthropology the understanding of man, rooted in the biblical idea of God, as being placed in question by God and relegated to inquire after God.

upon the history of Israel and of the Christian church itself. The history of religions appears in this light as a history of the questionableness and neediness of man, but also as a history of man's dealings with the reality of God, indeed, even as a history of the self-disclosures of the true God, which, to be sure, have been "held down in unrighteousness," as Paul says.

Man's inquisitiveness, which is able to proceed beyond every given situation and beyond every existing conception of God, cannot get beyond the biblical God himself because this God in his almighty freedom is not among the beings existing in the world, but is the Lord of the future, toward whose coming the world is moving. The biblical God is thus in fact – in the sense of Karl Barth's formula that at first sounds so paradoxical – the answer to the question of human existence which, as answer, does not put an end to the human question but for the first time really has freed it to proceed in openness. In this way Christian speech about God proves itself in relation to the limit-transcending openness of human existence, which is disclosed in its depths in this light and then in turn points back to the God of the Bible as its ultimate, unsurpassable fulfilment.

8

THE GOD OF HOPE

This essay is from the Festschrift *Ernst Bloch zu Ehren*, ed. Siegfried Unseld (Frankfurt, 1965), pp. 209–25.

Is THEISM dead? Looking back at the criticisms that have been leveled against the traditional ideas of God as the supreme being and a transcendent person, it is high time to ask about the extent of the impact of this criticism. Its point of attack has been, since Spinoza and Fichte, that the concept of a transcendent person necessarily includes the finitude of the human personality so that an "infinite person" would be unthinkable. Since the word "God" entails personalness, Fichte's criticism seems to have discredited the concept of God as such as the product of a misunderstanding. Fichte's later doctrine of the absolute ego could not repair the damage done by his earlier criticism. His arguments during the atheistic controversy prepared the way for Feuerbach's theory of projection. At any rate, Feuerbach elevated man as a species to the status of infinity so that, as had already been the case in Fichte, nothing remained for God but to consider him as the anthropomorphically masked husk of the concept of person. It is unnecessary here to go into Feuerbach's explanation of the motives for transposing the "fixed idea" of man, the properly infinite being, into something alien existing in an imaginary heaven. It suffices to point out that first the finitude and anthropomorphic character of the fundamental predicates of God, and then their derivation from merely man and nature have provided the lever which has toppled the traditional picture of God in the public eye. Today, the effects of this criticism have penetrated into Christian theology itself. In this case, in addition to the concept of the personality of God, what is involved is above all the idea of a transcendent being as such: theism has finitized God as a being alongside other beings. This argument, propounded by Tillich, likewise goes back to Fichte, who charged that the concept of a special divine "substance" is a reminiscence of the spatial mode of being of finite things. The idea of a God "in himself" as a particular being is rejected today on theological grounds, as well, because it deprecates God as a finite, "manipulatable" object alongside others. Every objectification of God as a being betrays the biblical idea of the almighty God as the all-determining reality (so Bultmann): it is not permissible to withdraw from any subject by means of an objectifying detachment. This theological argument, which is grounded in the inviolable sovereignty of God, coincides in result with the oppositely motivated atheism of freedom, which – in the wake of Nietzsche, espoused today by N. Hartmann, J.-P. Sartre, and Ernst Bloch – excludes the existence of a being equipped with omnipotence in the name of human freedom. In both cases, the result is the rejection of every attempt to retain God as the highest being. The difference between them is only that one side departs completely from all talk about God, whereas the other, the theologians, attempts to find new possibilities for speaking about God.

How do things stand here? Has the criticism simply shattered the shells of inappropriate concepts of God, or has it also freed the kernel which can provide the opportunity for some other kind of talk about God? What is the extent of the impact of this critique upon theism? In the first instance, it certainly does bear upon the finite and anthropomorphic character of concepts of God. The inexpungeable inadequacy of every human statement about God was something traditional theology and philosophy were also, for the most part, thoroughly aware. This is why Tillich can employ aspects of traditional metaphysical concepts of God against the theistic conception: God is not a being and thus neither is he a separate individual, a person, but rather Being itself, the ground and power of all being and of everything personal. To ask about the "existence" of God means to have already denied that God is the unity beyond the opposition of essence and existence. With such formulations, Tillich identifies himself as the champion of the metaphysical tradition against the theistic tradition that superseded it. It is a curious misunderstanding on the part of the Anglican bishop J. A. T. Robinson that he finds in Tillich a radical break with the traditional metaphysical concept of God as such. On the other hand, it is extremely doubtful that anything remains of this concept of God if God may not be understood under any circumstances as an independent being and as person. Does not the subject fall with the predicates, as Feuerbach showed? The references to the ground of being, the hidden depth and power that permeates all finite reality, especially the interpersonal realm, are hardly able by themselves – in view of that critique – to justify continuing to use the heavily weighted vocable "God". Romantic philosophies of nature can forthwith ascribe this depth, this breath of the infinite, to nature itself, and the transference of the infinite spirit over to the infinity of nature probably belongs among the presuppositions of Feuerbach's critique of religion. It is in fact not at all clear why the impersonal, fluid reality of this depth must be spoken of as a God. To be sure, we can no longer transfigure finitude itself – man and the world – with the aura of the infinite, as Romanticism and Feuerbach so casually did. The experience of finitude has become more radical since then. This is a sobering fact which cannot be trivialized as merely the reflection of a late stage in the development of the bourgeois economic system. The depth of being now appears as something enigmatic, as an absurdity. It is no longer experienced as an ecstatic expansion of our own being but as a painful limit. However, the word "God" is just as difficult to combine with the dark abyss of an empty transcendence as it is with the life-force in the depths of reality. Other grounds for speaking about God are needed if one is to justify the claim that there is some relationship between him and the supporting depth of being or the absurd groundlessness of existence.

It is useful here to keep in mind that the original Greek philosophical motifs of the traditional doctrine of God have often been of ambiguous value for the question of whether the world-ground has the independent existence and personal character of a God. In its conviction about the personal character of the world-ground, the traditional doctrine of God was influenced by the authority of the Bible more deeply than many of the fathers were aware. Can this conviction withstand the pressures that today seek to disperse the idea of God into the ether of some being shimmering in the depths of that which is? It can hardly do so as a block of supernaturally revealed truth, which is what the authority of the Bible has petrified into in Christian theology for the most part. Everything depends on whether the Israelitic, primitive-Christian understanding of God – to the extent that it proves itself to be a self-coherent whole precisely in its transformations – has any relationship to contemporary experience of reality. It is meaningful to ask this question because a specific understanding of reality corresponds to the God of the Bible. From the standpoint of this God, all reality is referred to the future and is experienced as eschatologically oriented. He has left his impression on the experience of the world and of the situation of man as the God of the promises, as the God who leads history into a new future, and as the God of the coming kingdom. The high point of his futurization of the experience of existence came with the appearance of Jesus. Here, the conviction about the nearness of the kingdom so intensified concentration upon God's future that alongside this everything transmitted from the past and all present reality lost any independent meaning, and God's future itself became determinative of the present. The rediscovery by Johannes Weiss and Albert Schweitzer of Jesus' eschatological understanding of reality had such a shocking effect upon the satiated feeling for life at the beginning of the twentieth century that it was hardly possible to face the utter strangeness of this Jesus except by presumptuous excisions and artificial reinterpretations. These novel interpretations are still alive today in the efforts to rob the eschatology of Jesus of its relation to time and to convert his passion for God's future into the presence of eternity in the momentary now. Perhaps Christian theology will one day have to thank Ernst Bloch's philosophy of hope for giving it the courage to recover in the full sense its central category of eschatology. A temporally understood future remains decisive for such a concept. Bloch has taught us about the overwhelming power of the still-open future and of the hope that reaches out to it in anticipation for not only the life and thought of man but in addition for the ontological uniqueness of everything in reality. He has recovered the biblical tradition's eschatological mode of thought as a theme for philosophical reflection and also for Christian theology. But how do things stand with the theological character of this eschatology?

According to Ernst Bloch, the "God-hypostasis" is untenable: as the messianic axis of the history of religions was progressively humanized, it was finally neutralized [*aufgehoben*] in the doctrine of the consubstantiality of Jesus Christ with God.[1] "God's glory became that of the apocalyptic Christ and his community."[2] The "religious heteronomy and its reified hypostasis are completely dissolved into the theology of the community. . . ."[3] From this standpoint, the atheistic critique of religion by Feuerbach and his disciples only completed the tendency toward a humanized fulfillment and sublimation of the history of religions which was already inherent in the public ministry of Jesus and in the Christian message. The utopia of the kingdom still remains – something Feuerbach misunderstood because of his "flat" anthropology of "a virtually inexpandable man-as-he-is-at-present [*Mensch-Vorhandensein*]."[4] But it is just this that supplants the "fiction of a creator God," since "where the great world-ruler holds sway, there is no room for freedom, not even the freedom of the children of God nor of the mystical-democratic figure of the kingdom that is found in the chiliastic hope."[5]

The "vacuum left behind by the demise of the God-hypostasis,"[6] which had been already presupposed as the "projection

---

[1] Ernst Bloch, *Das Prinzip Hoffnung* 2:1493ff.
[2] *Ibid.*, p. 1500. [3] *Ibid.*, p. 1408.
[4] *Ibid.*, p. 1412. [5] *Ibid.*, p. 1413.
[6] *Ibid.*, p. 1529.

space"[7] that made religious hypostatizations possible, is, for Bloch, no "chimera" like the figures of gods with which it has been populated by the religious imagination.[8] Without this space, not even the kingdom would be "intentionable" [*intentionierbar*].[9] Its true content is the utopia of the kingdom.[10] To this extent, the hope of the kingdom transcends every one of its particular but again surpassable realizations. The idea of the kingdom does not completely coincide with any social utopia[11] and remains "in itself a still to be attained classless society" that is "distinguished from the 'highest good' [*summum bonum*] of the religious-utopian kingdom by that leap which is posited by the explosive intention of regeneration and transfiguration itself."[12] But how is this hope of the kingdom grounded on its part? For instance, is it adequate to describe it from the standpoint of the present behavior of men, who project their wishes into the future? In this case, would not the psychology of man as he now is be installed as the criterion for judging the hope of the kingdom? Bloch's appeal to the potencies and latent aspects of the process are difficult to reconcile with his emphasis on the factor of novelty in the coming future. If the future is already laid out in these potencies and latent aspects of the historical process – in our case, in the wishes and hopes of man – then it cannot arrive with the suddenness and underivability of something whose novelty essentially transcends everything that was or is. Yet how would things stand if the hope of the kingdom were only the symbolic expression of the demonstrable psychological strivings of man? Obviously, it could then also be demolished by the fact that men had become satisfied and content with themselves and their present circumstances. If it were established only as an expression of human wishing, the hope of the kingdom could easily collapse into the triviality of a self-satisfied present. The primacy of the future and its novelty are guaranteed only when the coming kingdom is ontologically grounded in itself and does not owe its future merely to the present wishes and

---

[7] *Ibid.*, p. 1530.
[8] *Ibid.*, p. 1534.
[9] *Ibid.*, p. 1532.
[10] *Ibid.*, p. 1530; cf. pp. 1412f.
[11] *Ibid.*, p. 1410.
[12] *Ibid.*, p. 1411.

strivings of man. When the coming kingdom is designated in biblical terms as the kingdom of God, that is out of concern for the ontological primacy of the future of the kingdom over all present realities, including, above all, psychological states. This means that from the biblical standpoint the being of God and that of the kingdom are identical, since the being of God is his lordship. He is God only in the execution of this lordship, and this full accomplishment of his lordship is determined as something future. To this extent, the God to whom the hope of the kingdom refers is characterized in a radical and exclusive sense by "futurity as a quality of being" [*Seinsbeschaffenheit*].[13] We will return to this point later.

It has been shown that the theme of the idea of God has been by no means conclusively and convincingly explored by Bloch, since the question must be raised in relation to his own thought as to how it can guarantee the ontological priority of the coming kingdom over everything presently existing, including the men of the present and the hopes they harbor. It seems that this unsolved problem of his utopia of the kingdom has not escaped Bloch. Thus, he can lay it down that the projection of the kingdom "needed and needs even the sublimity of something over and above," and that the reverence that culminates in relation to man's humanity needs that "numinosity experienced in the face of the immensity of nature as a corrective in order to preserve his religious objectivity, that is, precisely in order to avoid failing to think of man with a sufficient sense of his nobility and mysteriousness."[14] With regard to the question of God, Bloch finds himself in an entirely different situation than Feuerbach. For the latter, the problem posed by the difference between the wretchedness and fragmentariness of the present state of man's existence and the grandeur of his human destination did not arise, because he was clever enough to clothe the man of the present – if not as an individual, then still as a species – with all the predicates of the infinite. Of course, in order to do this he had to ignore the individual and enervating question of his particular existence and destiny. And with that

13 *Ibid.*, p. 1458.   14 *Ibid.*, p. 1409.

he obscured the real situation of every human present, which is filled with conflict and often shocking and continual painful defeat for the individuals, and alongside which there is no room for a human species characterized by every conceivable excellence and untouched by the suffering of the individuals. In contrast to Feuerbach, Bloch has gone through the experience of the finitude of everything present, and therefore can find relief not in some fictitious idea of the species but only in the hope of a fulfillment that comes from the direction of an unheard of, victorious future. This newly emerged difference raises again the question of the ontological priority of the future over the present, and thereby reopens the theme of some kind of divine being transcending the present human race and the world: "Only in relation to the 'hidden God' [*Deus absconditus*] is the *problem* of what is at stake in the legitimate mystery of the '*hidden man*' [*homo absconditus*] kept open."[15] The primacy of the future, and therewith of the 'hidden God'" who is its ground, is necessary in order that man's humanity be protected against trivialization and continue to be summoned to its future possibilities.

The question now arises as to what the word "God" can still mean in this context. The criticism of the ordinary way of thinking of the "transcendent" God as a self-contained being alongside other beings still stands. A God conceived as a thing at hand, even as a thingified person, or a "reified hypostasis,"[16] is no longer credible. One may ask, however, whether such a characterization does full justice to the intention of the traditional philosophico-theological doctrines of God in the transcending, self-critical movement of their reflections upon the inadequacy of their own statements. Whatever the case may be, an absolute in the mode of being present at hand [*Vorhandenheit*] is no longer thinkable. For everything that already exists, all beings, can be fundamentally called into question and superseded. Therefore we must agree with Bloch that he has transposed the question of the most perfect being [*ens perfectissimum*] into a temporal mode, and turned it into "the highest utopian

---

[15] *Ibid.*, p. 1406.   [16] *Ibid.*, p. 1408.

problem, that of the end."[17] In this sense, his atheism is to be accepted. But the question of God arises once again insofar as the end must be conceived as being numinous in itself. In this connection, however, the question must now be concerned exclusively with the possibility of a God "with futurity as a quality of being," and therefore a return to the God of theism must be ruled out at this stage.

The idea of the future as a mode of God's being is still undeveloped in theology despite the intimate connection between God and the coming reign of God in the eschatological message of Jesus. What is the meaning of this intimate connection? For instance, is the future of his lordship, the kingdom of God, inessential to his deity, something merely appended to it? Is not God God only in the accomplishment of his lordship over the world? This is why his deity will be revealed only when the kingdom comes, since only then will his lordship be visible. But are God's revelation of his deity and his deity itself separable from each other? The God of the Bible is God only in that he proves himself as God. He would not be the God of the world if he did not prove himself to be its Lord. But just this proof is still a matter of the future, according to the expectations of Israel and the New Testament. Does this not mean that God is not yet, but is yet to be? In any case, he exists only in the way in which the future is powerful over the present, because the future decides what will emerge out of what exists in the present. As the power of the future, God is no thing, no object presently at hand, which man could detach himself from and pass over. He appears neither as one being among others, nor as the quiescent background of all beings, the timeless being underlying all objects. Yet, is being itself perhaps to be understood as in truth the power of the future? As the power of the future, the God of the Bible always remains ahead of all speech about him, and has already outdistanced every concept of God. Above all, the power of the future does not rob man of his freedom to transcend every present state of affairs. A being presently at hand, and equipped with omnipotence, would destroy such

[17] *Ibid.*, p. 1412.

freedom by virtue of his overpowering might. But the power of the future is distinguished by the fact that it frees man from his ties to what presently exists in order to liberate him for *his* future, to give him his freedom.

The power of the future and it alone can be the object of hope and trust. For the future is powerful in the present. It is the power of contradiction to the present, and releases forces to overcome it. Just for this reason is it alone able to rescue and preserve. Since the future has been powerful in the same way in every past time over what existed then, so everything that has come to pass, even in times long gone, has come about and also been changed once again through this same power of the future which decides over the present just as it has brought it forth. Thus, reflection upon the power of the future over the present leads to a new idea of creation, oriented not toward a primeval event in the past but toward the eschatological future. Ernst Bloch believed he must reject the idea of a creator-God in favour of the kingdom, as the still unrealized consummation,[18] because the former appears to him to be the expression of a "mythology of an opulent past."[19] Certainly one cannot deny the strong influence of such mythological conceptions of the primordial age upon the thinking of the biblical accounts of the creation. But the God of the coming kingdom had to become the occasion for an eschatological reversal of the idea of creation as soon as he was recognized – as happened in the message of Jesus – as the one who by the future of his lordship is alone powerful over the present world and decisive for its meaning, its essence. In the message of Jesus, creation and the eschatological future belong together most intimately. To be sure, theology has not yet recognized the task involved in this fact because its doctrine of creation remains within the confines of a thinking oriented toward the mythical origin of the primordial age, in contrast to the eschatological character of the message and history of Jesus.

This does not mean that the futurity of God excludes every possible idea of his eternity. For is the future not only of our

---

[18] *Ibid.*, pp. 1458, 1493, 1499f.   [19] *Ibid.*, p. 1500.

present but also of every past age. Nor has he been this in the actionless distance of something remote and receding ever further from the historical process; rather, in accord with what has just been said, he has been this in such a way that he has allowed every event and age to participate in his immediate historical future, which through its realization has ceased to be future. In this way, God, through the realization of the historical future at a given time, pushed this away from himself as power of the ultimate future and in this way mediated himself to it in his own eschatological futurity, If God is to be thought of in this way as the future of even the most distant past, then he existed before our present and before every present, although he will definitively demonstrate his deity only in the future of his kingdom. He existed as the future that has been powerful in every present. Thus, the futurity of God implies his eternity. But it is one thing to conceive eternity as timelessness or as the endless endurance of something that existed since the beginning of time, and quite another to think of it as the power of the future over every present.

The most difficult problem still remains untouched. To what extent are we justified in calling the power of the future, through which the coming kingdom has its ontological priority over the wishes of men, "God"? Do we do this only because it is in accord with biblical linguistic usage, or is it possible to find a basis for this way of speaking in the nature of the matter under discussion? As we pointed out earlier, the idea of the personal belongs inseparably to the word "God." Does the power of the future have any more personal character than the concept of a timeless ground of being in the depths of reality, in the background of the realm of being? And if that should be the case, would such a divine personality be defensible against the criticism, repeated ever since Fichte, that it is an anthropomorphic hypostatization? These two questions will decide whether we have been justified in using the word "God" as we have so far, or whether it has been fraudulently introduced. The resolution of both of these questions depends, however, on attaining deeper insight into the nature of the personal. The crucial point here is whether the idea of person is really derived from the human ego and then transported onto the object of religious experience, as Fichte and Feuerbach presupposed. If this assumption were to prove valid, then their criticism would remain unshaken: the idea of a personal God – and with this the idea of God as such – would have to be surrendered as finitization of an ostensibly infinite being, and as the projection of an anthropomorphic hypostasis. But it is doubtful that this assumption is correct. There is evidence for the view that the phenomenon of the personal was not first discovered in relation to man, but had its origin in religious experience, in the appearance of the numinous object, and was transferred to man only from there. This process already underlies the reverse procedure of anthropomorphic stylization of the gods. Alongside the findings of religious psychology that it really is the case that personality cannot be originally an anthropological phenomenon, there is also the primary character of the personal shape of the child's experience of his environing world, and the air of mysteriousness that cannot be erased from human personality. To this very day the human personality is still bound up with the religious theme and can be slighted where the latter disappears. The original phenomenon of the personal would then have to be sought in perhaps the impenetrability of the numinous power, which by no means remains vague but encounters one as having concrete pertinence. It is bound up with its holiness and inviolability. It is highlighted by the *freedom* of the power in relation to its form of manifestation, and this implies at the same time its freedom in relation to this particular form of manifestation. This, then, is perhaps the circumstance that allows us to understand man as personal, even in a time when the personal power of the other phenomena of nature has faced.

If in this way the personality expresses itself in freedom, then freedom itself presupposes openness to the future. Man is free only because he has a future, because he can go beyond what is presently extant. And so freedom is in general the power that transforms the present. This means, however, that futurity as a condition of freedom constitutes the very core of the personal; it is what "resonates" through the present form of manifestation and gives it its perplexing character as threat or enticement. It is also the thing that gives the present form of appearance its gravity as a pledge of the future. A power that remains in mere latency is impersonal – but to this extent it also loses its character as power and at best remains the world-ground as an impotent background phenomenon. Therefore the power of the future is personal in contrast to the mere depth of being because it touches every present concretely as its future in the possibilities of its transformation. As that which is powerful in the present, the future resonates through the forms of what presently exists. In this way it is also the power of being. Being is itself to be thought of from the side of the future, instead of as the abstract, most universal something in the background of all beings.

The power of the future has often in the history of religions been experienced as threatening (M. Eliade). This is understandable so long as the future is dark and uncertain and fails to provide incentive for meeting with a hopeful attitude the changes it will bring. In any case, in most religions men turn away from the future in order to seek refuge in something supposedly having existed since the primordial time. Therefore a mediating history is needed that will reveal the power of the future as the God of hope and displace the idols of present existence and their myths of the primordial time. Occasions for hope, for specific hopes, are needed in the present and in the historical heritage of man. The biblical writings are documents of this path that leads to knowledge of the God of Israel as the God of hope through the history of the promises which Israel received. The future announced itself in these promises, at first as still proximate historical goals, viz., in the promises of land, richer posterity, and invincible duration for the Davidic dynasty. But then the hope of the Israelites was extended beyond these preliminary objects of hope, beyond their fulfillment and beyond their announced failure, to the hope of a final act of Israel's God that would bring all history to its consummation in justice, peace, and everlasting life. This last hope for the

kingdom, for the lordship of God himself, arose out of the previous hopes, fulfillments, and judgments, and from the experiences Israel had undergone along the path these had marked
for it. Without this mediation, the rise of the hope of the kingdom would have been unimaginable. The lordship of God, whose
will and unique character Israel had experienced in its whole
history, was completely bound up in this history. The hope of
the coming Kingdom as that of the lordship of Yahweh attained its specificity only through its derivation from this history. Nevertheless, the concentration of the Israelitic hopes of
this final future in the message of Jesus could result in a revision
of the traditions of Israel itself in the light of the future of God
and his lordship. Trust in the coming reign of God now was
sufficient to link one to its salvation, without any further re-
quirements of traditional piety. Thereby the future of God –
of the God of Israel, to be sure – became the measure of all
things, even the measure of the history of its own past origins.
The Old Testament disclosures of God now, in retrospect,
proved to have been only portents and anticipatory presen-
tations of the future of God that was revealed and made accessible in the public ministry of Jesus and in the manifestation of
the eschatological glory in him through his resurrection from the
dead. Correspondingly, the Israelitic understanding of God's
form of existence appears in a new light as a result of the
eschatological turn toward the future of God as this has been
accomplished in the ministry of Jesus. For all their distinctiveness, Israel's concepts of God were still burdened with the
view the peoples of its surrounding environment had regarding
the manner of being of the divine as that of a power from the
primordial time. The numinous manifestations, which the early
traditions of Israel recount, were understood not as preap-
pearances of the future but as the appearances of some otherwise hidden but nevertheless real, present power, such as the
power of a stone or a tree. For this reason there was only an
external relation between the divine epiphany and the promise
mediated by it. It seems as if the promise was believed on
account of its divine author, who nevertheless remained distinct

from it. But was not the promise (or the threat), perhaps, in reality to have been believed because of the convincing power of its content? Was not the promise, perhaps, substantively the preappearance of the coming reign of God and so itself filled with the divine reality, which had been conceived and transmitted as something distinctive alongside the promises? Then the author and the content of the promises are ultimately one, and the future to which they pointed was a form of manifestation of God's future itself, the future of his lordship, whose power over what was then present proclaimed itself in the realization of the promises.

The unity of the promising God with his promise itself is consummated in the fulfillment of what was promised; for the fulfillment brings about the glorification of man and of the world, and thus their participation in the glory of God. The salvation that God promises is himself. This confirms the interpretation of Bloch that the "messianic" line of the history of religions and of the history of Israel finds its goal in the unity of God and man. Of course, this unity is "man's entry into religious mystery" only after the power of the future, the coming reign of God, has become influential in the present and has gripped man. Whoever has been gripped by God's future surely places himself, his trust, and his hope in it. But the ontological primacy of God's future over every presently existing form of human realization remains in force even here. For man will participate in the glory of God only in such a way that he will always have to leave behind again what he already is and what he finds as the given state of his world. Man participates in God not by flight from the world but by active transformation of the world which is the expression of the divine love, the power of its future over the present by which it is transformed in the direction of the glory of God.

Neither in the case of the consubstantiality of Christ with the Father, nor in the promised and, through the Spirit, anticipated fellowship of the believers with God, has unity with God involved a tensionless homogeneity. The Father is not displaced by the Son. For the consubstantiality of Jesus with God is grounded precisely in the fact that Jesus directed men wholly away from himself and refers them to the coming reign of the Father. Just this message was the means by which his own person became, for those whom he encountered, a decision regarding the lordship of God itself. The unity of Jesus with the Father is negatively communicated; it is accomplished in the unreservedness of the self-surrender of Jesus to the Father. Precisely in this way has he proved himself to be the *Son of the Father*. Thus, the difference between what is presently extant, and the future of God and his lordship, shows up in the personal relationship of Jesus to the Father. Only in that he acknowledges this difference, by placing himself completely in the service of the coming reign of God, and does not serve himself, is he one with God. Something similar to this was true of the Christians in whom the *Spirit* of Christ was at work. In that they serve God's future, his coming kingdom among men, they already participate in the sonship of Jesus; i.e., identity with him through the transformation of their own being at his initiative; participation in God's future only in going beyond the givenness of one's own existence and the presently existing world and acting to transform the world through love. Thus, the *doctrine of the Trinity* is the seal of the pure futurity of God, which does not harden into an impotent diastasis, a mere beyond contrasting with man's present, but which instead draws it into itself and through enduring the pain of the negative reconciles it with itself.